PREDICTING THE FUTURE:
Can We Do It? And If Not, Why Not?

A PRIMER FOR ANYONE WHO HAS EVER HAD TO
MAKE A DECISION ABOUT ANYTHING

GERARD G. NAHUM, MD

Copyright © 2014 Gerard G. Nahum, MD.

U.S. Copyright Registration Number TXu 1-898-942

All rights reserved. No part of this book may be used or reproduced by any means, graphic, electronic, or mechanical, including photocopying, recording, taping or by any information storage retrieval system without the written permission of the publisher except in the case of brief quotations embodied in critical articles and reviews.

Archway Publishing books may be ordered through booksellers or by contacting:

Archway Publishing
1663 Liberty Drive
Bloomington, IN 47403
www.archwaypublishing.com
1-(888)-242-5904

Because of the dynamic nature of the Internet, any web addresses or links contained in this book may have changed since publication and may no longer be valid. The views expressed in this work are solely those of the author and do not necessarily reflect the views of the publisher, and the publisher hereby disclaims any responsibility for them.

Any people depicted in stock imagery provided by Thinkstock are models, and such images are being used for illustrative purposes only. Certain stock imagery © Thinkstock.

ISBN: 978-1-4808-1106-5 (sc)
ISBN: 978-1-4808-1107-2 (e)

Library of Congress Control Number: 2014916460

Printed in the United States of America.

Archway Publishing rev. date: 10/30/2014

To my father, Lucien Nahum, whose incisive thinking, clear perspectives, humanitarian vision, and instructive good humor provided the tools that shaped my worldview.

CONTENTS

Prologue xi
Acknowledgment xiii

Background

Chapter 1   The Past, the Present, and the Future 3
Chapter 2   Predicting the Future: What We All Strive to Do 7
Chapter 3   Agency: Free Will vs. Determinism 15
Chapter 4   Causality: Linking Events Separated by Time and Space . 23
Chapter 5   Perception 37
Chapter 6   Consciousness 45
Chapter 7   Thought 51
Chapter 8   Knowledge 55

Technical Considerations

Chapter 9   Measurement: How Circumstance and Change Are
            Assessed 61
Chapter 10 Associations vs. Causality 77
Chapter 11 Logic and Inference 89
Chapter 12 Analysis 99
Chapter 13 Understanding 105
Chapter 14 Deductive vs. Inductive Reasoning 111
Chapter 15 Generalizability: Internal vs. External Validity 119
Chapter 16 Computability: Algorithmically Definable Calculations 127
Chapter 17 Continuity (Smoothness) vs. Discontinuity (Roughness) 137

Chapter 18   Stability vs. Instability: System Inertia and Resiliency ... 147
Chapter 19   Dynamical Certainty vs. Uncertainty: Trajectories 155

Fundamental Quantities, Relationships, and Limitations

Chapter 20   Thermodynamics: Laws Prohibiting the Spontaneous
              Reversibility of Physical Events 167
Chapter 21   Quantum Theory: Uncertainties of the Very Small 175
Chapter 22   Entanglement vs. Separability: The Locality Issue 185
Chapter 23   Many Worlds: Parallel Universes as an Explanation for
              Quantum Paradoxes 197
Chapter 24   Chaos Theory: Implications for Macroscopic
              Predictability 203
Chapter 25   Absolutes vs. Relatives: Relativity Theory 211
Chapter 26   Energy 223
Chapter 27   Information 227
Chapter 28   Energy and Information: Maxwell's Hypothetical
              Demon 233

Consequences and Practical Implications

Chapter 29   Modeling vs. Reality 243
Chapter 30   Where We Fit and What We Can Know 249
Chapter 31   Where Does All This Leave Us? 257
Chapter 32   Potential Theological Implications 267

Overview

Chapter 33   Summary and Conclusions 273

*Appendix (for chapters 20 and 28) 347

> "We must take care not to admit as true anything that is only probable. For when one falsity has been let in, infinite others follow."
>
> **Baruch Spinoza**

PROLOGUE

"In practical life we are compelled to follow what is most probable; in speculative thought we are compelled to follow truth."

Baruch Spinoza

This book is meant to be a practical guide for establishing what we can know, what we can understand, and what we can hope to predict about the future. To do this, it draws on several aspects of science and philosophy, but only to explain the relevant constraints that we face associated with our place in the universe.

The message conveyed is simple: the information that we can access, the knowledge that we gain as a result, and the understandings that we develop are what we use to make decisions about the way we believe the future is most likely to unfold. This, in turn, informs our perspectives, which informs our choices, and ultimately our actions.

Nothing about what follows is hidden or mysterious. The discussions of the following chapters suppose nothing more than a healthy curiosity about who we are and the kind of environment we live in. They are all rooted in scientific fact, but they are meant for the non-scientist. I have deliberately avoided the use of technical terms whenever possible. Any jargon is simply and explicitly defined by using ordinary dictionary definitions at the beginning of each chapter.

Since everyone reading this book has a wealth of experience making decisions, it may appear that its goals are trivial. This is not correct. It may be that we are all forced to make decisions on a routine basis, but this doesn't mean that we make them well. Although all of us necessarily decide things based on incomplete and fragmented information quite routinely, very few of us have any formal training in the intrinsic constraints associated with information availability, its quality, consistency, soundness, or completeness. Nor do many of us have a good appreciation of the circumstances that relegate us to the (constrained) environment we find ourselves in, or how to work within this limitation to guarantee that we ensure the best possible interpretations of information to influence future outcomes in the ways we want. At a practical level, this book points out what these constraints are, why they exist, why some of them are tractable, and why others are insurmountable—together with the best approaches for dealing with them.

So, why should you read this book? Because there is a wonderful utility in appreciating the limits of what is knowable. This is so as to (1) not waste time in searching for information that will never be either obtainable or useful and (2) have a good idea of when there is sufficient information available to make a decision.

Although this book addresses some admittedly challenging topics, it is notable that none of these is new. All have been investigated previously by scientists, philosophers, theologians, psychologists, logicians, mathematicians, statisticians, and social scientists, among others. What is quite remarkable, however, is that the bulk of the previous works in these different fields have not ventured to assemble all of these diverse perspectives into a single compendium that specifically addresses the key issue of what we can know and how this impacts our ability to predict the future.

Accordingly, although some of this book strays into theoretical territory, none of it presupposes any prior knowledge of physics, philosophy, psychology, physiology, mathematics, or statistics. All it requires is a degree of inquisitiveness, a willingness to weigh basic arguments, and a reasonable facility with ordinary language. It deliberately avoids the use of mathematics beyond that of simple arithmetic and basic algebra in the appendix.

As an aid to the reader, the final chapter of the book provides a brief synopsis of the salient material and conclusions from each of the preceding chapters. If a particular chapter is viewed as overly challenging, the reader should skip to these brief chapter overviews, which maintain the flow of the material while reducing it to its core elements.

If this sounds appealing, then by all means read on.

Gerard G. Nahum, MD

ACKNOWLEDGMENT

I would like to especially thank several individuals who reviewed early versions of this book and provided challenges and questions to help improve its accuracy, completeness, and transparency—Dr. C. Gerlinger (Germany), Dr. M. Kunz (Germany), and Dr. K.Q. Pham (United States—for providing technical assistance with several of the figures).

PART 1
BACKGROUND

CHAPTER 1
The Past, the Present, and the Future

The Past, the Present, and the Future

Past: Definition (Merriam-Webster Dictionary)

- Having existed or taken place in a period before the present: bygone
- Just gone or elapsed

Present: Definition (Merriam-Webster Dictionary)

- At or during this time: now

Future: Definition (Merriam-Webster Dictionary)

- That is to be
- Of, relating to, or constituting a time yet to come
- Existing or occurring at a later time

The past is unchangeable, the present is fleeting, and the future is difficult to predict. These are truisms to which everyone can relate. They make life a challenge. And we all spend much of our lives trying to orchestrate aspects of the present to make the future seem more certain.

Yogi Berra, the great American baseball legend, stated famously that "it is difficult to make predictions, especially about the future." We all try to predict what will occur in our lives. It is not for lack of trying that we cannot always control sequences of events, especially in the long-run but even in the short-term. In fact, we routinely orchestrate events in the present in an attempt to influence what we would like to see happen in the future. But despite our best efforts, everything doesn't always go according to plan. The question is why? The aim of this book is to provide a brief but comprehensive answer to this question.

It doesn't matter what we think about the future; regardless of whether we hope it will be the same or different, we routinely use the present as a "launching point" for assessing the possibilities that the future may hold. This requires us making a profound but little-appreciated assumption: that at least some aspects of the present are stable and will be carried through into the future unchanged.* Without stability as a backdrop, there is no benchmark for assessing change, and, therefore, there would be no way to establish the relationships among objects and events. Consider this: if everything were always in flux, it would be impossible to determine if any specific object (or event) was associated with (or causally related to) anything else. So, although we seldom dwell on it, we use the idea of stability as a starting point—a platform, if you will—to gauge the state of the future and to assess if it is the same or changed relative to the present and the past.

We all believe that we can influence at least some of the events that occur around us. Sometimes it appears that we are successful in doing this, and at other times it seems that all of our best efforts have no effect. We tend to categorize the first set of circumstances as falling within our *sphere of influence* and the others as being *outside our control*. But, the question is: Where is the dividing line? Does it really exist? And if so, is it hard and fast or is it malleable and potentially movable?

Importantly, how can we be certain if we ever truly influence future events or if they were always destined to occur in just the way they did despite all of our interventions? The other side of this same question is: How can we be certain that our actions—no matter how innocuous they might seem—*did not* affect the occurrences of the future, even if these are remotely separated from us in time or in space?

This book tries to provide a framework of explanation as to why we find ourselves in the situations we do concerning our ability (or inability) to predict and influence the future. It illustrates why the predicaments we run across often have much more to do with the fundamental physical constraints of the universe we live in than anything man-made.

The limitations concerning our ability to predict the future involve a core set of factors that can be briefly summarized as follows:

- the degree to which the universe is stable and smooth (as opposed to any predisposition it may have toward discontinuities and chaotic behaviors)
- the types and scope of the information we can access
- the intrinsic accuracy and precision—as well as the consistency and completeness—of the information we have to work with
- the accuracy and precision of the methods we use to process and analyze the information we possess
- the accuracy and precision of our interpretations of the information that is available to us
- how well we can place the information we work with into a complete context
- the opportunities we have for acting on the information we possess
- how well the results of our actions can be predicted, based on the intrinsic accuracy, precision, and completeness of:

    a) our information about the physical universe
    b) our analysis of the information to which we are privy
    c) our understanding of the results of our analyses
    d) the domains over which our understanding is applicable
    e) the degree of control we have over our actions
    f) the predictability and scope of the results of our interactions with our surroundings.

With regard to all of these, we are fascinatingly hamstrung by the physical constraints of our universe—much more so than we generally think about or would like to admit.

These issues compel us to ask other fundamental questions, among them:

- How much information about the universe is *accessible* to us?
- How much can we *know* about the information to which we have access?
- How much of what we know about this information can we *understand*?
- What is the *scope* of our understanding, and over what *domains* does it apply?
- How much of what we know and understand can we *act* upon?
- How much *choice* do we have over our actions?
- How intrinsically *precise* are the actions that we take?
- How *predictable* are the *consequences* of the events that we trigger by our actions?
- What are the *limits of* the *effects* of our actions?

All of these are weighty questions, but they are all approachable and answerable, at least to an extent that should make us feel comfortable.

By the end of this book, the reader should be able to address the following three questions successfully:

1. What can we *know*?
2. If there is an external *Truth* (with a capital T—i.e., one that is independent of our perception of it), how does what we know (and believe) relate to it?
3. How does our *understanding* of what we know help us to *predict* the *future*, as well as the *impact* of our *actions* upon it?

If the reader can address these questions and arrive at a successful conclusion for each, then the goal of this book has been accomplished.

> *Or, if they are changed, that they are at least changed in a way that is predictable, such that they can act as a legitimate point of reference.

CHAPTER 2
Predicting the Future: What We All Strive to Do

Predicting the future: Is it an art, a science, or something else?

Predict: Definition (Merriam-Webster Dictionary)

- To declare or indicate in advance; *especially*: foretell on the basis of observation, experience, or scientific reason

We all want to have some degree of comfort regarding certainty in our lives. Whether or not we like it, everyone has needs and desires; these compel us to *assess current circumstances, establish future goals* (sometimes short-term, sometimes in the long-run), and *devise plans* (i.e., *actions*) to make the future unfold in the ways we want it to. To do so requires making *predictions*.

This is not to suggest that we need to be clairvoyant or omniscient about what is to come, only that we count on many occurrences to happen in a fairly predictable fashion. Most of us don't think about it much, but our predictions presuppose a backdrop of *stability* in the environment that surrounds us. Though most of us would agree that it is harder to predict events a long time into the future than in the near-term, we nevertheless like to believe that we have some kind of a handle on events that are yet to come. Sometimes, we even employ sophisticated analytical schemes or place *confidence limits* around what we believe the *range* of *possible future occurrences* might be.

For instance, we all expect that the sun will rise in the morning every day for the next year—and in essentially the same way that it did yesterday, the day before that, and for each day of many millennia beforehand. And we also count on the likelihood that any future disaster (e.g., a devastating earthquake, volcanic eruption, meteor strike, etc.—all rare events) will not be global enough in its impact to completely destroy all of the earth's long-established structures and ecosystems. Likewise, we generally believe (except in extraordinary cases) that whatever desirable aspects of our own social circumstances we wish to maintain will remain more or less the same tomorrow as they are today, although we may expect (or even plan) that there will be some changes. But in general, we don't expect that these changes in our lives will be so dramatic as to make our existences tomorrow completely unrecognizable compared to the way they are today.

We count on all of these and other circumstances about the future implicitly. And we make our plans around them happening (such as the sun rising) or not happening (as in the case of a cataclysmic tsunami) with a degree of assurance that depends on our confidence in carrying *past* events and circumstances *through* the *present* and into the *future* in a *smooth* fashion.

But the question is: What allows us to do this? Is it simply that the alternative sets of circumstances constitute historically low-frequency events that—despite their having a potentially large impact—occur so *rarely* that we can *ignore* them? Or is it because we believe that the "playing field" where we operate (i.e., our universe) is of an intrinsically smooth nature that is sufficiently stable (i.e., non-chaotic) to avoid such outcomes? Or perhaps is it that we believe our knowledge about current circumstances and the way that these existing states transition from the present into the future is so accurate, precise, and predictable that we can detect something amiss long before it happens, thereby providing us with an opportunity to take corrective actions to avert undesirable outcomes?

The latter proposition is obviously not true at a universal level—we generally do not, and cannot, plan in advance for serious accidents, deaths, natural disasters, political upheavals, economic calamities, etc. But we generally tend to behave in our day-to-day lives as if these types of turmoil (i.e., *discontinuities*) do not occur. Some people (and institutions) that specialize in disaster planning attempt to do this. But, they can only make plans for certain sets of contingencies that are well-characterized—i.e., those that fall within certain well-defined limits. For instance, consider the example of trying to "earthquake proof" buildings in California. This is a laudable goal that has a long history, but what does it actually mean? For those of us who are not structural engineers, earthquake-proofing standards are difficult to interpret, so a hypothetical example will suffice: Let us say that buildings are mandated to be constructed to resist the forces that can occur in a strong earthquake of up to a magnitude 7.0 (on the Richter scale, which is one type of a logarithmic scale that grades the magnitude of seismic activity). This provides a well-defined framework that is easily interpretable. But, what if an earthquake of magnitude 8.0 were to occur (i.e., one ten times more forceful)? The answer is that no degree of earthquake proofing for a magnitude 7.0 earthquake would be good enough to systematically resist the larger forces that would occur under those more dire circumstances. They simply fall outside the bounds of what was planned for. The consequence is that many of those earthquake-proof buildings would tumble.

Interestingly, the opposite of what I have just outlined as our general operating procedure—that of making predictions based on the belief of smoothness that carries through from the past, through the present, and into the future—is not how we view the universe. Most of us (professional disaster-planning specialists aside) do not plan our lives around the occurrence of calamities. We prefer to operate within smooth domains—those that are readily predictable and where small changes in inputs result in commensurate changes in outputs, with a minimal impact to the overall *system* (i.e., the larger platform where everything occurs).

In fact, most people shun the opposite circumstance, where disproportionate responses occur in the face of small changes. We routinely try to protect ourselves against such unexpected intrusions into our otherwise stable lives—whether natural or man-made. Most of us regard such unbalanced responses as unsettling, if not frankly disruptive.

However, there are many examples of disproportionate responses to incremental changes. A good example involving human intervention is when someone inadvertently nudges a glass off a table so that it goes crashing to the floor and shatters (figure 1). It takes only a very small force to tip the glass off the edge of the table, but the initial (interventional) force is multiplied dramatically when the potential energy of the glass is converted into kinetic energy (by gravity acting upon it over the distance of the height of the table from the floor). Even if the intent was to move the glass a small distance, it was not to have it fall off the table and break. When this happens, it represents something unexpected—and the result is a *discontinuity*. The sequence of events precipitates an *irreversible consequence*, in the sense that the glass cannot be made to come back together again spontaneously (for a further discussion concerning the reasons for this type of irreversibility, see chapter 19, entitled "Dynamic Certainty vs. Uncertainty: Trajectories," and chapter 20, entitled "Thermodynamics: Laws Prohibiting the Spontaneous Reversibility of Physical Events").

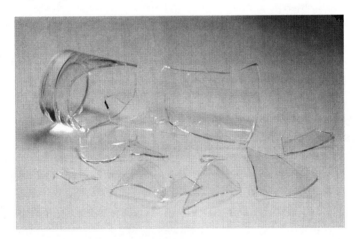

Figure 1: Example of a discontinuity
The result of a glass falling on a solid floor—it shatters.

Another example can be cited from the social realm, where the consequences of current events are often less predictable than we would like. One such arena involves political negotiations, where there are frequently complicated and overlapping issues. Here, there can often be *unintended consequences* associated with decisions and agreements, sometimes resulting in inconsistencies that precipitate the need for further negotiations (in the best of circumstances) or wars (in the worst).

I will argue later that these types of circumstances do not occur simply as a result of incomplete information regarding the situations under discussion or their intrinsic levels of complication (although these may certainly prove contributory in specific cases). In addition, they are related to:

1. the intrinsic *imprecision* of available *information*
2. *inexactitudes* in the *methodologies* used for *describing* and *encoding information*
3. imbedded *inconsistencies* due to the *incompleteness* of information
4. the *limits* of *logic*-based *analytical* techniques
5. the *restricted context* we have for making *interpretations*, and
6. the *limited understanding* we have of both *current circumstances* and the *consequences* of our *actions*.

Despite these constraints, most of us expect to have surety and stability about the future, especially concerning ourselves, our families, and our communities, as well as our health, employment, finances, homes, and climate—to name just a few. And, whenever this does not happen, we tend to search for explanations as to why an "aberration" occurred—not the other way around.

Our expectations about the future are predicated on several core assumptions, including the following:

- The *present* (i.e., the initial condition) is *well-known* and *well-characterized*;
- *Initial conditions* can be used as a *starting point* to predict the future;
- *Causality* (i.e., consequences resulting from interactions among physical entities) is the *universal instrument of change* that dictates the direction, pace, and outcome of all that will occur in the future;
- The universe is *intrinsically stable* (i.e., the place where we exist is not prone to large or recurrent discontinuities and divergences that are intrinsically unpredictable); and

- We *know* and *understand* both the *initial conditions* (i.e., the starting points) and the *rules of change* (i.e., the physical laws) where we operate—at least well enough to account for all the factors that might influence our ability to predict what will happen next.

In sum, what these assumptions mean is that if we *know* the *present conditions accurately* and with sufficient precision—and if we *believe in causality* as the universal instrument of change—then we can *predict* how the present will *evolve* into the future. This was the view of the universe espoused by the great French thinker René Descartes and other rationalist philosophers—one where the universe was likened to a finely tuned watch, with change occurring into the future in a deterministic, predictable, and unmodifiable way. In essence, the schema is that once all of the initial conditions (i.e., the *states*—the positions and momenta of all matter) and *forces* in the universe are defined precisely at any particular instant, there is no longer any ambiguity about the future (or the past)—it is determined in accordance with the *initial state* of the universe at any particular time, and it can be run either forward or backward in time with equal predictive accuracy. If this were the case, then the implication (by analogy) would be that we would be reduced to mere pawns on a chessboard, being moved around in arcane ways to accomplish a master intent without us knowing the overall plan and without any regard for our (individual) safety or purpose.

As simple as some of these assumptions about the universe may appear, the implications associated with their not being satisfied are actually quite complicated. They result in our having inaccurate reflections of reality, both individually and collectively. I will point out later that these assumptions and other related issues are much more idealizations than they are realities. They are not things that we can know—or can even hope to have information about (in some cases)—with the required degree of accuracy and precision that would be necessary to use them to predict the future successfully. These limitations apply both to the measurement of *things* (i.e., physical *objects* and *events*) and to the *rules* (i.e., *physical laws*) that govern their evolution.

Why is this important? Quite simply, it is because it influences each and every facet of our lives, bar none. These considerations do not simply constitute an academic exercise or "science for science's sake." They have implications far beyond the domains that are typically included under the rubrics of both empirical and theoretical science. In fact, they have a profound impact on what we can know about who we are and what we represent (now), in addition to what we can *expect* (in the future).

We all make predictions each and every moment of our lives. We do so when we walk (so we don't misgauge the surface underfoot and fall down), drive a car (so we don't crash into other traffic), lift a saucepan (so we don't spill its contents), plan a vacation (so we get to where we want to go and enjoy what we hope to experience). We also do it when we choose a spouse (we expect happiness and fulfillment), pick a career (we generally expect gratification and a certain degree of remuneration), or have a child (too complicated to describe!). In each instance, our reasoning revolves around an individual calculus that is complex but always involves predictions about the future. To accomplish this, we depend on what we *know* at this moment in order to construct (i.e., *deduce*) other *truths* that we then depend on to decide on our proper course of *action*. These are then designed to influence the course of subsequent events and outcomes (i.e., the future).

What has just been described is a game of prediction that we cannot ignore. Although it has sometimes been described as a set of direct one-to-one cause-and-effect relationships or correspondences, it actually represents a much more complicated matrix (i.e., web) of interactions. The questions are: Can we do it? What do we rely on to do it? And how can we do it better?

CHAPTER 3

Agency: Free Will vs. Determinism

The freedom to make choices: Do we have it or not?

Agency: Definition (Merriam-Webster Dictionary)

- A person or thing through which power is exerted or an end is achieved

Free Will: Definition (Merriam-Webster Dictionary)

- Voluntary choice or decision
- Freedom to make choices that are not determined by prior causes or divine intervention

Determinism: Definition (Merriam-Webster Dictionary)

- The quality or state of being determined
- A theory or doctrine that acts of the will, occurrences in nature, or social or psychological phenomena are causally determined by preceding events or natural laws
- A belief in predestination

The image of the universe constructed by the rationalist philosophers of the seventeenth century was akin to a finely tuned watch: once the nascent universe was first set into motion, the natural laws of the universe completely determined its future trajectory. Underlying this was the notion of *causality*—that one set of events causes the next, which causes the next, and so on, which made this outcome seem both necessary and inescapable (see chapter 4, entitled "Causality: Linking Events Separated by Time and Space," for further discussion).

From a practical standpoint, this means that if one could assemble all the information about the universe at any particular instant (i.e., the precise *positions* and *momenta* of all objects) and also knew all of the *rules* concerning the physical interactions among them (i.e., the effects of all of the *forces* acting on them), then constructing an accurate view of the future would be reduced to an exercise in mere *calculation* (at least in principle). Such a schema would make the future (and the past) both entirely transparent and predictable.

This mechanistic view of the universe was championed by the rationalist French philosopher René Descartes. It was subsequently adopted by many other philosophers, mathematicians, and physical scientists, including the inventor of classical mechanics, Sir Isaac Newton. It has proved to be an extremely useful way of viewing the universe; it has been used to successfully describe and accurately predict the planetary motions, as well as the evolution of many other physical systems.

This *deterministic* view constitutes one of the major underpinnings of classical physics. It has some very appealing features, including its wide-ranging success as a tool to both model and understand the relationships among objects and events, especially as they evolve over time. Because of this, it has come to serve as the basis for scientific inquiry and scientific standards of proof. However, despite its many practical successes, it also creates a major issue as a by-product: How can this deterministic view be reconciled with the idea of *free will*? The very notion of free will presupposes a *freedom to operate* that is unconstrained by mere physical precedent and the necessities arising from well-defined physical interactions.

This apparent contradiction can be reduced to two opposing questions:

1. If the universe is *deterministic*, then how can there be room for any type of *choice*, which represents the hallmark of *free will* (because this would necessarily violate the principle of determinism)?
2. If there is *free will*, then how can the universe be *deterministic*, as there are choices that if made differently would unavoidably *alter* future *trajectories* (which is not permitted in a deterministic universe, as everything depends precisely and predictably on the state that occurred immediately prior, ad infinitum)?

To make these two arguments concrete, consider the following examples.

First, if the universe is deterministic and if we are faced with a situation where we believe that we have the free will to make a choice, then when we ultimately make the choice, how can it ever be construed that it was really a free choice at all? In other words, since the consequences of having made the choice differently would be that the universe would have necessarily evolved along a different path, was the choice we made merely an *illusion* when, in fact, we were always predestined to make the one that we ultimately made?

This type of a schema would provide for the *illusion* of *free will*—as well as the *perceived necessity* for making a *choice*—without violating the basic tenants of determinism (i.e., we did exactly what we were meant to do all along despite having the ill-founded feeling that we had the ability to do something else if we had really wanted to). If this were the reality for our universe, novelty and spontaneous action would be real only from our own (myopic) *human point of view*, but not from the perspective of the universe as a whole, where they were determined and *always known*.

This perspective is not as fanciful as it might seem. For instance, since the idea of free will ultimately depends on thought, we must consider what the underlying processes are in our minds that allow us to perceive it in the way we do.

There are cells in our brains (called *neurons*) that act upon each other (generally through the release of neurochemicals) to allow for the integration of incoming information. This results in minute transmembrane ion fluxes that generate small localized membrane depolarizations. When a minimum threshold of depolarization is reached via the time-dependent integration of these incoming signals, a self-perpetuating depolarization sequence is initiated that propagates down the long axis of the neuron (its axon) and on to junctions with other cells. This latter step occurs via a standardized moving *action potential*, which results in the signal being passed to other cells for further integration and processing. This last set of events is typically accomplished through the release of chemicals across *synapses* between these excitable types of cells. The net effect of these manipulations of incident information is to place it into forms in our brains that are ultimately responsible for everything we characterize as mental phenomena (i.e., recognition, emotion, memory, ideation, etc.) and (finally) thoughts—including those that we have about the issue of free will.

Thus, our brains represent complex *information processing systems* that are a hybrid between *digital transmission* systems (i.e., via the axonal transmission of all-or-none action potentials) and the more flexible *analogue-type* of *signal integration systems* that exist at the level of postsynaptic cell membranes (where there is local integration of small depolarizations that result from neurotransmitter-mediated ion fluxes). All of these steps are describable in rigorous scientific terms, making them examples—at least in principle—of *deterministic* processes. If this is the case, then it would seem to be an inescapable conclusion that all of our *thoughts* are *deterministically based*—with one resulting from the last, which resulted from the one before that, etc.—in a sequence of completely predictable precedent, as well as future occurrences.

All of this raises an important question: Is what we *think* (and *believe*, including our presumption of free will) just a highly scripted deterministic set of processes to create a *mind-set* (or a set of *illusions*) that includes the concept of free will? Or, alternatively, are we really free to make choices and do as we please? The challenge here is that to distinguish between the two possibilities of "imagined free will" on the one hand versus "actual free will" on the other, we would need to design some type of a test. But, both these varieties of free will would (1) be perceived by us in exactly the same way and (2) result (ultimately) in us performing precisely the same sets of actions as a consequence of our (same) thoughts. So, what could be imagined as a test (i.e., a gold standard) to allow us to distinguish between the two? What hypothesis, exactly, could we attempt to falsify? Since we would ultimately be designing an investigation to test ourselves—the thinking beings who must also act as the final arbiters to make a determination of which of these two circumstances is actually the case—this is a task that involves circular reasoning, which makes it very difficult to accomplish, if not impossible.

Consider the following: If free will is real, and if we wish to make sure that particular events occur, then why are we so often constrained by the *rules* of the universe (i.e., the laws of physics), which routinely thwart our sincerest desires and intentions? Aren't the physical rules of the universe that are at odds with our desires somehow acting to constrain and impede our free will, which shouldn't be constrained at all if it were truly free? And, if so, aren't the rules that do this type of constraining ultimately outside of our control, inviolable and, therefore, deterministic?

The preceding arguments would seem to suggest that it is more difficult to defend the concept of free will than determinism. They also suggest that it is difficult to imagine a middle ground between the two. Both the ideas of determinism and free will seem to be incapable of independently explaining what we perceive to be reality or to admit of the other as a possibility. However, both conceptualizations may merely be flawed idealizations of a reality that is more complex.

To explain this, I will describe two scenarios that appear to blur the seemingly sharp distinction between these two worldviews.

The first is a consideration of perspective. What if there is simply a *local information deficit* that denies us as individuals the necessary information to recognize the deterministic structure of the greater universe? From our current knowledge of the physical universe, it appears at both a theoretical and a practical level that we cannot have access to all of the information that exists (see chapter 25, entitled "Absolutes vs. Relatives: Relativity Theory," for further discussion). Given this constraint, every decision point at a local level would arise from local indeterminacy, at least part of which would result from the limitation of local *information incompleteness* and not because of any universal lack of determinism. Thus, determinism could be operative at a universal level while our more local view might admit of a seeming need to make decisions due to an entirely *locally perceived need* to *choose*. Despite this *illusion* at a local level, there is no actual such need because the ultimate outcome is already fully determined and known on a universal scale; however, it is *unknown* on a more truncated local scale until it actually occurs.

The second issue that makes reality more complex relates to *idealizations* of our view of the physical universe, including mathematical idealizations such as the concept of *points*, the ability to perform physical *measurements* to *arbitrary limits of precision*, and the presumption of *smoothness* (i.e., continuity) as governing the relationships among objects and events. Each of these has implications for whether the universe is deterministic (including with respect to ourselves!) or if there are alternatives that allow for free will (i.e., choice). As has just been outlined, if the underlying structure of the universe is deterministic, but there is no way for us to have access to sufficient information about it to be able to accurately predict the ways in which it will operate, then it would appear to us that it were not deterministic and that we had the ability to change (i.e., impact) outcomes (i.e., events) as a result of actions we could freely choose. Each of these items (i.e., mathematical idealization, the idea of arbitrarily high precision in measurement, and continuity) has implications for whether there is determinism versus free will, and each will be discussed in more detail in the chapters that follow.

The question that results from all these considerations can be framed as follows: What if the idea of *deterministic trajectories*, which is the universal underlying presumption of classical (i.e., Newtonian) mechanics, is an idealization that has no single corresponding physical incarnate, but rather that *sets* of trajectories exist and simply *average* to the single values that we measure? We might be blinded to this circumstance because of our inability to resolve the different underlying spectrums of trajectories, which would deny us the ability to view them as composites with separate underlying components. If this were the case, it would mean that there is actually no single deterministic set of temporally ordered events that would result from a series of prior interactions, but rather an ever-increasing number of sets of possibilities that would expand (if they were divergent instead of convergent) with each event in the sequence. If this were so, then which of the panoply of possible states would be most likely to occur at each juncture going forward? Would this reduce to simply a statistically-weighted version of single trajectory determinism, or would there be divergences and *non-normalizable* conditions that would make the process give rise to something fundamentally different, thereby creating entryways into more uncertain (i.e., incalculable) or *chaotic* domains? If so, would this open the door for the concept of free will as a consequence?

Beyond these considerations, there are additional theoretical and practical limitations concerning (1) the inability to collect all of the information about the universe in a single place at a single instant (due to the local inaccessibility of portions of the universe's information for all observers), as well as (2) being unable to analyze available information any faster than the universe itself evolves and moves forward (because of the relativistic prohibition against processes progressing at faster than light speed—see chapter 25, entitled "Absolutes vs. Relatives: Relativity Theory," for further discussion).

If all these constraints, both theoretical and practical, result in impossibilities from a physical standpoint, then what does this say for the possibility of determinism and free will? Can it be that it is precisely due to these physical constraints and limitations that the idea of *universal determinism* on the one hand and of *local free will* on the other are not at odds with each other and may be able to coexist?

The aim of this chapter has been to outline potential paths forward toward the reconciliation of the apparent conflicts between the two concepts of determinism and free will. It has shown why neither is a self-sufficient theory for explaining all that we perceive to be the reality of our universe, or our roles in it. The chapters that follow will shed more light on the additional factors that bear upon this issue.

CHAPTER 4

Causality: Linking Events Separated by Time and Space

Are events related to one another in causal chains (or webs) that depend on interactions?

Causality: Definition (Merriam-Webster Dictionary)

- The relationship between a cause and its effect or between regularly correlated events or phenomena

Time: Definition (Merriam-Webster Dictionary)

- The measured or measurable period during which an action, process, or condition exists or continues: duration
- A nonspatial continuum that is measured in terms of events which succeed one another from past through present to future
- The point or period when something occurs: occasion

Space: Definition (Merriam-Webster Dictionary)

- A boundless three-dimensional extent in which objects and events occur and have relative position and direction
- A limited extent in one, two, or three dimensions: distance, area, volume
- Physical space independent of what occupies it—called also absolute space
- A set of mathematical elements and especially of abstractions of all the points on a line, in a plane, or in physical space

The idea of *causation* is simple: it is that one event has an *effect* on another. The concept is important because it undergirds the belief that individual events do not occur in isolation. This implies that they are somehow connected to each other and that events can have consequences (i.e., effects on other objects and events). This notion may appear simple but it is extremely important. It relies on other assumptions that are often overlooked, many of which are neither simple nor obvious.

Without the idea of causation, there is no obvious way to link or *connect* objects and events in the *present* to others that will occur in the *future* (or have occurred in the past). Accordingly, the concept of causation is a fundamental principle in Western philosophical thought. As such, it serves as a basis for scientific inquiry and explanation, which represents a cornerstone in the way that Western cultures routinely perceive objects and events to relate to each other (notably some other cultures, especially in the Far East, have philosophical traditions that have embraced other types of relatedness and interaction paradigms).

More technically, the term causation describes the nature of the relationship existing between two distinct objects or events when they are *linked*. One is referred to as the *cause* and the other the *effect*, with the second considered a consequence of the first. Importantly, for a causal relationship between two events to be possible, the two must be *separated*. This separation involves the interposition of either time or space (or both). Although we most often think of causally related events as separated in time, such events can also occur contemporaneously. In this latter case, they are separated from each other by an intervening distance (i.e., space).

When causally-related objects or events are separated in time, the first (the *cause*) necessarily precedes (i.e., exists before) the second (the *effect*). In cases where objects or events occur contemporaneously, the lack of temporality in the relationship makes it uncertain which of the two should be considered the cause and which the effect. In these cases, it must be asked whether they are simply associated with each other, or if one is the cause of the other.

The idea of *temporal causality* is easy, because we all understand and have direct experience with it. However, *contemporaneous causality* is not something that we typically think of in the same way. As an example, consider a suspension bridge. Such bridges have a large number of components, such as foundations, towers, cables, roadways, etc. Each of these contributes to the internal integrity and supports the overall structure, such that the bridge is able to maintain its strength, configuration, etc. All of these different elements are discrete, yet they interact on a contemporaneous basis to ensure the maintenance of the overall structure. They all represent only parts that have various functions, not the totality of the bridge. What they do is act together—in concert and contemporaneously—to "cause" the suspension bridge to occur. And if any of these critical elements were to be taken away, it would compromise the integrity of the greater structure of which they are a part (the bridge), which might very well result in its collapse.

For *causality* of any type to be established, a stringent set of criteria must be fulfilled beyond those required for a mere association (for a detailed discussion of this distinction, including the classical temporal causality criteria promulgated by Sir Bradford Hill, see Chapter 10, entitled "Associations vs. Causality"). This is because, even in the case of sequential events, it is often uncertain whether the occurrences are merely associated with each other (albeit in a temporal sequence), or if the first actually caused the second.

Conflicting opinions regarding the issue of causality extend as far back as Aristotle, with many of these remaining unresolved today. For the current discussion, our working definition of causality is that well-circumscribed objects and events can have effects (i.e., *outside influences*) on others. The full extent of these effects may not be known, but they are generally thought to have their largest impact over other objects and events that occur *locally* (i.e., those that exist nearby in time and space, making them *accessible*).

This last idea concerning *locality* represents a lingering final vestige of pre-quantum mechanical philosophical thought that will be examined in more detail in subsequent chapters. Although the idea of locality may appear to be self-evident at a practical level, it may nonetheless be ill-founded and incorrect (see chapter 22, entitled "Entanglement vs. Separability: The Locality Issue," for further discussion).

By explaining the idea of causality in this way, a key question concerning its premises arises: Just how separable are objects and events into discrete entities, such that they can be considered intrinsically distinct (i.e., where does one object or event "end" and another "begin")? This, in turn, brings up the idea of what separates objects and events from each other. From this, two additional notions arise, both of which have already been mentioned: those of time and space.

The idea is simple: for any particular event (or object) to have an effect on any other, the two must be distinct, which means that they must be separate (otherwise they would merely be a continuation of one-in-the-same thing). And, by definition, the separation that occurs between well-circumscribed events (and objects) must arise as a result of something that intervenes—time, or space, or both.

There is a long history of philosophical and scientific thought concerning the nature of time and space. For our current purpose, it is sufficient to know that time and space were once thought to be fundamentally separate entities but that this view changed during the early twentieth century with the advent of Einstein's special theory of relativity. This theory has since been experimentally verified to a very high degree of accuracy. One of its core elements is the idea that differences in time can be *traded* for differences in space, and vice versa (all according to certain well-defined rules). These trade-offs depend only on the particular inertial frames of reference of different observers (see chapter 25, entitled "Absolutes vs. Relatives: Relativity Theory," for further discussion).

Based on current theory, time can be treated as simply another dimension that is analogous to those of space. Accordingly (and consistent with experimental findings), these can all be either dilated or foreshortened as a consequence of the relative motions of different observers. Because of this, ideas concerning which events are *simultaneous* and which follow others can be different depending on the particular point of view that is taken by individual observers. However, there is a great equalizer that is a universal constant: the speed of light (which refers to its speed in a vacuum). As long as this speed is not exceeded (which relativity theory asserts that it cannot), it is not possible for any causal event that occurs prior to a consequence to be viewed as occurring afterward in any frame of reference.

This is reassuring, to say the least. If this were not the case (i.e., if it were possible for causally-related events to occur in *reverse order* for observers viewing them from different frames of reference) then it would be impossible for any object or event to be causally related to anything else from a temporal point of view. And if, in the end, we cannot believe in temporally dependent causal relationships—the idea that antecedent events are what cause others to happen subsequently—then what other ideas remain for us to have confidence in? This question is worth pondering because if temporal causality were to be negated as a concept, then what else might we believe in as an alternative? This notion is so ingrained in Western philosophical thought that if it were to be expunged, there would likely be little else to replace it (at least nothing that is immediately obvious or that comports with our common sense experience or the findings of scientific experiments).

From both a practical and theoretical standpoint, it is seldom (if ever?) that a single event is the only one that has an effect on what occurs subsequently. Given that there are generally many events occurring simultaneously (in at least some inertial frames of reference) and that many (if not all) can have influences on others, the idea of a *causal nexus* has arisen to describe when collections of objects and events (i.e., causes) converge to produce some type of *resultant effect*. Such causal nexuses can *converge* in multiple ways at the same time, and in different ways at different times, to affect many other events. This idea can be imagined as a web of interacting causal factors that have a net set of outputs that affect other objects and events (or phenomena) at particular times.

Another interesting aspect concerning causal relationships is that even though they *can* track uniformly in a particular direction in either time or in space, there is nothing intrinsic to the idea of causality that says that they must. If, instead, they "loop" around rather than project straight ahead, then they can have the potential to completely circle back upon themselves. This is referred to as a *causality loop*.

Some confusion exists about the idea of causality loops. For instance, there are "positive" and "negative" *feedback loops* that have been described in natural science, engineering, psychology, economics, politics, etc. These are different than causality loops, because the so-called feedback loops are not truly complete *loops*, which makes the choice of terminology unfortunate. The positive and negative feedback loops can be thought of as "helices that advance through time". In the diagrammatic representation of this concept (see figure 2), the central axis of the helix represents the progression of time, and the helix itself represents the evolution of events as they wind around the time axis (thereby providing a "corkscrew-type" of evolution that represents the time-dependent evolution of events). The key here is that time always marches forward and never backward, so that events cannot land back upon some preexisting "inciting cause" to modify it. This means that the sequence of events is not a true loop (in time), but a forward-moving helix of non time-overlapping events that exist in a causally linked chain. These sets of sequential events can sometimes appear very similar, but they are not time-identical events, as each step in the process advances inexorably in the forward direction of advancing time.

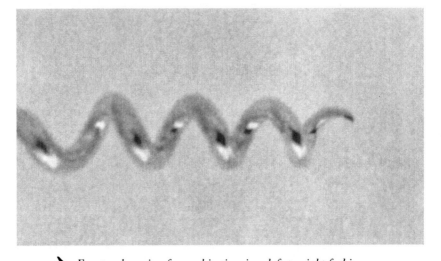

⟶ *Events advancing forward in time in a left-to-right fashion*

Figure 2: *Helical representation of events as they progress forward through time*

Any "feedback" that involves prior states does not go backward in time. All such effects result from interactions that progress monotonically forward with advancing time (in the left to right direction).

An example can be cited of a so-called *positive* or *negative feedback loop*: if event A causes event B, and event B causes event C, and event C causes a *new* event A_1 (similar in all respects to event A), then these events are said to be in a feedback loop. In this case, as long as all of the events march along in a forward direction in time, sequential (i.e., iterative) feedback occurs (either positive or negative), but there is no (backward) "time looping" as part of this process.

This rather straightforward idea of an ordinary feedback loop is fundamentally different from the previously described *temporal causality loop*. The two should not be confused. In this latter case, a specific *inciting cause* also becomes *a consequence* of the events that it affects (see figure 3).

⟶ *Time advances in a forward direction in a left-to-right fashion*

Figure 3: Temporal causality loop

Events advance forward in time in a left-to-right fashion and recede backward in time in a right-to-left fashion. In a temporal causality loop, the effect (shown on the right of the diagram) that occurs in response to an inciting cause (shown on the left of the diagram) feeds back in time to affect its own original cause, which can have an impact on the effect.

Temporal causality loops can be imagined as going forward and then backward in time, forming closed time-like curves. These paths have been referred to as *worldlines* through the combined dimensions of space and time (which is also referred to as *space-time*). Solutions exist to the equations of general relativity to describe space-times that contain these types of closed time-like curves (e.g., Gödel space-time), but the physical plausibility of these solutions is uncertain. Nonetheless, the worldlines that emerge from these solutions constitute closed time-like loops, which have the effect of permitting the consequences of events to return to their own past. To date, these are only theoretical (i.e., there is no experimental evidence for their existence), but this type of a loop effectively has events feeding circularly backward, so that they go backward in time.

Although ordinary feedback loops can be readily imagined when causally related objects and events march ahead together in time (or when they occur contemporaneously with a separation in space), the concept is much more difficult (and less certain) when they form a temporal causality loop. If these latter types of loops were to occur, then the objects and events themselves would be separated in time, but they would exist in a closed time loop that could be, nevertheless, non-recurrent. This would admit the possibility of potential *contradictions* (i.e., that some objects and events could both occur and not occur at the same time).

As an example, if the event A that occurred in the past was the accidental death of a person, then looping back to event A would necessarily involve looping back to a time where there is a (potential) risk of changing what occurred previously (i.e., changing past events—in this case, that the person might emerge from the accident alive instead of dead). If that occurred, an event in the present would feed back to change an event in the past, thereby creating a so-called *temporal causality violation*. If such types of temporal causality violations were to occur, they could result in inconsistencies and paradoxes (one of which is referred to as a *predestination paradox*—see below for an example).

Can such temporal causality violations actually occur? The simple answer is: probably not. There are physical laws that impose directionality on temporal sequences of events, and these would appear to preclude such time-reversed situations from occurring. One such constraint is the second law of thermodynamics,* which states that whenever (real) processes proceed *spontaneously* in the forward direction (in time), there is always the creation of increasing amounts of *entropy*. The idea of entropy can be likened to the idea of disorder, such that when events occur spontaneously (i.e., in the forward time direction), they create an increased overall state of disorder for the *combination* of the thermodynamically isolated system (i.e., the system under consideration) *plus* its surrounding environment. The reverse cannot occur spontaneously, because an increased state of order must be generated to re-create the original circumstance; this requires the expenditure (i.e., addition) of outside energy to the system, which must come from the surrounding environment (see chapter 20, entitled "Thermodynamics: Laws Prohibiting the Spontaneous Reversibility of Physical Events," for further discussion).

As a tangible example of why it is not possible for causality to "run backward," imagine again a glass falling off a table and shattering on the floor. The intact glass on the table represents a highly ordered structure with relatively low system *entropy* and relatively high *potential energy* (note: both the system entropy and potential energy are always *relative* to other states that the system might assume, and not something absolute—for a further discussion, see chapter 26, entitled "Energy"). The shattered glass on the floor has fragments that are less well ordered than in the original intact glass resting on the table, representing higher system entropy and a lower potential energy state.

If this sequence of events were to run in reverse, all of the broken shards of glass would come back together to re-form the unshattered glass. This is not something that has ever happened spontaneously, either in our commonplace experience or in scientific experiments, and for good reason: the forward direction of the glass shattering results in the release of free energy into the environment and the creation of increased system entropy (i.e., a more disordered state for the glass) relative to the previous state (i.e., the intact glass). This is as opposed to the backward direction, where the process would require the addition (i.e., the incorporation) of free energy into the glass system (from the surrounding environment), so as to allow it to reassemble and become more ordered, thereby lowering its internal system entropy. This latter process is not something that can just "happen" spontaneously from an energetic standpoint; it requires something else, which is the addition of energy from the outside environment to the "glass system."

Thus, physical laws such as the second law of thermodynamics prohibit "reverse causality" from ever occurring from a purely energetic standpoint. This is good, because if temporal causality loops could occur, temporal causality violations would be possible, which would mean that the past would be forever changeable. This would have very difficult and potentially irreconcilable consequences for the present, because changes in past sequences of events could occur in a way that could create inconsistencies. A well-known example of this is the *grandfather paradox*.

In the hypothetical situation of the grandfather paradox, an event occurs now as a result of a person's actions (event A) that feeds back into the past (via a hypothetical time-like worldline) in a way that results in his grandfather's death before he meets his grandmother (event B). If this were to happen, then the birth of his mother (or father) (event C) would never have occurred (because it is contingent on the occurrence of event B). Thus, his own birth (event D) could also never have occurred (i.e., the person who caused the event that changed the past to result in his grandfather's early demise could not have been born), which is necessary for event A to occur. Thus, the person who precipitated event A could never have existed at all and, therefore, the event "from the future" could never have occurred to cause his grandfather's untimely death. This would, therefore, allow for (1) his own birth, which would (2) result in his grandfather's early death. Hence, there is an inconsistency that precipitates an unresolvable paradox: because (a) his grandfather cannot be both alive and dead at the same time (in the past) and because (b) he himself cannot both exist and not exist (in the present), these constitute irreconcilable contradictions.

Albert Einstein, when confronted with the possibility of these types of issues, weighed in by saying:[†]

> The assertion: 'B is before A,' [does not make] physical sense... if there exist point-series connectable by time-like lines in such a way that each point precedes temporally the preceding one, and if the series is closed in itself [Einstein is referring here to a *closed time-like curve*]. In that case the distinction 'earlier-later' is abandoned for world-points which lie far apart in a cosmological sense, and those paradoxes, regarding the direction of the causal connection, arise.

Some physicists have suggested that these types of paradoxes can be avoided by appealing to some type of universal constraint against altering the past in ways that would affect the future (one of these is known as the Novikov self-consistency principle). Others have considered the idea that there might be an infinite number of branching, non-communicating universes (i.e., so-called *parallel universes*), such that every version of mutually exclusive trains of events exists *somewhere* (for a more detailed discussion of this interpretation of quantum theory, see chapter 23, entitled "Many Worlds: Parallel Universes as an Explanation for Quantum Paradoxes"). The contemporary theoretical physicist Stephen Hawking has also promulgated a *chronology protection conjecture* that suggests that the fundamental laws of nature prevent the occurrence of such paradoxes. But, quite disappointingly, this conjecture's validity cannot be verified without a theory of quantum gravity (i.e., one that joins quantum mechanics and general relativity into a single, unified theory), and this has proven elusive thus far.

Having effectively dispensed with the idea of temporal causality loops, we can now go back to the more typical loops that don't violate temporal causality. These constitute ordinary *feedback loops* (i.e., positive and negative feedback loops) and so-called *coproduction loops*. These generate three other concepts: *vicious circles*, *virtuous circles*, and *emergent phenomena*, the last of which can give rise to unintended consequences.

When a feedback loop or coproduction loop produces an effect that is considered desirable, the system change is described as a *virtuous circle*; when it produces an undesirable effect, the system change is described as a *vicious circle*. When these involve interactions in a complex system, they can also produce unpredictable consequences that are termed *emergent phenomena* (for a more detailed explanation, see chapter 17, entitled "Continuity (Smoothness) vs. Discontinuity (Roughness)," and chapter 24, entitled "Chaos Theory: Implications for Macroscopic Predictability"). Although such consequences are unintended in the sense that nothing about the components of the system deliberately intends for them to occur, they nevertheless are the result of complex system changes (for additional discussion, see chapter 18, entitled "Stability vs. Instability: System Inertia and Resiliency"; chapter 19, entitled "Dynamical Certainty vs. Uncertainty: Trajectories"; and chapter 24, entitled "Chaos Theory: Implications for Macroscopic Predictability").

But what if the idea of causality—even as a concept—is wrong? One consequence would be that our universe would then allow "anything to happen," such that nothing could be reliably predicted. We don't typically recognize this in our everyday experience, so we generally reject the idea that the universe operates in such a way. But this type of purely experiential and empirical reasoning doesn't rule out the possibility that this could be the case. Only a well-conceived proof that would deny this as even a possibility could rule this out. To date, no such proof exists.

Another perspective regarding the idea of causality is also possible: that all combinations of possible interactions and outcomes that can occur actually do—*somewhere*. This represents the so-called *many worlds* interpretation of quantum theory. It posits that every possible combination of events happens (i.e., in a very large, possibly infinite, regress of non-communicating *parallel universes*), each taking a *different direction* at every decision point of reality (for a more detailed discussion, see chapter 23, entitled "Many Worlds: Parallel Universes as an Explanation for Quantum Paradoxes"). But because this theory also postulates an intrinsic inability to communicate with any of the alternative universes that evolve according to the divergent series of events, it is unverifiable as a possible alternative to the ideas we use to underpin our standard notions of causality.

The aim of this chapter has been to introduce the concept of causality and to emphasize its importance in Western philosophy, as well as to the scientific approach to inquiry and explanation. In addition to providing a definition and the underlying basis for our general belief in causality as a concept, I have attempted to outline the premises that are the necessary prerequisites to believe in its existence. This is particularly important with respect to its dependence on the notion of separability, which itself depends on notions of time and space (see chapter 22, entitled "Entanglement vs. Separability: The Locality Issue," for further discussion). All of these issues will be addressed further in the chapters that follow.

---

* The second law of thermodynamics was discovered during the nineteenth century. It helps to define the *arrow of time* by providing an explanation for how causes differ from effects from an energetic standpoint. The salient feature can be summarized as follows: the *sum* of the *states* that constitute the *effects* (encompassing both the thermodynamic system under consideration and its surrounding environment) can *never* have *lower composite entropy* than the *sum* of the *states* that constitute the *causes*. Thus, if one set of events has a lower composite entropy than the other, the *higher composite entropy* must be associated with the sum of the states that exist *downstream* in *time* (i.e., the *effects*) and the *lower composite entropy* with the states that exist *upstream* in time (i.e., the *causes*).

† Paul Arthur Schilpp and Albert Einstein, *Albert Einstein: Philosopher-Scientist* (1st ed. Evanston, Ill.: Library of Living Philosophers, 1949).

CHAPTER 5
Perception

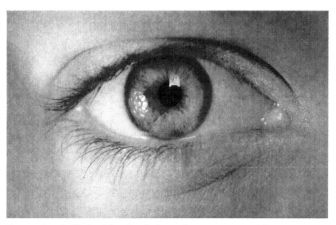

Perception is limited by the design of our senses and how we process information.

Perception (Perceive): Definition (Merriam-Webster Dictionary)

- To become aware of through the senses; see, observe
- Awareness of the elements of environment through physical sensation
- A result of perceiving: observation
- Physical sensation interpreted in the light of experience

For us to know about objects and events, we must first *perceive* them. This is because if they exist, but we have no way of knowing about them, it would be to us as if they did not exist (i.e., they would be effectively *invisible* to us). As a result, the only objects and events that we can know about in a non-speculative way (i.e., one that is not part of our imaginations) are those that are presented to us by some kind of *information* that we can access about them.

When this type of information is available, it is provided to us via *perception*, which occurs by way of our *senses*. Perceived information is referred to as *phenomenological*, which is distinct from the notion of actual *things-in-themselves* (a notion that was championed by the influential eighteenth-century German philosopher Immanuel Kant, but that dates back to ancient Greek philosophy).

Some objects and events that we can perceive are outside of ourselves, whereas others are an internal part of us. Some examples of perception are the images that we have of the furniture in a room (i.e., a *visual* image of objects external to us) or the positions of our arms when we are in bed (i.e., a sense of the position of our limbs, which is referred to as *proprioception*). But in both instances, no form of perception just "happens." All perception requires some sort of an *apparatus* to *transduce* the *information* coming to us into a form that can be (1) *detected* and then (2) *communicated* internally (i.e., transmitted), such that we can recognize it and ultimately *sense* and appreciate it.

Thus, the information we have about objects and events (i.e., which mirrors their phenomenology) is not necessarily reflective of what they *really are* (i.e., the things-in-themselves). What we can access is restricted to *representations* conveyed to us by discrete pieces of information about them; this then allows us to construct a mental image of what they *look like*. This distinction is key: what we are able to perceive is only what we were *designed* to recognize, and nothing more. Anything else is simply beyond our capability to access and to be aware of.

For instance, it is clear that different types of organisms can (and do) perceive different facets of their environment even when it is identical. An example is provided by the nighttime desert: Under a dark and moonless sky, a man may curl up in a sleeping bag on the desert floor and sleep unnoticed by other men who scan the surface with their eyes. But, to a rattlesnake, the motionless man lights up like a beacon, because the snake's visual apparatus is designed to detect infrared light (i.e., heat), which the sleeping man emits passively and without any ability to control.

Thus, for one class of sensing beings (men) there is no perception of an object that exists (a sleeping man) in this particular environment (the desert), but to another (a rattlesnake) there is the ability to detect him, which makes it immediately obvious that he is there. Thus, for different types of beings with varying types of sensory apparatuses, there are very different perceptions of the thing-in-itself (the sleeping man). Each being's perception is predicated upon a different type of (phenomenological) information that is gleaned about the man by sensory apparatuses of different design and sensitivities.

Pressing this example further, other important issues can be noted. In the case of human vision, for example, there are arrays of light-sensitive cells at the back of the eye (the retina) that act as the primary receptors for light perception. Each of these cells either detects sufficient light (within the visual spectrum to which it is sensitive) or it does not. When it does, it causes a signal to be sent to the brain (along the optic nerve after some local integration). Thus, there is a *threshold effect* for the light *stimulus* to be *recognized* as present; above a certain level it is perceived as a signal, but below that level it isn't. Thus, if a stimulus is present but is below the threshold, it goes unrecognized and is necessarily ignored.

The human retina is, therefore, an example of a *non-continuous* type of receiving apparatus. It has both (a) a *response threshold* and (b) a *"pointillist type"* of *grid* over which it locally receives and then integrates information, both over time and space. This description of the peripheral design of the human visual system serves as an example for all known sensory apparatuses that serve as the first step in allowing perception to occur, all of which are predicated upon analogous types of design constraints.

An important corollary arises that applies to all sensory systems as a result of these universal types of design constraints: there are times when an incident stimulus (i.e., incoming information) will be received, but the degree of the effect on a sensory receptor will be insufficient (i.e., below the design threshold) for a signal to be either generated or propagated. In the case just cited, this was what happened when men were unable to perceive a sleeping man in the desert, which was due to the low level of visible light that was incident upon their retinas. In such cases, even though a signal may be received (a *stimulus*), there is no recognition of it, and there can be no (downstream) perception of the sensory event.

Additionally, and again using the human visual system as an example, because each cell in the retina has very large dimensions compared to the range of wavelengths that comprise the visible light spectrum, another corollary is this: the seemingly continuous bands of light that impinge on the retina are transduced to only *points* of on-off type cellular recognition (i.e., *local* "yes" or "no" signals). This means that even if the light that falls upon the retina were continuous in nature (which we may temporarily accept as being the case), the processing of the primary information by the retina turns it into a *coarse mosaic* of points—just as a pointillist-school painter might do in interpreting the continuous image of a landscape onto a canvas.

Thus, the retinal representation of what is perceived will be fundamentally different (i.e., more *granular* and *coarse*) than anything that is continuous. In addition, each of the tiles of the mosaic that comprises the coarse representation is merely a sampling of the total spectrum of the incident input, being generated by less-than-completely-efficient light-sensitive receptors that are triggered by only a fraction of the signal that bears upon them. Finally, the signal that is recognized is a *sum* (or *average*) over both space (i.e., the *finite dimensions* of each of the receiver cells) and time (i.e., the *finite time* over which the incident signal is summed by each cell).

Thus, based on these considerations, the *signal* that is ultimately perceived by us is all of the following:

A. a particular *representation* of the phenomenological information received about objects and events, not the actual "things-in-themselves";
B. the result of a *specific type* of *information* gleaned from objects and events;
C. a composite that represents an *integrated signal* over both a finite period of time and a finite amount of space (i.e., something that is summed or averaged); and
D. a *pointillist-type image* (i.e., one that is ultimately coarse and granular at small scales) of what is assumed to be—and ultimately imagined by us to be (by interpolation, smoothing, and reconstruction of information)—something that is continuous.

The aim here is not to provide an exhaustive overview of the different types of sensory apparatuses that are possessed by various types of beings. Neither is it to provide a detailed explanation of all of the transduction and transmission mechanisms used to communicate this information to more central processing units (i.e., central nervous systems). It is simply to highlight that, whatever type of sensory apparatus is used to glean information about particular facets of the universe, whether it is something native to us or a very sensitive device designed for a particular purpose, it is limited by intrinsic and unavoidable physical design constraints. What's more, such types of devices can provide only an incomplete and averaged representation of the particular characteristics that they detect concerning what is "really out there." The result is neither a comprehensive nor a real image of what is observed. It is rather a fragmented, time-averaged, and space-averaged representation (i.e., a coarse and pointillist-type of grid) of what is imagined to be a more fine and continuous external *emitter* of the information. Furthermore, it is constructed only of signals that have exceeded a particular threshold limit that permits their recognition.

This conclusion should make us take pause; our senses can and do lie to us about what is around us, and they do so all the time. This is because they are only capable of providing a limited and incomplete view of our external (as well as our internal) environments. In many ways, they can be likened to monitoring systems that can be installed on mechanical devices to check key aspects of their status and function; these may be designed to focus in on particular operating features and conditions, but they do not (and cannot) provide sufficient information about the device to be able to fully reconstruct it in its entirety. This is not what they were designed to do.

As an example, consider a typical thermometer: it is specifically designed to monitor the ambient temperature of the local environment where it (i.e., its probe) is placed (figure 4). When properly constructed, it can be very accurate in discerning the temperature within its prescribed operating range (but not at temperatures outside that range—for instance, at thousands of degrees, it would melt and cease to operate). However, the ability of a thermometer to distinguish temperature differences is not infinite (e.g., a particular thermometer may be able to accurately distinguish the difference between an object at 40 degrees versus 41 degrees, but this does not mean that it also has the ability to distinguish between an object at 40.00 degrees versus 40.01 degrees). So thermometers can be designed to be very accurate for measuring and communicating local (average) temperatures with a high degree of *precision*, but this and their intrinsic ability to *resolve* temperature differences are characteristics that are deliberately designed into them. The better ones have increased accuracy and precision over a particular operating range, but in all cases (a) the *operating range* is prescribed and well defined (i.e., it is relatively *narrow*) and (b) the degree of expected accuracy and precision is also well defined (i.e., not infinite).

So we can conclude that thermometers can be constructed to be very accurate devices for measuring local (average) temperature, both properly and reproducibly. But what if we were also interested in knowing the local level of visible light to be able to distinguish between daytime and nighttime? Or the local noise level to know when to protect our ears? Because of the way that thermometers are designed, they are functionally incapable of discerning these other types of information directly. They are designed (appropriately) to measure something else (temperature). In effect, thermometers are *blind* to both visible light and to noise levels; they simply don't incorporate a mechanism to directly measure changes in either of these other two types of phenomena.

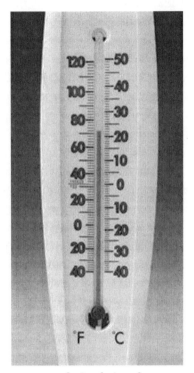

Figure 4: A thermometer: a device designed to measure temperature

A thermometer is designed to measure and display temperature accurately, but it is not designed to detect other local phenomena, such as visible light, noise, etc. To measure these, different types of detectors would be required.

We can conclude that any monitoring systems we design—in direct analogy to the limitations of our own senses—can only provide us with information about items that are within the boundaries of their detection and operating limits. Accordingly, they can only provide information about what they were designed to measure. Because of this, they are very likely to "miss" the great majority of what is "out there"—and they do so all the time.

Thus, we can neither claim that we experience all there is to know about the universe (i.e., other objects and events) or even that what we do recognize and experience is complete, accurate, or precise. It is merely all that we can know about using the sensory apparatuses that we possess (together with whatever potential technological "extenders" we may have, in the form of man-made devices and sensors). Other characteristics of objects and events remain unrecognized and "shielded" from us—making them, therefore, unknown. We might speculate about what these other characteristics might be and what other types of underlying traits they might be associated with, but we cannot know them; we simply do not have access to the primary information that would be necessary for us to do so.

So no matter how many external or auxiliary "sensory systems" we might choose to construct (i.e., different types of mechanical apparatuses that are specifically designed to be more sensitive than we are ourselves for detecting certain types of signals), we can never be certain that we've covered it all—there may always be other items remaining that we haven't imagined that are outstanding and uninvestigated beyond the (extended) domains of the various devices we devise. This poses a daunting limitation because—as the old adage goes—we simply *don't know what we don't know.*

But despite this, sensory input encompasses all the information about the universe that we have to work with. Whether we like it or not, this is a limitation that we cannot do anything about and that we must accept. Simply put, we must (1) make the best use of the admittedly fragmented and incomplete information that we can obtain about the universe through the use of our senses, (2) draw conclusions from it, and then (3) use the resulting constructs that we devise to our best advantage.

CHAPTER 6
Consciousness

Consciousness allows us to be aware, which permits us to be able to know.

Consciousness: Definition (Merriam-Webster Dictionary)

- The quality or state of being aware, especially of something within oneself
- The state or fact of being conscious of an external object, state, or fact
- Awareness
- The state of being characterized by sensation, emotion, volition, and thought
- The upper level of mental life of which the person is aware as contrasted with unconscious processes

For those readers who are hoping for a detailed explanation of the phenomenon of consciousness, this chapter will likely be a disappointment. It does not attempt to define the origins of consciousness, nor does it try to elucidate its complete scope or purpose. Instead, it will draw attention to only one fact: *consciousness* is an *absolute prerequisite* for the type of non-vegetative *mental activity* that follows from the ability to *register inputs* (e.g., representations of objects and events)—whether they are internal or external.

Consciousness is required for us to have an appreciation of anything. It is the phenomenon without which life would be vegetative. It is often equated with *awareness*, which serves as the basis for what we term individual *subjective experience*. Importantly, consciousness refers to what is *experienced* internally by *sentient entities* (i.e., what sentient beings "know about"), which in turn leads to the notion of *self*. Such experiences can either have their origins externally—with their existence being communicated via some type of perceptive apparatus (see chapter 5, entitled "Perception," for further discussion)—or they can arise internally (such as with de-novo *thoughts*, for which there is no need to reference anything external).

Because consciousness is an *internal phenomenon*, it does not have any requirement for external manifestation. As such, it is based on *internal changes* in *physical states* that occur *within sentient beings*. Such internal physical changes are required because, without them, there would be no physical correlate of informational change and, therefore, no internal "register" to catalog changes. All such information requires a physical representation in order to exist (see chapter 27, entitled "Information," for further discussion). Simply put, there must be something to be aware of in order for awareness to occur; this necessitates an internal change that is represented by an internal physical correlate of informational change.

By using this type of a functional definition, consciousness can be regarded as a platform—essentially a *baseline state of being*—against which *inputs* of various sorts can be *registered*. Comparisons are then made to other contemporaneous states (which serve as metrics), or to historical (i.e., past) states (which can also serve the same purpose). Accordingly, consciousness is *dependent* on the *maintenance* of a *well-defined internal state of order*. It represents a quasi-steady state that serves as a *point of reference*—a comparator for other states—and not a stand-alone state or condition.

From this description, it is apparent that consciousness is intrinsically tied to the underlying *maintenance* of *internal system stability* within sentient beings. This stability provides the necessary underpinnings for the continuity of what can be characterized as a single entity over time, thereby providing for the commonplace notion of a single *self*. In all cases, ongoing energy expenditure is required to maintain such a *pseudo-steady state*.

Although the two concepts of *consciousness* and *self* are non-identical (i.e., a conscious entity might be imagined without an associated concept of boundaries to self), it is difficult to imagine how *awareness* could exist without a notion of self-identity. This is because it is unclear how a sentient being might be aware without harboring some concomitant notion of being a "central entity" to appreciate "other things" (most of these being external, but with the same considerations applying to internal subdivisions of itself). In addition, it is similarly difficult to imagine what the utility of consciousness might be without the concomitant ability to be aware.

Importantly, the idea of *self* serves as a de facto division (i.e., limiting barrier) between who each of us is (as a sentient being) and our surroundings (the outside environment). As a result, there arises the potential for us to influence objects and events outside of ourselves (i.e., to manifest *agency*) and also to (perhaps) exercise *free will* (see chapter 3, entitled "Agency: Free Will vs. Determinism," for further discussion). Nonetheless, although consciousness is a necessary antecedent for (volitional) acts, it does not require that *external* actions actually occur.

The reason that consciousness is an important topic for this book is that it is a prerequisite for both the *awareness* of the objects of perception (which depends primarily upon garnering information either from outside or inside of ourselves) and *thought* (which is also an internal phenomenon that similarly has no requirement for any overt external manifestation—see chapter 7, entitled "Thought," for further discussion). Both are fundamental to defining who we are and how it is ultimately possible for us to know about anything.

The conclusion is that consciousness presupposes a baseline state of internal *stability* within sentient entities, which is embodied by the presence of order. In addition, there must be something that changes (internally) for awareness to even be a possibility (i.e., there must be an internal informational change with some type of a physical representation).

Finally, the notion of consciousness can be potentially confounded by a number of other phenomena. It is helpful, therefore, to state not only what consciousness is, but also what it is not. Consciousness should not be confused with other separable mental phenomena, such as attention, memory, processing capacity, information access time, processing tempo, etc. All of these are functions that relate to accessing, processing, storing, transferring, and analyzing information. They may depend on the existence of consciousness for their relevance, but they are ultimately subordinate functions that interact with consciousness, making them functionally "mechanical" in nature. The examples listed here are non-exhaustive, but by pointing them out it is hoped it will become evident what falls within the scope of consciousness *per se* and what does not.

Thus far, our discussion of consciousness has left unaddressed a fundamental physical issue that may appear technical, but it is not. This relates to the notion of *internal* versus *external* phenomena and their manifestations (i.e., events that occur *within* a *sentient being* versus those that occur *beyond* its *delimiting barrier* in the *outside* environment). It is instructive to consider how such a distinction is made. At a gross (i.e., macroscopic) level, it may appear that the *outputs* of a sentient entity can be readily defined (i.e., that they occur when the entity expends some of its internal (free) energy to deliver a *force* from within, and that this force then precipitates a motion (such as of an appendage, limb, body, etc.). This motion can then result in *downstream effects* on objects and events that reside in the surrounding *environment* (i.e., the universe outside of the sentient entity itself).

In principle, the foregoing should provide an acceptable working definition of what a sentient entity *does* when it acts, as opposed to simply being *internally aware*. However, several additional questions arise. For instance, *how much* motion is required to be able to recognize that a sentient entity is *exerting* an *external effect*? Since small motions can (and do) occur randomly (i.e., some degree of *statistical fluctuation* occurs in all real systems with temperatures above absolute zero), how much force must be exerted to determine that its application has occurred purposefully? This reduces to the following question: "*How much* of an *influence* on the external environment should count as being a deliberate *external manifestation* attributable to a conscious entity?" This presents a qualitative distinction that ultimately depends on a seemingly arbitrary quantitative cutoff. It also raises an additional question: "Is there ever a change in the internal state of things-in-themselves (sentient or otherwise) that would not be detectable (upon suitably sensitive interrogation) to the 'external environment' that resides outside of it?"

Stated otherwise, this last question can be recast as: "Is it ever the case that a sentient entity is entirely *isolated* from its surrounding environment, such that the *changes* in its *internal state* (i.e., those necessary for awareness) are completely *uncoupled* from its *surroundings* and can go entirely unrecognized?" This is equivalent to asking: "How completely can any system (sentient or otherwise) be *thermodynamically isolated* from its surrounding environment, such that there is absolutely *no cross-communication* of *energy* and, hence, information between them?"

Fortunately or not, there is an absolute requirement for the cross-communication of *black body* (or, more practically, *gray body*) radiation among all objects that are not at equal temperature, so the notion of complete thermodynamic isolation is an idealization that can never be realized (see chapter 20, entitled "Thermodynamics: Laws Prohibiting the Spontaneous Reversibility of Physical Events," for further discussion). This would suggest that sentient entities are always affecting their surroundings as a consequence of their internal physical changes—including those small changes that are associated with consciousness—albeit in very small ways and irrespective of any desire (or lack thereof) to do so.

An important implication arises: unless there can be absolute isolation of a sentient entity from its environment, the notion of a complete *separation* between *internal events* and *external manifestations* must be considered *impossible*. Of particular relevance is that the premise regarding absolute thermodynamic isolation would violate a primary condition required to support the maintenance of a sentient being's own pseudo-steady state—the throughput and consumption of *external energy resources*—which is absolutely necessary to maintain the organization and internal homeostasis of sentient beings. This is because all such entities are *highly organized, open biological systems* that exist *far from* an *equilibrium state*, which makes continuing energy consumption an absolute requirement for them to maintain their structure and function.

From this last consideration, there arises the possibility that "everything is connected to everything else," which is a fundamental concept that also arises from quantum entanglement (see chapter 22, entitled "Entanglement vs. Separability: The Locality Issue," for a detailed discussion). This may have profound implications for the localization of consciousness as a phenomenon (i.e., it may be that although consciousness may appear to exist at a particular place and time, its actual locality may be more diffuse).

However, for the purpose of this book, which is concerned with what we can know and how it can help us to predict the future, the absolute location of consciousness *per se* is of only limited consequence.

It is hoped that this chapter has provided (1) A flavor for the different factors delimiting the key issues related to the underpinnings of consciousness, (2) why this is important for being able to detect and be aware of changes (both external and internal), and (3) how this relates to what we might ultimately have the human capacity to know.

CHAPTER 7
Thought

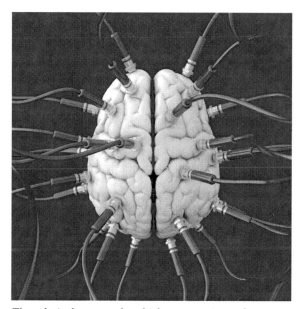

Thought is the means by which we organize and represent information within a given context.

Thought (Think): Definition (Merriam-Webster Dictionary)

- To form or have in the mind
- To form a mental picture of
- To reflect on; ponder
- To devise by thinking
- To determine by reflecting
- To call to mind; remember
- To exercise the powers of judgment, conception, or inference; reason
- To have the mind engaged in reflection; meditate

The notion of *thought* spans a wide range of mental activities. In all cases, it involves the *representation* and *manipulation* of *mental objects* and their *relationships*. These can pertain either to *physical* objects or events (i.e., those existing either outside or inside of us, such as rocks or gallbladders), or to wholly *mental constructs* (i.e., unicorns on the one hand or emotions on another). Its hallmark, however, is that it is something that only conscious beings have the capacity to do (see chapter 6, entitled "Consciousness," for further discussion). And, like consciousness, thought is an *internal phenomenon* that does not have any routinely observable outward manifestations.

The renowned German philosopher Immanuel Kant pointed out in the eighteenth century that thought necessarily incorporates presupposed notions of *space* and *time*. Our understanding and interpretations of these entities have changed since he first promulgated his theories (see chapter 25, entitled "Absolutes vs. Relatives: Relativity Theory," for further discussion), but even today our routine, working notions of them do not conform to what modern physics suggests they are (i.e., modern physics has determined that space and time are intrinsically coupled, but most of us still think of them as separate and standing apart from the objects and events that transit them). Nonetheless, they still serve as a *stage* for the occurrence of all events and the basis for our mental manipulations of the imaginary objects and events of our thoughts.

By the term *imaginary*, it is important to recognize that thoughts are *representations* and not the actual objects and events they reflect (as an example, think about your mother at the time of your birth—she existed then and can be thought of now, but she does not exist now in the same way that she once did).

So it can be concluded that not all the objects and events that are encompassed by thoughts have a separate physical existence outside of the thoughts themselves. As an example, we can think of unicorns, but there are no such real animals. But, irrespective of whether the objects of thought have any external existence, for thoughts to occur, they must be somehow *coded* into *mental representations*. This is important, because all such mental representations are only that and not the objects or events that the thoughts are about. This brings up the key issue of how such mental *images* are constructed and where they reside.

No one knows exactly where thoughts are housed. The best scientific evidence suggests that they reside in our brains (not in our hearts, as many incurable romantics might like to believe!). At a practical level, this is supported by the observation that people who suffer injuries to their brains (i.e., as a result of trauma, strokes, tumors, degenerative diseases, etc.) often have cognitive deficits that involve changes in thought patterns. But, it is unknown just how many of our brain's neurons (brain cells) are involved in creating the representations necessary for the mental embodiments that we refer to as thoughts. In addition, it is not known precisely where these neurons are located, if thoughts are represented solely by patterns of neuronal excitation, or if there is something else that resides deeper within the physiologic structures of the individual neuronal cells themselves (e.g., microtubules)—or perhaps in their specific connections to other cells—that allows thoughts to become manifest. It is even unclear if thoughts are represented as a diffuse type of brain phenomenon that is global in nature (analogous to holographic representations), or if they are entirely confined (physically) to specific brain areas.

Not surprisingly, thought is sometimes confused with memory (or recall), which is a separate type of retrieval process. Although thoughts can arise de novo, at other times they have occurred previously and are reconstructed through recall. However, this latter phenomenon of memory is likely to represent a separate and subservient function that can help to provide the substrates (i.e., mental objects) of thought (as do, for instance, the inputs of perception), but it is not intrinsically necessary for thought itself to occur. As another medical example bears out, people with certain types of dementias have significant short-term memory loss (and often long-term memory deficits as well), but they still often retain their capacities to think, imagine, reason, etc.

Something else about thoughts is unknown: How much information is necessary to define a single thought? Do some thoughts encompass more information content than others? One might suppose that there could be differences in informational content depending on the complexity of thoughts, but this has never been shown (and it would be extremely difficult to construct a scientific experiment to examine this issue without relying on some other type of non-rigorous surrogate indicator or measure!).

There is substantially more known about the acquisition and processing of sensory information than about the construction and manipulation of thoughts. This is because thoughts are intrinsically more abstract in both their origin and nature. Neurologists, neurosurgeons, neurophysiologists, and neuroanatomists understand quite well that there are particular areas of the human brain (for instance) that have both primary and secondary responsibilities for processing different types of afferent sensory signals. There are also particular tracts in the brain that are responsible for the transmission and processing of such incoming signals. Many of these are involved in the integration of signals from both cortical and subcortical brain structures (such as the thalamus, basal ganglia, and the limbic system), and these can ultimately result in different types of motor outputs. But, the connection between these types of *tangible representations* of *sensory inputs* and the types of more *abstract information* that constitute *thoughts* is uncertain. Thoughts require more than mere perception to occur; they require that there be some level of conscious awareness, such that they can be appreciated. This means that they must be placed within some type of a larger context. It is only then that thoughts can have existence, which gives them at least the potential to have relevance.

At a minimum, thought is a complex phenomenon that requires the presence of all the following: *information* (whether it originates externally or internally), *coding* (i.e., internal representation of the available information), *processing* (i.e., the manipulation of the information), *awareness* (i.e., the *viewing* of the information), and, ultimately, *consciousness* (i.e., the phenomenon that allows us to *appreciate* the information). Often, the *process* of thought *uses* the *substrates* of *thought* (i.e., *ideas*) to perform comparisons of some objects (or events) to other objects (or events) that are of analogous type. This means that the mental objects of thought (after processing) are being checked for their consistency—or lack thereof—to other information. The other information may be either contemporaneously received, or it may be historical in nature (i.e., the result of recall). To accomplish this, thought must presuppose some basic underlying notions of both space and time.

In summary, *thought* constitutes a *higher-level function* that *requires* the presence of *consciousness*. It lies at the basis of our being able to compare and contrast information so as to establish *knowledge*. And, as such, it serves as the basis for our being able to ultimately reach what we call understanding—both about objects and events in the universe beyond ourselves and about what we represent and who we are as individuals.

CHAPTER 8
Knowledge

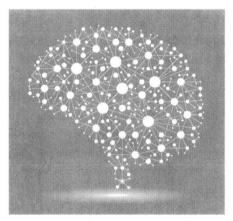

What does knowledge represent and how do we come by it?

Knowledge: Definition (Merriam-Webster Dictionary)

- The fact or condition of knowing something with familiarity gained through experience or association
- The fact or condition of being aware of something
- The range of one's information or understanding
- The circumstance or condition of apprehending truth or fact through reasoning; cognition
- The fact or condition of having information or of being learned

We depend on *knowledge* to inform our decisions. Knowledge includes discrete packets of information that are often characterized as *facts*, which also encompasses the *relationships* among *objects* and *events*. In all cases, knowledge constitutes circumscribable objects of thought, which can occur only in conscious beings.

The origin of knowledge must be either *native* or *acquired*, or both. When it is *native* (as is the case for inborn *instincts*), then it is derived exclusively from within. In this case, it must arise from the structures and associated internal functions that exist within conscious beings themselves (i.e., this type of knowledge can be regarded as *hard wired*). For example, experiments have shown that some types of bird hatchlings that are kept without external adult inputs are able to sing species-specific songs without any exposure to them. Alternatively, when knowledge is *acquired*, then some appeal must be made to information that is only available in the surrounding environment (i.e., information from the *outside* universe that is *external* to the conscious being itself).

Based on current theory and experimental evidence, it appears unlikely that knowledge is derived exclusively from one or the other of these two sources (contrary to the opposing positions of the rationalist and empiricist philosophers). As the influential German philosopher Immanuel Kant proposed during the eighteenth century, knowledge is more likely to arise as the result of the abilities of the *receivers* of information (i.e., conscious beings such as ourselves) and what types of inputs they are both *capable* of receiving (i.e., ones that they possess the proper sensory apparatuses to recognize) and *prepared for* (i.e., ones that they can also properly incorporate, process, and interpret). Being-specific factors then act to "filter" the information that is *accessible*, so as to form thoughts from the changes that occur in internal states that are reflective of outside conditions. Kant referred to this hybrid category of knowledge as the so-called *synthetic a priori*.

As an illustration, consider once again the example of rattlesnakes. They have light-perceiving organs (i.e., eyes) that are designed to function in a range that allows them to see *infrared light*. This permits them to identify *hot* objects in the dark. Humans do not have visual capabilities in this portion of the electromagnetic spectrum, so for people the infrared information characterizing the outside universe goes effectively unrecognized. The result is that although the information exists for all to detect, it is as if it does not exist for humans, because we cannot perceive it. As another example, dogs can hear sounds at higher frequencies than humans, so that they cringe in response to high-pitched wails that humans merrily ignore; this is because people have no sensory apparatus to inform them that the offensive noise is occurring.

Because all such information is *received* by conscious beings via some sort of *perceptive apparatus* (i.e., sensory systems that are designed to detect light, sound, touch, taste, smell, heat, cold, pressure, pain, etc.—all within certain circumscribed *operating ranges* beyond which they are not designed to function; see chapter 5, entitled "Perception," for further discussion)—there is some degree of *primary interpretation* of the sensory *signals* by the apparatus that first receives them, regardless of if it arises from an internal or external source. In addition, all such sensory apparatuses are ultimately *granular* in their ability to detect a signal, because they have (a) a grid of receptors to capture incoming signals (typically), (b) space and time dimensions over which they integrate information and (c) *thresholds* that must be exceeded in order to *recognize* that a *stimulus* has occurred. It is only then that they communicate (typically with an *all-or-none* type of signal that is *digital* in nature) from the periphery to a central nervous system for further processing (see chapter 5, entitled "Perception," for further discussion). What is important is that the inputs and outputs—both in quality and quantity—are necessarily granular in nature rather than continuous.

However, an interesting phenomenon occurs after the primary stimuli are first recognized. Because the universe is viewed by us as being *continuous* rather than granular, this means that our *minds* constantly *interpolate* (and sometimes extrapolate) these types of fundamentally discontinuous inputs, so as to *fill in the gaps*. This allows us to arrive at a more continuous (i.e., *smooth*) representation of the information in a way that permits us to analyze it more easily once it has been (automatically) reformulated. Although this is a *convenient representation* of the discretely assembled primary information that we receive, it is only an *idealization* that is fundamentally *incorrect*. In fact, it is only a *construct* that is derived from the discrete and *intrinsically discontinuous* packets of *information* that constitute everything that we can perceive (i.e., experience).

These issues have profound implications for the types of information that we can know about. Based on limitations arising from the *discrete nature* of the *information* that comprises the basis of knowledge, the *limited ability* of our perceptive apparatuses to acquire the *full scope* of this information, and intrinsic limitations associated with the *mechanisms* we have for *processing* and *interpreting* it, there are significant *restrictions* that apply to both the *scope* and *veracity* of what we call *knowledge*. As will be explored later, this is the result of significant limitations that arise due to the *truncated* nature of the information that is available to us, the limited *accuracy* and *precision* of the information that we have access to, as well as the *methods* that we employ for its subsequent *analysis*. Ultimately, this limits both the knowledge that we can have about the universe, as well as our interpretations of it.

PART 2
TECHNICAL CONSIDERATIONS

CHAPTER 9

Measurement: How Circumstance and Change Are Assessed

The way we measure determines how much confidence we can have in the results.

Measurement: Definition (Merriam-Webster Dictionary)

- A figure, extent, or amount obtained by measuring
- The act or process of measuring

Change: Definition (Merriam-Webster Dictionary)
- To become different
- To undergo a modification of
- To make different in some particular: alter
- To make radically different: transform
- To give a different position, course, or direction to
- To undergo transformation, transition, or substitution

Measurement forms the basis of all that we can know, first by identifying and categorizing items of interest (i.e., objects and events), and then by cataloguing changes in them, as well as their relationships.

To obtain information about the environment, there must be an *interaction* between us and the outside universe to gain access to it (see chapter 5, entitled "Perception," for further discussion). These (energetic) interactions provide us with *empirical data* that are gained through *experience*. Because these data are measured directly, they do not need to conform to any particular theory.

Investigations involving empirical data vary depending on whether they are observational or interventional in nature. The difference between the two can be summarized as follows:

For *observational* investigations:

> Objects and events of interest are *measured* together with their relationships, typically in cross-section with respect to time; these are then *tracked* (over time, without intervention) to catalogue their *evolution*. Measurements are made again and *compared* with *starting values* to assess the extent of *change*. The intent is to gain insight into the strength and interdependencies of the relationships among the various elements under observation and to infer any *connections* that might exist among the different objects and events (via some kind of a *model*).

For *interventional* (i.e., *experimental*) investigations:

> Objects and events of interest are *measured* together with their relationships, typically in cross-section with respect to time; after some (external) *intervention* is imposed, they are *tracked* with subsequent measurements over time. From this *before-and-after* assessment, the *extent of change* is determined *compared with* the *starting values*, but the effect of the intervention is still not certain. For a causal attribution to be made, a *control* experiment is necessary; this is identical to the original experiment except

that there is no intervention. The *differences* between the changes measured in the interventional and control experiments are then assessed, and these are (causally) *attributed* to the *intervention*.

Observational studies are much *weaker* than interventional ones in their ability to establish *causal* relationships; the best they can do is document the evolution of a system from some starting condition to a subsequent one at a later time. Such studies aren't designed to elucidate precisely what in the system caused something else to happen within it; they just catalog what the changes happened to be.

In the case of *experiments* (i.e., interventional studies), there is a clear intention to provoke measurable change by means of an external intervention that is meant to perturb the system. Together with the use of a control experiment, this allows the measurements to quantify the extent of the interventional effect (see the example depicted in figure 5).

Experimental Plant *Control Plant*

Figure 5: Plant growth

An example of a controlled experiment: if we want to know if the addition of a specific (external) fertilizer increases a plant's growth rate, one way would be to measure the growth of two identical plants under the same conditions (i.e., with the same soil, degree of moisture, amount of sunlight, etc.), with the only difference being the addition of a specified amount of fertilizer to the experimental plant and none to the control plant. The difference in the measured growth between the two plants (i.e., their size after a specified period of time as compared to the original size) is then attributed to the only difference between the two experiments—the addition of the fertilizer (i.e., the intervention).

Models are often constructed after empirical data are assembled to try to make sense of the information. Subsequently, the *predictions* of these models are tested (i.e., either verified or disproved) by making additional measurements in observational studies or experiments (see chapter 29, entitled "Modeling vs. Reality," for further discussion). Perhaps not surprisingly, the history of science is notable for instances where models built from empirical data (and others built on theoretical considerations) could not be adequately tested because the measurements necessary to either confirm or refute their veracity could not be made with sufficient *accuracy* and *precision*. Thus, the practicality of conducting particular empirical investigations has often depended on the *accuracy* with which certain measurements could be made.

An example of this is what occurred in an experiment designed to measure the speed of light in the seventeenth century. The famous Italian scientist Galileo Galilei proposed that it could be measured by observing the *time delay* between uncovering a lantern and the perception of its emitted light at a distance far away. Using lanterns separated by about a mile, the experiment was conducted in Florence in 1667. No discernible time delay was observed. But, the real conclusion was that no delay *could be detected* because the methods used to ascertain it were inadequate (i.e., they were not *sensitive* enough because they lacked the necessary precision). We now know that the time delay associated with light transmission in the experiment was on the order of microseconds. This delay is measurable using modern techniques (i.e., those in place since the end of the nineteenth century), but it is much shorter than could be measured using the technology available when the experiment was conducted.

This conclusion is an important one and is generalizable: it is *not possible* to *measure changes* that are so small that they *fall below* the *discrimination threshold* of the techniques used to measure them. Happily, technological advances have often improved the ability to measure ever smaller quantities with increasing degrees of accuracy and precision. However, this is not always the case, and, more importantly, this expectation cannot be presumed to be limitless.

In fact, there are very small scales below which differences cannot be resolved and, hence, not known. This is where small changes simply have no chance of being detected, because the information necessary to recognize them is not obtainable. Particularly important is that this is not due to deficiencies in existing technologies. Instead, it is due to fundamental scale limits below which more precise measurements cannot be made (see chapter 21, entitled "Quantum Theory: Uncertainties of the Very Small," for further discussion). This means that there is a theoretical limit—and not just a practical one—to "how well" objects and events can be measured. Given that everything that we can *think* of involves information (i.e., more than just empirical knowledge), the implications extend well beyond empirical investigations.

Importantly, all information represents some type of a *quantity*, and measurement is required for its quantification. Thus, the inability to measure extremely small differences represents a crucial limit to what it is possible to gain information about and what it is possible to know.

The need for measurement to define information extends beyond empirical data to theoretical quantities where there may be no known physical embodiment or representation of certain constructs (the objects of string theory, for example). Regardless of whether information is empirically derived or originates internally, it must be quantified. In all cases, the primary description and subsequent manipulation of information depends on its *quantification*, which allows for it to then be compared and contrasted. Accordingly, it does not matter where the information originates—in some part of the universe external to us or as part of our own abstract thoughts; for it to be known to us, a measurement is required.

For many readers, the implicit need to quantify all information via measurement may not have been immediately obvious. This is because it has traditionally been taught that there is a difference between *qualitative* and *quantitative* information. In the first instance, there is the representation that there can be a qualitative description of objects and events without quantification, whereas in the latter case quantification is necessary by definition.

Traditionally, *quantitative* data is regarded as being of *higher quality* than qualitative data. This is based on the following:

1. *Quantitative* data is regarded as *better structured* and *richer* (i.e., more *exact*) because it is more *countable* at a finer level of detail; this makes it *better defined, more precise,* and more *nuanced* (i.e., it is more finely *localizable* and more *granularly definable* on *smaller time-distance scales*, etc.).
2. *Qualitative* data is *less precise, less well defined* and, consequently, *less exact*, meaning that what it describes
    a. falls into one *category* or another (e.g., that some *quality* about it either exists or does not exist—making it *"nominal"* in character); or
    b. belongs to *some class* of objects or events that fall along a *gradient* (e.g., the color of a traffic light that may be one of three sequential colors of red, yellow, or green—making it *"ordinal"* in nature).

As reasonable as this hierarchy of informational "quality" may seem, it generates questions that relate to the nature of and the necessity for measurement. For instance: How can we *know* that something exists or that it doesn't (i.e., a seemingly qualitative distinction)? Ultimately, the only way we can learn this is by

- defining something unique about the object or event that we are searching for (e.g., some special attribute); and
- making a measurement to see whether it is present.

If it is present and the attribute is unique, then we say that what we are searching for exists. But if it is not (i.e., if it is either not there or it falls below some predefined level of detectability), then we say that it doesn't. (Note: For this to be the case, the unique trait being measured must be (i) *unfailingly present* when the item exists, (ii) *not* present when the item does not exist, and (iii) *accurately measurable* in all cases [which would give it both 100 percent *positive-* and 100 percent *negative-predictive value* for identifying what is of interest]). Thus, to make the distinction between existence and nonexistence, a measurement is necessary to allocate what we are trying to detect to either inclusion or exclusion with regard to the category of the presence of a particular trait.

As an example, we can consider the case of the traffic light. How do we know if it is green? Ultimately, we must have some way to (A) *detect* if any light is emitted from it (i.e., the light must be incident upon a receptor in an amount greater than the threshold for it to be detected) and then (B) *measure* the *wavelength* of the light (to within certain predefined limits) to see if it is in the range we define as *green*. Despite the fact we might choose to classify "greenness" as a *quality*, both the processes of light detection and wavelength assessment involve making quantitative measurements.

The data derived from such quantitative measurements are then allocated to one of the following types:

1. *Nominal* (something that can be placed into distinct categories)
2. *Ordinal* (such that there is an order to the variable, but the precise magnitude or significance of differences associated with the order is not consistent or not well defined), or
3. *Continuous* (these are either *interval variables*, where the intervals between values have a well-defined meaning, or *ratio variables*, where the ratios between values have a well-defined meaning).

The first two types of data have already been discussed and are often equated (incorrectly) with the idea of being *qualitative*. The third (continuous) type is equated with the idea of being *quantitative*. (Note: A middle category is thought by some to fall somewhere in between—*semi-quantitative*, which appears to be a contradiction in terms!).

This type of a schema brings up something important about traditional data categorizations: they make implicit assumptions about

I. the continuous nature of space-time;
II. the continuous nature of our numbering system; and
III. the discrete and localizable nature of information.

These assumptions do not comport well with modern-day quantum theory (i.e., the ideas that *quantized values* are discrete and generate *quantum uncertainties* that cannot be circumvented). As a result, they give rise to limitations for such types of classification schemes that will be addressed in subsequent chapters (see chapter 21, entitled "Quantum Theory: Uncertainties of the Very Small," and chapter 22, entitled "Entanglement vs. Separability: The Locality Issue," for further discussion).

For data that are considered to be qualitative, the measurements performed to obtain them are simply *less accurate* and *less precise* (or, alternatively, they are recorded with less precision) than for quantitative data. But, because there is no hard and fast dividing line between the types of information that should be considered qualitative versus quantitative (as exemplified by the previous example of the color of a traffic light), the distinction between them can be challenged as both artificial and arbitrary. This is important because the implicit assumption is that more precise measurements provide an ability to gain greater knowledge about the universe, whereas less precise measurements result in "lesser quality" data that allows us less knowledge; the imbedded notion is that qualitative data are "good enough" to make categorical distinctions, but not good enough for quantitative analysis.

This is not the end of the issue, however. Quantitative data relies on a highly accurate measurement. Yet, without at least some reasonable degree of precision, there can be no hope that a measurement will have meaningful accuracy. As an example, if the precision of a measurement is so poor that it is "all over the map," then any attempt to define a meaningful *center* of the measurement (i.e., by using some measure of central tendency, such as an average) is functionally useless for most real purposes. This is because such summary measures (e.g., a *mean*, a *median*, a *mode*, etc.) tell us very little about what the *real* values of all the measurements actually are, since they were actually measured to be "all over." [Note: Statisticians have developed methods to describe the overall distribution and degree of dispersion of such measured values, but these rely on probability and are themselves only summary descriptions]. So measures of central tendency must be regarded as mere *idealizations*, and *not* accurate reflections of *reality*. This has implications for both classical (i.e., macroscopic) measurements as well as for measurements involving submicroscopic objects and events (i.e., at quantum scales).

Despite these issues relating to data quality, empirically derived information is viewed as useful for validating *a priori* notions that we have about *truths* concerning the universe. As such, they constitute the *raw data* upon which scientific experiments rely for performing tests to assess the validity of hypotheses. If such data is derived *internally* (e.g., *a priori* thoughts that do not depend on any direct reference to anything outside of ourselves), accurate measurements must also be made, and the same considerations apply if subsequent manipulations of the information (and the deductions made from them) are to be considered valid. Thus, accurate measurement is required regardless of whether data is based on *external* experience or is generated *internally*.

After data is obtained through measurements, some type of *processing* generally follows. Such manipulations are designed to *extract useful information* from raw data via *analyses*. This injects yet another level of complication, which typically occurs routinely: any *errors* (i.e., *inaccuracies* and/or *imprecisions*) that were imbedded in the original data are prone to being compounded by these transformations. If the initial quantification of information is improper (i.e., incompletely determinate), then the implications derived from the measurements cannot be made more determinate (i.e., clearer) as a result of analysis. This means that analyses of measured values that are inaccurate or imprecise cannot be reliably expected to yield insights that are either correct or useful; in fact, any additional conclusions can only become more muddled. This has been summed up in the widely known colloquial data-processing adage of "Garbage in, garbage out."

The conclusion to be reached is that neither the accuracy nor the precision of a measurement can ever be improved via analyses that are performed during the post-measurement period. If such types of refinements are accomplished, then they must depend on assumptions and generalizations based on other "like objects and events" about which other (supplementary) information is known. The assessment as to whether these are "like enough" to be regarded in the same way requires invoking additional criteria and analyses, but it depends on auxiliary information that is not contained within the original measurements (i.e., it is not intrinsic to what was measured). As such, the (external) validity of the auxiliary information must always be questioned with regard to its applicability to the measured information (i.e., the primary information being processed), as well as the ultimate veracity of any results generated via its use (see chapter 15, entitled "Generalizability: Internal vs. External Validity," for further discussion).

An example of this may be found in mathematical algorithms (i.e., computer programs) that are used for enhancing images. In such cases, images of intrinsically poor quality can be "made clearer" by means of a set of well-defined image enhancement rules that have been gleaned from prior analyses of other pictures of higher quality. Thus, it may be that pixels adjacent to some others should fall into line with a certain set of previously established and well-defined standards (i.e., rules) and, if they don't, they are modified to come into better conformance with those constraints. This makes the image clearer and crisper. But, the additional precision imparted to the original (low-quality) image to make it appear of higher quality is not native to the original image (i.e., the initial measurements). It is simply additional information (i.e., precision) that is imputed and superimposed (i.e., "added in" to make it conform to rules that were established previously for higher-quality photographs). This provides it with higher resolution that makes it "look better." However, there is no reason to believe—other than on the basis of precedents gleaned from other photographs—that the result is actually a true representation of the original scene that the image depicts.

Thus, "adding" new precision of this type has no basis for being considered either true or false. In fact, if there are a large set of possibilities about what the original image might have contained if its natively higher resolution were more properly captured, the likelihood is much greater that the enhanced image will be more inaccurate with regard to portraying the "real image" that the original photograph tried to capture. The result is that the enhanced image is sharper, but this is ultimately nothing more than the result of the application of rules gleaned from other, unrelated observations to generate informed guesswork (i.e., create a probabilistically guided result that is based on past experience).

From this, it can be seen that precision encompasses the fundamental idea of "How good is the measurement?" This is closely related to the notions of "How granularly definable is it?" and "How reproducible is it?" (i.e., from an experimental standpoint, measurements should be both "exact" and reliably reproducible if they are "good"). However, neither the precision nor the reproducibility of a measurement should be confused with the idea of its accuracy. Another example illustrates this distinction: if an archer shoots arrows at a target and each time he hits exactly the same spot at a position along the periphery, then his marksmanship is both precise and reproducible (he keeps hitting the same mark each time), but it is not accurate (as he is aiming for the center of the bull's eye, but he hits the outer edge of the target—meaning that he missed!).

This last example demonstrates that the *accuracy* of measurements is important if we are to know the *true state* of what we are measuring. But just as important, the *precision* of such measurements should be within tight bounds, or the notion of (average) accuracy becomes too diffuse and inexact, making it functionally meaningless. The idea of precision is bounded at two ends: the first on the "less good" side (total imprecision) and the second on the "excellent" side (complete fidelity with what is being measured). We can imagine that increasing imprecision ultimately leads to such large degrees of uncertainty that individual measurements become effectively devoid of meaning. But what about the other side of the spectrum? How good must a measurement be in order for it to be perfect? More to the point, can it ever be so?

This depends on the nature of the tools used to make the measurements. For example, if we use coarse tools (such as a yardstick to measure short distances), then it will not be possible to discern small differences even in principle (e.g., those that are on the order of fractions of an inch). In such cases, there is a mismatch between what we are trying to measure and the tools we have chosen to do the measuring.

To illustrate this point, the question can be asked "How long is the coastline of Maine?" If, to arrive at an answer, one were to reference a satellite image, the coastline could be measured using appropriate tools and a (proper) answer would be generated from that perspective (i.e., from outer space). However, if one were to then ask a team of ground-based workers to measure the coastline using yardsticks placed end to end—thereby accounting for the "cragginess" of the coastline more accurately—a different (and longer) distance would result. If, after that, we asked for the same exercise to be repeated using twelve-inch rulers, there would be more precision in accounting for the cragginess, and the result of the overall measurement would be longer still. If we then asked for the measurement to be repeated using small strings of one inch in length, it would be even longer.

So which of these results is correct? The answer is that they all are with respect to how the measurements were made (with the proviso that they are all properly reproducible to within certain limits—which they should be). They were simply obtained using different tools, which defined the limits of the precision (and, ultimately, the accuracy) that could be obtained in each case.

So which tool is the "right" one to use in any particular instance? Because the measuring device was left unspecified in the original question concerning the length of Maine's coastline, insufficient guidance was provided to arrive at a unique answer. To properly do so, the question must be recast more specifically with regard to methodology, which would generate a question of the type "How long is the coastline of Maine if it is measured using 'technique X'?" Technique X would then need to be specified together with all of the parameters for its proper description, including the type of measuring device to be used, its intrinsic precision, who would be doing the measuring, how the measurement would be performed, how many times the measurements would be repeated (to ensure reproducibility), how the information would be recorded, etc.

This still begs a crucial question: Which measurement technique should be considered the "gold standard"? Some might answer: "I don't care—pick any appropriate methodology, so long as it's 'good enough' to provide the 'right' answer." This presumes, of course, that there is a single right answer and, if so, that there is more than one appropriate methodology for determining it. However, as illustrated by the example of coastline measurement, there would appear to be many "right" answers depending on the choice of different methodologies. In addition, each result has some plausible degree of utility from a practical standpoint. This would depend on the intent for the use of the result (e.g., whether it is meant to be used for the purpose of advertising coastal vacation opportunities to Maine visitors, apportioning federal funds for coastal improvements, determining how many harbors to build along the coast, etc.). All of the methodologies will generate answers that have certain intrinsic limits. The real question becomes, "Is there any methodology that does not have a limit with regard to its accuracy and precision, such that it is an absolutely *true* reflection of reality and cannot be improved?"

For instance, what if we were to choose the incredibly small dimension of a specific wavelength of visible light to make a new measurement of the length of Maine's coastline? This would account for the cragginess of the coast at a very tiny scale and provide an answer of extraordinary length compared to the previously described methods. But, even if this could be considered the right answer, what practical utility might it have? And what if quantum uncertainties ultimately limited the precision and reproducibility of the measurements that could be obtained using this type of a technique as well (see chapter 21, entitled "Quantum Theory: Uncertainties of the Very Small," for further discussion)? What then?

Clearly, all of these issues present significant challenges for making accurate measurements. But, even if it is impossible to know which measurement technique would result in the sought-after gold-standard result, there might still be another approach to arrive at the right answer. This would involve using the admittedly imprecise results from the full panoply of different measurement methodologies, ranking them in terms of their precision (relative to each other), and then using extrapolation techniques to "triangulate" to the correct value. By using this type of an approach, the presumed (and hypothetical) *true* value might be definable, even if it could not be measured directly. This method is indirect, but it is interesting and has some significant intellectual appeal. Essentially, it would *infer* the right (i.e., accurate) answer with absolute precision by merely collecting imprecise real data and then employing analytical techniques to identify the true value rather than needing to make the absolutely accurate and precise measurement directly. Thus, it has the potential to point to the true value without ever needing to measure it!

As an example, this type of approach was used to impute the value of the lowest temperature believed to be possible, which is known as *absolute zero*. No one has ever been able to cool anything to as low a temperature as absolute zero or to measure it directly (minus 273.15 degrees Celsius, a temperature that has not been physically attainable using any type of experimental device). But its value was inferred (initially) from the relationship between gas volume and temperature, with all measurements made at temperatures higher than absolute zero (while holding pressure constant).

When gas volume is extrapolated back to the temperature at which it would be zero (i.e., where there is only quantum mechanical zero-point energy and thermal motion decreases to a minimum), this is the value defined as absolute zero. Thus, even though absolute zero has never been measured, it has been imputed by measuring the behavior of gases at higher temperatures. This leaves open the question of the degree of accuracy intrinsic to the estimate that has been made for absolute zero, but current indications are that it is quite good.

Other issues arise with this type of approach that relate to the reliability of the methods used to analyze data. These are themselves analogous to the current limitations that pertain to measurement (see chapter 11, entitled "Logic and Inference," and chapter 12, entitled "Analysis," for further discussions). Thus, if inferential approaches are used, it simply has the effect of "kicking the can down the road"; it puts the blame of the limitations previously associated with making accurate primary measurements on the accuracy and precision of post-measurement analytical methods instead. These are separate issues, but they result in the same types of limitations regarding the accuracy and precision that can be expected from making real measurements.

Ultimately, measurements determine the accuracy with which we can know about objects and events, their relationships, and their interactions. Although measurements provide the basis for all information and human knowledge, there are significant limitations concerning what can be measured and how accurately this can be accomplished. Critical issues relating to predictability depend on the degree of accuracy and precision of physical measurements (see chapter 19, entitled "Dynamic Certainty vs. Uncertainty: Trajectories," for further discussion), which in turn depend on what is being measured and the tools used to accomplish the task. Because of these limitations, there is a fundamental limit to the precision—and accuracy—of what we can know, whether it relates to the external universe or to ourselves.

In summary, by measuring objects and events we attempt to obtain information that allows us to

- create the basis for *knowledge* that can then lead to an *understanding* of their "intrinsic" *essence*; and

- catalog their *relationships* to—and *interactions* with—other objects and events to try to *understand* them.

Unfortunately, if the processes used for performing measurements are themselves limited or flawed—or if they are an intrinsic function of other factors (or connections) that stand outside of what is being measured—then by the mere act of measuring, we may be generating context-dependent approximations that are *misleading* at best and (quite possibly) delusions at worst. If so, then the chance that our measurements represent a proper reflection of reality will be drowned out by the much higher probability that their imbedded approximations will lead to increasing degrees of error, inconsistency, and misunderstanding. However, there is no choice. Our need to rely on measurement to gain information cannot be circumvented. It is a constraint that we must live with, whether we like it or not.

CHAPTER 10
Associations vs. Causality

How can we differentiate if objects and events are merely associated with each other or causally related?

Association: Definition (Merriam-Webster Dictionary)

- The process of forming mental connections or bonds between sensations, ideas, or memories
- The act of associating
- The state of being associated: combination, relationship

Causality: Definition (Merriam-Webster Dictionary)

- The relationship between a cause and its effect or between regularly correlated events or phenomena
- A causal quality or agency

The idea of *causality* is simple: it is that one object or event has an effect (or influence) on another.

Causal effects can occur over time, so that something existing (or occurring) now has an effect on others that occur later. But, causality can also involve objects or events that exist simultaneously (i.e., where something that *exists* or *occurs now* has an effect that allows for the *contemporaneous existence* of something else).

It is useful to outline the latter case of *contemporaneous causality* in more detail. As an example, the case of a suspension bridge will again be cited. Such a bridge has a large number of discrete components—foundations, towers, cables, roadways, etc. Each of these contributes to the internal integrity and support of the overall structure, such that the bridge is able to maintain its configuration, strength, etc. All of these different elements are distinct, yet they interact on a contemporaneous basis and are essential components that "participate" in both creating and maintaining the overall structure. If any of these elements was removed, it would compromise the integrity of the bridge. And should any critical components be absent, the bridge might very well collapse—causing it to no longer exist.

These ideas of temporal and contemporaneous causality are different in principle from associations. *Associations* "run together" (i.e., occur in *clusters*), but they do not affect or influence each other. They do this either in space (i.e., by being arrayed in some way *around* each other) or in time (i.e., by having some kind of temporal relationship or *sequence*). The key to the difference between associations and causal relationships is that with associations there is no dependence of one object or event on the others for it to either exist or to occur, whereas in the case of causality there is.

Although associations and causal relationships differ in this crucial respect, they are often lumped together and confused. As a result, errors of various types can occur. In this chapter, the differences between these two classes of relationships are defined, and criteria are presented for establishing whether a relationship should be categorized as belonging to one versus the other.

The confusion between association and causality is understandable. Even as infants, one of the primary means by which we learn about our surroundings (and ourselves) is by making associations between objects and events. As an example, there may be an association between urinating (a good feeling) and subsequent discomfort (due to wetness), or recognizing that when our mother enters the room (initially a neutral feeling) we then get fed (a satisfying feeling). Often, these types of associations can lead to the recognition of patterns, both in space and over time. Such types of associations guide us to an appreciation of what is happening around us, and they allow us to anticipate what is *most likely to occur*.

However, an important distinction between associations (i.e., patterns) and causality is often overlooked: The first are merely sets of *concordances* (in space) or *sequenced aggregations* (in time) of objects and events to which we can anchor our thoughts, feelings, and (ultimately) our understanding. However, the second—the idea of causality—implies that some occurrence (e.g., an object, a circumstance, or an event) is *responsible for* (or engenders a *predisposition to*) another object, circumstance, or event, which may be either now or in the future. There is an important consequence to this difference: whereas associations and patterns do not permit the idea of *agency* (i.e., the capacity for acting or exerting power to achieve an end), the notion of causality does.

A useful way to view the difference between associations and causal relationships is that associations can be thought of as *aggregations of objects (or events)*—either in space or over time—without any interaction, whereas causal relationships have some type of an interaction that connects them to each other. This difference is important because it implies that with *causality* there is a *mechanism* at work between objects (or events) that produces linkages with *consequences*. This means that causality is ultimately rooted in a mechanistic view of interactions (i.e., that *chains of events*—or *causal webs*—are in operation) that are either spatially or temporally related. In the case of temporal causality, this implies that sequences of events have well-defined *trajectories* and that one event determines the next, which determines the next, and so on.

There is a profound implication whenever such *mechanistic models* of *causality* are invoked: the causally-linked chains must be envisioned to extend backwards in time, and, by so doing, there cannot but be imagined an *iterative regress* to a *first cause*. This conclusion appears inescapable, especially for non-probabilistic models of causality (and for many, probability-based theories of causality seemed to be a contradiction in terms, at least until recently). As witness to its resilience, causality has independently arisen as a prime tenant within Western mathematical, physical, philosophical, and religious thought, comporting with the theories of Cartesian rationalist philosophy.

The implications of classical causality-based reasoning are fundamental and wide-ranging. In principle, once the rules for causality-based interactions are identified and defined (i.e., if they are assumed to be constant or, alternatively, if they are known to change in predictable ways over time—both of which cannot be adequately tested!), a sequence of causal interactions can be inferred that extends in *both temporal directions*—back into the past (i.e., to define a sequence of events that completely describes prior history), as well as into the future (to predict all that is yet to come). Thus, classical causality-based interactions serve as the basis for the doctrine of determinism (see chapter 3, entitled "Agency: Free Will vs. Determinism," for further discussion). Without causality, deterministic thinking (which underpins Newtonian mechanics, as well as virtually all of classical physics) would have no theoretical or practical basis. Because of these considerations, it is essential to determine if the relationships among objects and events are causally related or if they fall into the category of mere association.

Associations themselves are also intriguing. They often fall into the realm of *concurrent presence* (i.e., whenever a particular object or event is present, something else is present, too). More interestingly, however, they also fall into the realm of temporally dependent sequences (i.e., whenever a particular object or event occurs, then something else follows in time). In the former case of contemporaneous association, if two objects or events are present at the same time, but neither of them caused the other, they still may be *interdependent* in terms of their interactions (i.e., objects or events may still depend on each other as elements of a larger structure, even if they didn't cause each other to occur—as exemplified by the case of the previously mentioned suspension bridge).

An interesting question arises from this line of reasoning concerning the issue of separability, which can be formulated as follows: if two objects (or events) are intrinsically interdependent for the existence of something else, but neither of them causes the other, then should they be regarded as two separate objects (or events) or just a single one that is more expansive with multiple (internal) components? Depending on definitions and context, the answer to this question may be either. So for objects and events that exist concurrently, there may be an interdependence between them of some type but no causal relationship (per se).

In the case of *temporal causality*, a *sequential association* is necessary for an object or event to be potentially causally related to another, but this criterion—in and of itself—is insufficient to establish that it is actually responsible for causing another to either exist or to occur. An example illustrates this: as an infant, we may notice that when the door to our room opens, our mother comes in, and we get fed. Depending on the consistency and uniqueness of the association and for how long it goes on, this sequence of events can become a very strongly ingrained expectation (i.e., we can become *conditioned* to accept this sequencing of events as being the norm), which represents an example of classical Pavlovian-type conditioning. However, despite the rising set of expectations for the repetition of the same sequence that we learn to associate from these sets of events, if we were to conclude that the opening of the door somehow caused our mother to come in and then to feed us, this would be wrong. There is nothing about the door opening—in and of itself—that causes our mother to come in, and there is nothing about our mother coming in—in and of itself—that causes her to feed us. This is merely a sequence of events that has been repeated consistently in the past (i.e., it has occurred repeatedly with the same—or similar—*pattern*). This is the hallmark of an association. It can be characterized as a "habit"—a habitual set of associated events. But, it is not causality.

One criterion that is often used to assess the possibility of a causal relationship is the notion of plausibility (i.e., "How is it that object (or event) A is capable of causing object (or event) B?)" This line of inquiry quickly evolves into the idea of mechanism, which is one of the basic questions addressed by science. However, establishing a plausible mechanism is neither an absolute requirement for the presence of a causal relationship nor proof of it. There are many examples where the mechanisms that have "connected" object (or event) A to object (or event) B have not been readily evident or transparent at the outset of a discovery, only to be discovered later.

One such example is the eighteenth century demonstration by the Scottish physician James Lind that consuming citrus fruits can treat scurvy (he wasn't the first to suggest this, but in 1747 he was first to study the effects of citrus fruits on scurvy via a controlled experiment, representing one of the first clinical studies in medicine). To do this, he divided twelve sailors with scurvy into six groups; all ate the same basic diet, but they also received the following daily in addition: Group 1—cider (a quart), Group 2—sulfuric acid (twenty-five drops of elixir), Group 3—vinegar (six spoonfuls), Group 4—seawater (a half pint), Group 5—two oranges plus one lemon, and Group 6—a spicy paste plus barley water. After six days, one sailor in the orange-lemon group was fit for duty while the other was nearly recovered. The only other group showing some positive effect was the cider group. Initially there was no known mechanism of action to link the consumption of citrus fruits to the successful treatment of scurvy, but on subsequent and more detailed evaluation (in the twentieth century), this was found to be due to the vitamin C that these fruits contain.

Alternatively, science is replete with cases where purported mechanisms were considered to imply a plausible causal linkage between objects and events that were ultimately determined to be mistaken or incorrect. An example is the supposed connection between "direct human contact" and the transmission of yellow fever—a potentially life-threatening infectious disease. This was subsequently discovered to be caused by a virus transmitted by mosquitoes! Nevertheless, without the identification of a mechanism (i.e., a mode of interaction whereby one object or event is able to act upon another), causal relationships are often considered to be both suspect and unproven.

The difference between associations and causality can be summed up as follows: many occurrences are associated with other objects and events, but if they do not cause them to happen, then they are merely "innocent bystanders" that "hang around"—perhaps even consistently—but this is different from them being causal. Occurrences of this type are merely associated with other objects and events and do not have any direct effect upon them. On the other hand, in causal relationships there is a direct relationship between objects and events that is mediated by some type of interaction and (at least) one of them is necessary to either (a) allow for or (b) dictate that something else will occur. In the case of temporal causality, the "something else" occurs "downstream" in time. In this latter case, without the occurrence of the causal objects(s) or event(s) as antecedents, the subsequent event (or object) won't occur.

As clear as this distinction between mere associations and causal relationships may sound in principle, it is often very difficult to discern in practice. There are many reasons for this. One is that many associations tend to run together very consistently. As an example, imagine the case of fish and water: whenever we identify fish in the wild, they are always found together with water. Water may exist without fish, but there are no (true) fish that exist outside of an aquatic environment. Thus, upon repeated observations by countless observers over millennia that fish exist in water, one might be tempted to conclude that there is a causal relationship between the two (i.e., that water can somehow "spawn" fish that then live in it under the right conditions). Or, even more fantastically, because fish are always found surrounded by water, we might imagine that fish somehow "create" water and are the underlying source for it. As absurd as these ideas may sound to educated people in modern societies, there was something analogous that was widely held by educated people and scientists for millennia—a long-standing doctrine known as the *spontaneous generation* theory.

The idea of a spontaneous generation can be summarized as follows: living organisms can arise from inanimate materials if the local conditions are such that they predispose to it. The doctrine originated from observations in antiquity that particular types of living beings (e.g., maggots), appeared to arise spontaneously in places where inanimate conditions "fostered" their generation (e.g., rotting meat). The principle had its most coherent expression by Aristotle, who held that life arose from inanimate matter under the proper conditions as a matter of course. Subsequently, this idea became entrenched and was widely believed for two millennia. The theory was ultimately disproven by the "goose-neck flask" experiments of Louis Pasteur during the nineteenth century, who showed that no such sequence of events occurred under suitably controlled conditions. It was only then that the idea of spontaneous generations was supplanted by modern-day cell theory.

Analogously, we now understand that water is a necessary condition for fish to live, but that it is insufficient to promote the de novo generation of these creatures from inanimate materials (i.e., merely placing water in containers will not result in the spontaneous generation of fish). However, if we were to rely only upon empirical *observations* instead of testing specific hypotheses that underlie this purported cause-and-effect relationship in an *interventional* way, we could not distinguish the veracity of one of these hypotheses over the other (association versus causality). This is an argument in favor of the testing made possible by scientific methods (i.e., using interventional experiments to test hypotheses that are potentially falsifiable—see chapter 9, entitled "Measurement: How Circumstance and Change Are Assessed," for further discussion). Without such a rigorous system of testing, we could be easily deceived into believing that the recurrent presence of a mere association (e.g., between water and fish) could, in fact, be causal—either in one direction (i.e., water spawns fish) or the other (fish create water).

The other side of the coin is that many objects (or events) that may actually be responsible for causing others to happen are either unrecognized or "hidden" from us, often because we have not yet discovered them or because we simply do not have the sensory apparatuses (biological or mechanical) to detect and properly identify them. This constitutes a large portion of the substrate for the investigations conducted in both the realms of theoretical and empirical science, but it also allows for *beliefs* in (possible) relationships between objects and events that have not (yet) been proven.

For instance, the medical literature is replete with examples of associations that were once thought to be causally related. This occurs commonly and is often the result of *confounding*. A good example comes from twentieth century medicine: during the 1980s, evidence emerged for a relationship between the use of intrauterine devices (IUDs) in women and an increased incidence of pelvic infections. This relationship was posited to be causal, resulting in both costly litigation and a downward spiral in IUD use. Upon closer examination, it turned out that even though it appeared that women who used IUDs had an increased incidence of pelvic infections (compared to nonusers), this was due to systematic differences in the average number of sexual partners for the women in each group (users versus nonusers). Accordingly, the causal relationship turned out to be between the number of sexual partners and the risk of pelvic infection, and not with the IUDs themselves.

In this case, there was a user bias in the studies. The IUDs turned out to be "innocent bystanders"; they were interventions that permitted a higher level of sexual activity among their wearers (or, alternatively, they were worn more often by the women who were intrinsically more sexually active), thereby placing these women at an increased risk of pelvic infections for that reason. The real culprit (i.e., the actual causal relationship) was between the number of different sexual partners and the risk of pelvic infection. Thus, the outcome of interest (pelvic infections) was not the fault of the IUDs, but it *was* causally related (i.e., the fault of) systematic differences in sexual behavior between IUD wearers versus non-wearers.

Another example comes from a common realm we deal with all the time—marketing. The objective of marketing products comes down to this: creating an image that makes potential users want to use them. This is accomplished in sometimes ingenious ways: marketeers depend on creating an illusion of causality (i.e., the idea that "if you use this product, then you will become like this or that") when, in fact, they are merely conjuring up in people's minds an image that represents an association of desirable attributes that they want (e.g., a cluster of beauty, relaxation, youth, energy, sex, etc.). The effect is to make the potential users believe that if they were to buy the product, they would automatically gain all of those other attributes as well. This type of association is portrayed in a way so as to project causality when it does NOT exist! As such, it rests behind the rationale for using a beautiful model to show the positive effects of women's makeup (an effect that is largely attributable to the model and not to the makeup!), the raw "manliness" associated with using a mud-strewn pick-up truck to move heavy, dirty objects (an effect attributable to the images of tall, muscular men, but not to the truck itself), the rough-hewn sexiness of a cowboy smoking a cigarette (an effect associated with the open-spaced, devil-may-care appearance of the cowboy roaming the range on horseback, and not to the cigarette itself), etc.

Given the need for practical guidelines to clarify the difference between associations and causality, a schema for assessing the difference was outlined in the 1960s by Sir Austin Bradford Hill of England. The rules he enumerated reflect a set of minimal conditions regarded as necessary to provide adequate evidence for a (temporal) causal relationship between a cause and a consequence. The following nine considerations are derived from Hill's original criteria to distinguish temporal causality from mere associations:

1. **Temporal relationship** (The cause must precede the consequence.)
2. **Strength of association** (The correlation, relative risk, odds ratio, etc. should be large.)
3. **Consistency** (The consequence should be seen to follow the cause repeatedly.)
4. **Response gradient** (The strength of the consequence should be related to the strength of the cause; i.e., there should be an "intensity-response" relationship.)
5. **Experimental evidence** (Well-controlled experiments should support the cause-and-effect hypothesis.)
6. **Specificity** (The consequence does not occur when the cause does not occur.)
7. **Plausibility** (A mechanism—or pathway—can be envisioned whereby the cause could result in the consequence.)
8. **Coherence** (The cause-and-effect relationship is consistent with other existing knowledge or evidence.)

9. **Analogy** (The cause-and-effect relationship is similar to other known relationships that have been proven previously.)

The first five criteria are considered the most important. The sixth criterion (specificity) is very reassuring if it is satisfied, but is seldom the case (i.e., there is often more than one "cause" that can precipitate a particular "outcome," but this—in and of itself—does not substantially weaken the case for the cause-and-effect relationship for any specific cause). The seventh criterion (plausibility) has been discussed previously; it can be falsely reassuring if it is deemed to be present, and falsely undermining if the underlying causal interactions are either undetectable or not yet discovered. The eighth and ninth criteria (coherence and analogy) are both reassuring if they are present, but they cannot be present if the discovery is truly new (i.e., first-in-class); this makes their necessity inconsistent and, therefore, weak.

The intent of this chapter has been to highlight the differences between *associations* (i.e., *clusters* or *patterns*) and *causality*. The difference is often difficult to establish, but to do so is crucial: by mistaking associations for causal relationships, we can be fundamentally misled with regard to the relationships between objects (and events). To misconstrue such relationships means that we can develop a flawed understanding of them. In the worst of circumstances, this can make us believe that there are connections between objects and events that do not actually exist. Or alternatively, it can make us believe that there are no causal relationships between objects and events when there actually are.

The real danger in believing in these types of falsities is that we might think that we can act with the intent of influencing something else (i.e., impact the probability of a downstream event), when no relationship between the two is even remotely possible. An example might be giving distilled water to cancer patients in the hope of curing their disease, when there is no plausible reason for a cause-and-effect relationship to exist between distilled water and the cure of cancer. Then we might commit energy, time, and resources to something that is impossible while depriving patients of other (effective) treatments without even recognizing it—and be surprised when the outcome isn't what we thought it would be. The opposite is also true: if we believe that there is no causal relationship between objects (or events) when there is, then we might do something to influence what we consider to be only an "innocent bystander" association that did not have any potential for downstream impact on the events of interest, only to discover that there are unintended and distressing consequences that we never anticipated.

Thus, before choosing to *act*, it is best to determine if the relationships between objects and events are *causal* or simply mere *associations*. Otherwise, there is a risk of going astray with any intervention, the effects of which can either be devoid of any impact or magnified by unintended consequences to an extent that may not be reasonably predicted or controlled.

CHAPTER 11
Logic and Inference

Logic is an approach used for making inferences and drawing legitimate conclusions.

Logic: Definition (Merriam-Webster Dictionary)

- A science that deals with the principles and criteria of validity of inference and demonstration
- The science of the formal principles of reasoning
- Interrelation or sequence of facts or events when seen as inevitable or predictable
- A particular mode of reasoning viewed as valid or faulty

Inference: Definition (Merriam-Webster Dictionary)

- The act of passing from one proposition, statement, or judgment considered as true to another whose truth is believed to follow from that of the former
- Something that is inferred; especially a conclusion or opinion that is formed because of known facts or evidence

- The premises and conclusion of a process of inferring
- The act or process of inferring

Logic is the term used to denote a system for determining the *validity* of an inference (i.e., conclusion) *deduced* from *two* or more *statements*. Statements are *premises* that comprise the substrates of arguments. The focus of logic is *not* on what the premises state (i.e., the *content* of the statements), but on the *structure* (i.e., the form) of the argument that is mounted by using them.

More than two millennia ago, the Greek philosopher Aristotle addressed the subject of logic in a systematic fashion and originated the theory of *syllogism*. In his work *Prior Analytics,* he defined syllogism as a logical argument in which one proposition (the *conclusion*) is *inferred* from two or more others (the *premises*) by stating that it was "a deduction in a discourse in which, certain things having been supposed, something different from the things supposed results of necessity because these things are so." Aristotle's influence permeated widely through Western culture, but not to the same extent through cultures residing in the Far East.

For any system of logic to be *valid*, if the *premises* are *true*, then the *inferences* derived by using them—also called the *logical consequences*—must also be *true*. To accomplish this, there are three *principles* that underpin classical (Aristotelian) logic:

1. **Identity**: An object is the same as itself (i.e., "If you have A, then you have A" or "If a statement is true, then it is true"). This is a tautology (merely a repetition of the same idea).
2. **Excluded middle**: For any proposition, either the proposition is true, or its negation is true (i.e., a statement must be either true or false).
3. **Non-contradiction**: A statement cannot be both true and false at the same time (e.g. the two propositions "*A is B*" and "*A is not B*" are mutually exclusive).

Using this set of principles, rules can be constructed for making inferences to mechanically derive conclusions from premises. When these *rules of inference* are codified to make a *formal language,* the resulting system is referred to as a system of *formal logic.*

Why should we go to this length to make a formal logical system?

Because the expectation is that it should work. At best, such a system should allow for the deduction of all the *truths* from an initial (minimal) set of complete truths (i.e., premises, also known as *axioms**). But at the very least, such a system should never lead us astray; that is, it shouldn't take us (incorrectly) from an initial set of true premises to an untrue (i.e., false) conclusion. If it did, then we would be faced with untrue conclusions that would be inconsistent with the true premises from which they arose, thereby creating falsehoods that could result in *paradoxes* (i.e., an apparently true statement that leads to a *contradiction* or a situation that defies logic or intuition). Obviously, this would not be good and, if it occurred, it would cast doubt on both the validity—and, thereby, the utility—of the entire system.

Many paradoxes have cropped up in *mathematics*, which is perhaps our most relied-upon system of formal inference. These have made mathematicians question its consistency. David Hilbert, the renowned early twentieth-century German mathematician, was so concerned about these inconsistencies that he proposed a way to fix it. His plan required going back to basics, by which he meant that mathematicians should charge themselves with two fundamental challenges: first, ensuring that all mathematical *theorems* (i.e., statements that have been *proven* on the basis of previously accepted *axioms*) be based on a *finite* and *complete set* of *axioms* and, second, that they construct a *proof* to show that *all* of these axioms are *consistent*.

It is important to note that all systems of formal logic—with mathematics representing a prime example—are *not* designed to validate the truth of the premises (i.e., axioms) they use as substrates. The premises themselves are simply meant to be accepted (i.e., *given*) without proof. The idea behind formal inferential systems is that they operate according to a basic underlying assumption of the following type: "If we accept this set of premises to be true (at the outset), then we can infer the following additional truths as a result." The clear implication is that the *additional truths* that are uncovered are somehow *imbedded within* the greater truth of the original premises that are accepted as true to begin with.

There is a flawed logic with regard to this procedure of discovering truths. This is because the truth of the initial axioms used as premises is established outside of the formal logic system that is designed to operate on them. This means that the system can only infer additional truths after the original ones are accepted as being true without proof. This underscores a fundamental fact that delimits the truth of any conclusion that can be drawn: because there are other means by which the primary determination of truth is made with regard to the premises themselves, the truth of the conclusions from any inferential system can *never* be any *better than* the *truth value* of the *original premises*. Thus, if the truth of the original premises is flawed, then the truth of the conclusions has a very high potential to be flawed also (except if we are very "lucky" by chance).

Although this is so, it is curious that there are no well-defined rules to establish the truth of the initial axioms that underlie logical arguments as substrates. The term *self-evident* is often used to describe the method, which means "evident without proof or reasoning." But, this raises further questions: Self-evident to whom, under what conditions, within what context, etc.? Unfortunately, none of these questions have well-defined answers. Therefore, the original premises (i.e., substrates) that are used by formal systems of inference rest on squishy ground. This is not good, especially if one intends to use a formal system of logic to arrive at true conclusions as outputs.

These concerns arise not just in an effort to foster an academic discussion concerning the underpinnings of truth. These issues reach to the core of why we believe what we believe. The first limitation we must accept is the fact that the truth of the original premises we believe in rests on considerations that lie outside of the formal systems we use to bridge from them to other (imbedded) truths. But, even if we are correct in our original assumptions regarding the truth of the starting premises, a second limitation arises that revolves around the inherent reliability of the formal logic systems we use to make our inferences.

Mathematicians have made very serious attempts to prove that the mathematical systems of formal inference will lead exclusively from true premises only to true conclusions, but they have never seriously attempted to test the truth value of the premises used as the inputs themselves (aside, perhaps, from addressing their consistency—physicists are the ones who are most concerned about the truth of the premises as they relate to the universe). Often, this has been reduced to the question of whether a formal logic system is capable of generating *contradictions* (which would violate the third of the three sacrosanct principles of Aristotelian logic).

So, leaving the issue of the truth of original premises (axioms) aside, several questions can be examined surrounding the usefulness of inferential logical systems themselves. Two famous proponents of attempting to formalize such systems were David Hilbert and Kurt Gödel.

In the early 1920s, David Hilbert promulgated the goal of establishing a secure foundation for all of mathematics. To accomplish this, he envisioned that the following minimal elements needed to be assured:

- **Formalization**: All mathematical statements needed to be written in a *precise formal language* and manipulated according to a well-defined set of *rules*.
- **Completeness**: A proof was needed to demonstrate that *all* true mathematical statements could be *proven* within the formalism.
- **Consistency**: A proof was necessary to show that *no contradiction* was possible within the formalism; this proof should use only *finite* reasoning (preferably) about finite mathematical objects.
- **Decidability**: An *algorithm* was necessary for deciding the *truth or falsity* of any mathematical statement.

Hilbert's program was ambitious, but he viewed it as both a necessary and fundamental step for setting out the pillars of an unassailable system of formal inference, of which mathematics was the ultimate example.

However, it was shown soon thereafter that most of the goals of Hilbert's program were not attainable, because they could not be assured simultaneously. In 1931, Kurt Gödel—then a German graduate student—developed his *incompleteness theorems* demonstrating that *any consistent theory* powerful enough to encode for the basic underpinnings of mathematics *cannot prove* its *own consistency*. Specifically, Gödel developed two theorems that showed the following with respect to Hilbert's objectives:

- **Formalization**: It is *not possible* to *formalize all* of *mathematics*, as any such attempt will *omit* some *true mathematical statements*.
- **Completeness**: Mathematical theories are necessarily *incomplete*, because there is no complete, consistent extension of a recursively enumerable[†] set of axioms.
- **Consistency**: Even a simple mathematical theory (such as *arithmetic*) *cannot prove* its *own consistency*, such that the consistency of any more powerful theories (e.g., set theory) cannot be proven.

- **Decidability**: *No algorithm exists* that can decide the *truth* (or *provability*) of statements in any consistent extension of arithmetic.

The conclusions of the theorems are both clarifying and devastating. They set out the theoretical limits of the utility and applicability of all logical systems of inference by showing that it is *not possible* to obtain an effectively (i.e., *algorithmically*) generated, *complete* and *consistent theory* in mathematical logic (at least in certain important cases). What this implies for all meaningful, nontrivial logical systems is that:

1. *If* a *logical system* is *consistent*, then it *cannot be complete* (i.e., there are true statements that lie outside of the system's ability to prove them).
2. *If* a *logical system* is *complete*, then it *cannot be consistent* (i.e., there are statements that can be shown to be both true and false within the system at the same time).

Specifically, Gödel's first incompleteness theorem states that *no consistent set* of *axioms* whose theorems can be listed by an *effective procedure* (i.e., an *algorithm* of the type that might be executed by a computer program) is *capable* of *proving all* the *facts about them* (in the case of Gödel's theorem, all the natural numbers). This means that for any such system, there will *always* be *statements* that are *true* but that are *not provable* within the system. The second theorem states that if such a system is also capable of proving certain basic facts about the premises, then a *particular truth* that the system *cannot prove* is the *consistency* of the *system itself.* Together, Gödel's theorems are widely interpreted to mean that *enumerating* a *complete* and *consistent set* of *axioms* for *all* of *mathematics* is *impossible*.

So, what can we conclude from this discussion? Two items that we must presume are quite fundamental:

- The *truth value* of *premises* (i.e., *axioms*) that we use in logical systems to infer (i.e., deduce) additional truths is something that falls *outside* of the *logical systems* themselves; in other words, we must *accept without proof* the *initial premises* that we believe to be true in order to use the inferential systems that we then depend on, thereby

relying on something other than logic itself to determine what we believe to be true in the first instance.
- The *logical systems* that we use to infer additional (i.e., imbedded) truths about the premises we believe to be initially true are fundamentally limited in their scope and applicability, as they *cannot* be *both complete* and *consistent* at the same time (i.e., if they are consistent, then they must necessarily be operating over a limited domain that does not consider the implications of factors that lie outside of their realm of operation; or if they are complete, then they necessarily embody intrinsic inconsistencies that can lead from true premises to contradictions).

The first of these pertains to the fact that we must rely (initially and primarily) on the truth of *self-evident axioms* that we simply believe are true *without formal proof.* This generates questions about the reasons we have for our beliefs, as they fall outside the realm of logic. The second pertains to the way that this axiomatic information is subsequently *manipulated* within our *logical systems* to arrive at *additional truths* (i.e., those that are *deduced* or *imbedded*). Based on what has been presented, both of these would appear to be inexact and, therefore, subject to *error.* This should give us pause, because even small errors can be multiplied considerably through subsequent (i.e., iterative) usage. This can occur inadvertently and unknowingly, especially if there are no external standards or benchmarks by which to judge outcomes. Because of this, they can explode into large errors quite readily and routinely (see chapter 24, entitled "Chaos Theory: Implications for Macroscopic Predictability," for further discussion). We must, therefore, consider not just if the premises that we believe in are actually true, but also if the conclusions that we can draw from them by using systems of formal logic are true as well.

Another issue bears mention that revolves around one of the fundamental principles of Aristotelian logic: the validity of the second principle of the *excluded middle.* This operation contends that everything in propositional logic can be dichotomized into either "yes or no," "true or false," "is or is not," or "this or that," etc. In effect, it deliberately leaves no room for anything to bridge the gulf, to connect the dots, or to be *BOTH* this *and* that at the same time under any circumstances. The question arises: Is this a reasonable approach and is it an accurate reflection of reality? Is it true?

Are there particular circumstances under which objects and events *both* "are and are not"—all at once and under the same circumstances, without any internal contradiction?

The Aristotelian perspective about this issue has been permeated throughout most of Western thought and modern science, but it is not similarly embraced within many Eastern cultures. What is the *middle* itself that Aristotle deliberately chooses to exclude? If it contains any useful information (as would be the case, for instance, for any continuous variable), then the process of dichotomization into two opposing *big bucket* categories of either/or serves to *discard* the *useful intervening information* (i.e., if there is a *continuum* that includes a *middle*, and it is arbitrarily *divided* into *two categories*, then the additional information that constituted what was intervening is discarded even when it contains non-superfluous additional structure and information). As already mentioned, even small perturbations to otherwise predictable systems can sometimes *tip them over the edge* without warning—thereby producing large and discontinuous effects that are the hallmark of unstable systems (see chapter 17, entitled "Continuity (Smoothness) vs. Discontinuity (Roughness)"; chapter 18, entitled "Stability vs. Instability: System Inertia and Resiliency"; and chapter 19, entitled "Dynamic Certainty vs. Uncertainty: Trajectories," for further discussions). Thus, the assumption that the wanton disregard of even small amounts of information is permissible without effect—as is done with the Aristotelian operation of excluding the middle—becomes indefensible, because the ultimate *downstream effects* of including such additional information can, in fact, be very large.

Many of the questions posed in this chapter are easier to ask than to answer. But, they should nevertheless inject some degree of *uncertainty* (and discomfort) into the ways that we routinely assemble, categorize, process, and interpret the information we are able to access about the universe. Systems of logic and inference are often useful, but those that we have at our disposal are far from flawless. In fact, they are all prone to *error*, which means that they can break down—often quite quickly and unexpectedly. The chapters that follow build on these uncertainties and provide a further basis for understanding why they exist and what this means regarding our ability to predict the future.

*Axioms (or *postulates*) are those *sentences* (or *propositions*) in formal logic that are considered to be *true without proof* (i.e., *self-evident*). An axiom's truth is taken for granted and serves as a starting point for deducing (i.e., inferring) other (theory dependent) truths that are *imbedded* within them. Thus, axioms define and delimit the realm of any analysis. The following are true of axioms:

- An *axiomatic set* is *complete* if, for any statement in the axioms' formal language, *either* that *statement* or its *negation* is *provable* from the axioms.
- An *axiomatic set* is *consistent* if there is *no statement* such that *both* the *statement* and its *negation* are *provable* from the axioms.
- In a *standard system* of first-order logic, an *inconsistent axiomatic set* will *prove every statement* in its language (this is sometimes referred to as the principle of explosion), and is thus *automatically complete*.
- In contrast, a (theoretical) *axiomatic set* that is *both complete* and *consistent* will *prove* a *maximal set* of *non-contradictory theorems*.

†A set is *recursively enumerable* if an *algorithm* can *mechanically enumerate* (as would occur in the case of a computer program) *all* the *members* of the set. The algorithm's output is simply a list of the set members. The algorithm may run forever, if necessary.

CHAPTER 12
Analysis

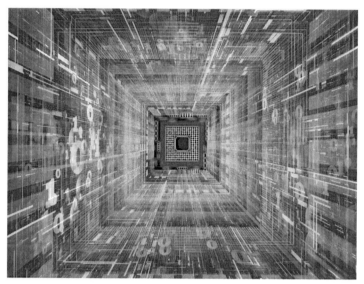

Analysis refers to the types of techniques used for processing the information we acquire.

Analysis: Definition (Merriam-Webster Dictionary)

- An examination of a complex, its elements, and their relations
- Separation of a whole into its component parts
- A method in philosophy of resolving complex expressions into simpler or more basic ones
- Proof of a mathematical proposition by assuming the result and deducing a valid statement by a series of reversible steps
- A branch of mathematics concerned mainly with limits, continuity, and infinite series: calculus
- The identification or separation of ingredients of a substance

The idea of *analysis* can be traced back to the ancient Greek philosopher Aristotle, who taught that its goal was to *dissect* objects and events into their component parts. The idea was that if these could be broken up into their most basic building blocks (i.e., *constituents*), there would be a better appreciation of how each exists and behaves separately. Then, by using this knowledge about the components as a starting point, it should be possible to examine all of them individually and in combination to reconstruct the whole. By going through this exercise of dissection followed by reconstruction, it should be possible to gain a deeper understanding of what objects (and events) are, how they function, what they mean, and—ultimately—why they exist (or occur).

At a practical level, a wide variety of approaches can fulfill this type of analytical schema. In fact, many different methodologies have been used to perform analyses in varying disciplines. Often, these have depended on the types of objects and events being analyzed (or, more properly, the data that we have about them). The approaches taken to dissecting apart some types of objects (i.e., physical bodies such as elephants, or biological subsystems, such as the human brain) have been quite different from those taken to analyze other physical systems and occurrences, such as the environment (i.e., the atmosphere and its weather patterns), man-made objects (i.e., bridges, airplanes, etc.), natural events (i.e., birds flying, volcanoes erupting, tsunamis overrunning coastlines, etc.), or human thoughts and ideas (i.e., feelings, abstract mathematics, economic theories, political ideologies, etc.).

Analytical approaches have also tended to vary widely depending on the type, size, scope, and quality of the available data. These include the different methodologies employed by the social sciences on the one hand versus the so-called hard sciences on the other. However, in all cases the goal is the same: to gain a deeper understanding of what is being analyzed.

Different approaches to analysis have had varying degrees of success due to their differing intrinsic limitations. The intent is not to describe them all. Instead, it is only to point out that all methods of analysis involve performing particular types of operations on the information we have about objects or events. In general terms, these are the following:

- *breaking* them up (physically or mentally) into the *smaller parts* (i.e., into their *components* or constituents); and
- *assessing* the *intrinsic nature* of the *components*, as well as their *relationships* and *interactions*.

After coming to conclusions, we often attempt to *project* and/or *generalize* our findings, to *other times* (i.e., a hundred, a thousand, or even a million years ago), *other places* (i.e., other parts of the world, other planets, etc.), and to *other objects* (and *events*) that we consider to be of *like type* (i.e., those that we regard as being similar based on a myriad of potential matching characteristics). Through this process, we hope to be able to *explain* why objects and events are the way that they are, including not only what they are now, but also what they had been in the past and what they will become in the future.

It is useful to point out another, more modern dimension of analysis that goes beyond the original Aristotelian idea of evaluating the component parts of objects and events: by extension, it functionally reverses the original process by assessing *aggregations* of *separate objects* and/or *events* in collections to make up *larger wholes*. An example of this might be in the field of cosmology. There, once a working knowledge concerning some of the cosmological subsystems is gained (i.e., of stars, planets, comets, galaxies, interstellar gases, etc.), an "aggregative analysis" can be performed to "build up" to a larger structure. The intent is to see the implications of putting all of these subsystems together as a whole—even if the boundaries are arbitrary or incompletely known.

Thus, in the instance of *aggregative analysis*, the original idea of Aristotelian analysis is applied in reverse: the subcomponents of the overall object or event under consideration (e.g., stars, planets, comets, galaxies, interstellar gases, exploding supernovas, etc.) are better known and understood than the whole (i.e., the cosmos). Accordingly, they are used as the starting point for building up to the greater system when the full extent, behavior, meaning, and purpose of the larger, overarching system is unknown.

When analyses are performed properly, they allow us (in principle) to better appreciate the following:

1. *How* what was analyzed (i.e., an *object* or *event*) is *internally organized,* as well as how it "operates" and *interacts* with other objects and events; and
2. *How* to *construct like objects* and *systems* in ways that they can act similarly to the object(s) and event(s) that have been analyzed.

The next question that is potentially addressable is *why* the object or event exists at all (i.e., what it *really is*, what it is *supposed to do*, and, ultimately, what it is *here for* in more than simply a functional sense). The answers to these questions depend in large part on the *context* (i.e., the greater environment within which the object or event finds itself) which, importantly, provides additional information for helping to define the *intent* of its existence (in an overall sense). Addressing these issues is typically not the primary goal of analysis, but they represent metaphysical questions that are often approached through the results of analysis.

From this discussion, it can be seen that all methods of analysis rely on either the *deconstruction* of *wholes* or the *assembly* of *aggregates* (whether they are physical or "imaginary" objects and events)—or both. The hope is to then be able to *reconstruct* them and demonstrate that there is a sufficient working knowledge to "put them together" and make them operate in the way that was intended. Thus, analysis provides a framework for ultimately developing and coming to a degree of understanding about what has been investigated (see chapter 13, entitled "Understanding," for further discussion).

As a starting point for any type of formal analysis, a set of rules or procedures must be adopted and adhered to. These can be either physical or mental in nature (i.e., such as establishing reproducible procedures for making measurements on the one hand, or a hierarchical set of approaches to thinking about objects and events on the other). These rules then constitute the framework for a particular type of analysis, and they help to define its scope and limitations, as well as the applicability of the results. When these constitute a step-by-step prescription of a well-defined list of procedures (or operations) that describe how to go from a starting point (i.e., inputs) to the end result (i.e., outputs) of the analysis, this set of instructions is referred to as an *algorithm*.

The idea of formal analysis depends on a well-defined method of this type (i.e., an algorithm) to "crank through" a sequence of steps using some initial inputs to arrive at a conclusion. At a practical level, it is predicated upon three fundamental premises:

I. The existence (and discovery) of an appropriate algorithm that can "do the job"
II. The appropriate application of the algorithm (i.e., ensuring that all the assumptions necessary for its proper use are fulfilled)
III. Having the algorithm's execution result in a finite number of well-defined steps that can be carried out within a finite period of time.

All three items must conform to a standard methodology, and they must be conducted in a manner that can be reproduced.

The execution of algorithms of this type can be thought of as resulting in some sort of a *calculation*. In some circumstances, the results of these calculations can be a prediction of the expected circumstances or conditions that will occur at other times and places, which necessarily involve making predictions by extension about unrealized circumstances.

Depending on the size and scope of the objects or events under analysis, there may be a dizzying number of subcomponents and interactions that need to be identified and accounted for. This often depends on the extent of what is considered to be a *smallest component part* and a *smallest level of interaction* between objects and events, but it is often *unclear* what the *size* and *delimiting boundary* of any particular part or interaction actually is, thereby making this distinction arbitrary. This is relevant because it means that at a practical level, the idea of analysis is useful only for relatively small, well-defined systems (i.e., those for which the numbers of discrete components and interactions is tractable). This is because once the numbers of components and interactions increase beyond a certain limit (a number that is relatively small), the overlapping *nonlinear behaviors* of some of the subcomponents of *large systems* often makes the downstream description of events and circumstances intrinsically uncertain due to the emergence of *chaotic phenomena* (see chapter 24, entitled "Chaos Theory: Implications for Macroscopic Predictability," for further discussion).

Unlike the common understanding of the term *chaos*, its usage here denotes a system behavior that is deterministic, but that simply cannot be known in advance of "reaching that point" by either cranking through the analytical sequence or allowing the system to evolve to observe the results; this is because there are immediately adjoining, well-defined trajectories that result in discontinuities (e.g., bifurcations) that generate non-identical (i.e., competing) downstream results. All of the differing consequences of the cascade of bifurcation "decisions" at each step are possible, and these can be markedly divergent as a result of starting conditions that are only very marginally different (at least potentially—see chapter 19, entitled "Dynamic Certainty vs. Uncertainty: Trajectories," for further discussion). These divergences conspire to make the net result of all such interactions intrinsically unpredictable in advance, even in principle.

Because of these constraints, analysis very often does not culminate in well-defined, stable results that are reliable and reproducible. As a consequence, it can only provide us with approximations that cannot be used to routinely generate accurate or precise predictions. Therefore, as much as we would like for analysis to provide us with additional insights and understandings to help us to make accurate predictions about the future, it very often cannot.

CHAPTER 13
Understanding

Understanding allows us to make sense of the knowledge we derive from information.

Understanding: Definition (Merriam-Webster Dictionary)

- A mental grasp; comprehension
- The power of comprehending; the capacity to apprehend general relations of particulars
- The power to make experience intelligible by applying concepts and categories
- Explanation; interpretation

Many reputable thinkers have attempted to define what is meant by the term *understanding*, but none has produced a definition that is entirely satisfactory. Despite this, there can be general agreement that the idea of understanding is functionally testable: we typically suppose that we have a proper understanding of events and their relationships when we can *think through* a set of events in advance of observing their occurrence and accurately *predict* what they will be. So, although the necessary ingredients as well as the actual basis for understanding may both be nebulous, this type of a functional evaluation of whether understanding exists rests with a practical assessment of *predictive utility* as the test for whether or not we have it.

This means that if the events of the future can be properly predicted by (1) the use of previously available information (i.e., knowledge) via (2) the application of some type of a process (e.g., analysis), then there can be a presumption that some level of understanding exists (see chapter 8, entitled "Knowledge," and chapter 12, entitled "Analysis," for further discussions). This is the result of two factors: (A) An understanding of the prior information itself (which is derived from the past) and (B) confidence concerning its extended (i.e., generalizable) utility (i.e., a presumption that it applies to *like situations* everywhere, both in the past and in the future). This allows predictions to occur properly, which flows not only from the utility of the prior information itself, but also from the application of *rules* that allow it to be applied meaningfully and with utility to other situations, including those of the future.

This type of a test involving the future applicability of previously assembled knowledge depends on

- the application of *deductive reasoning* to like types of objects and events (i.e., those that have already existed or occurred in the past), so as to dissect them apart and use this extracted/ dissociated information to construct more generalized *concepts* that are then assumed to have extended (i.e., universal) applicability, and
- employing *inductive reasoning* to apply these assembled concepts to predict the future (see chapter 14, entitled "Deductive vs. Inductive Reasoning," for further discussion).

Importantly, the opposite is also the case concerning understanding: if predictions made using previously assembled knowledge together with the application of analytical tools results in an incorrect description of what is actually observed, then we must conclude that we had an incomplete or insufficient understanding to be able to predict correctly.

Thus, our *beliefs* concerning the presence or absence of *understanding* ultimately depend on the results of a *functional test*, which is based on *observations* made *over time*. If predictions concerning future objects and events and their relationships are accurate based on past knowledge and subsequent analysis, we believe that we possess a *valid* understanding of what we have knowledge about (see chapter 15, entitled "Generalizability: Internal vs. External Validity," for further discussion). As long as predictions continue to hold true, we believe that our understanding is valid based on a model that we have constructed (i.e., an *operational schema* derived from *concepts*—see chapter 29, entitled "Modeling vs. Reality," for further discussion). This depends in turn on the extraction of knowledge and the generalizability of concepts based upon past specifics. But, as soon as future predictions fail to hold, we no longer believe that the previous model reflecting our understanding is complete (i.e., that at least in some circumstances it is invalid), and the presumption of our possessing a proper understanding is undermined.

Something obvious arises from this sort of a functional definition of understanding: its validity is the result of a *rolling assessment* of predictive value, making it limited to past testing experience, rather than to anything universal and permanent. This is because its validity always has the potential to be undermined by the next test. Clearly this is not what we are striving for, because there is no way to ever be certain of the *universality* of our understanding. Thus, although we would all like to believe that our understandings are absolute once we have them, the tests we use to determine whether they exist are ultimately functional, making their validity both temporally and spatially constrained. Therefore, they can provide only an ongoing suggestion (but not a proof) of *local* validity for understanding in both space and time (see chapter 22, entitled "Entanglement vs. Separability: The Locality Issue," for further discussion), but nothing more.

So what we can conclude is that to know if our understanding is proper (i.e., consistent and complete), an *infinite set* of *tests* would be necessary to ensure that our understanding is universal under all circumstances and in all potential environments (i.e., it is valid over all venues). Unfortunately, this is not possible due to the constraints of both (a) limited time and (b) the ever-evolving (i.e., changing) nature of the universe in which we live. Based on this, we must conclude that our understanding—however broad we may perceive it to be—is always limited and local, with its validity extending only so far as the scope of its testing allows. The question then is how limited and how local?

Thus, when a *model*—which represents an *operationalized version* of the *concepts* that underpin our understanding—results in *inaccurate predictions*, this *violates* its *universality*. Whenever this occurs, we must conclude that either our previous understanding is flawed or that our methods for processing and projecting it are incorrect and, therefore, *invalid*. Then we must search for a different construct (i.e., a different model, or possibly even a different concept) to refine our understanding (see chapter 29, entitled "Modeling vs. Reality," for further discussion). Sometimes the new model (or concept) that we construct is an extension of our previous one, but it can also be radically different.

So in the end, the notion of understanding reverts to something akin to the application of the *scientific method* on a universal scale. A first step toward establishing scientific understanding is to formulate *testable hypotheses* in such a way that they are both consistent with prior knowledge and also *potentially violable*. Preexisting knowledge can arise from several different sources, but it ultimately involves the measurement, description, and categorization of objects and events, either explicitly (e.g., for those having a physical existence) or implicitly (e.g., for those that we simply imagine or think about). Subsequent to hypothesis generation, there are often *mechanisms* that can be imagined to *explain* why they are the way they are. These are then reduced to a set of consistent and sometimes interlocking or interfacing concepts, which are ultimately further reduced to a set of existential and interaction *rules*. These rules are then imagined to be universalizable and the implications are then evaluated for—you guessed it—their future predictive value for events and circumstances that have not yet been observed but that are nevertheless *testable*.

Thus, our *understanding* can be best characterized as a set of *not-yet-violated beliefs, hypotheses, and operating principles*. This is in the best of circumstances, when everything for establishing both the underlying scope of relevant knowledge and the applicable analytical framework has been constructed properly. But the implication is that there cannot be anything about our understanding that is absolute, which means that there cannot be anything about it that can be assumed to have applicability to anything or to any domain other than those that have already been tested.

In addition, there is another limitation: because our understanding is established by means of functional tests that involve its utility for making predictions, it can only be evaluated for validity with respect to observations that have already been made. Its validity and applicability with regard to the future—where we would like for it to apply and where we want to use it—is always in question and cannot be tested prospectively, requiring that we wait until future events actually occur before we can evaluate it for continued accuracy.

Because understanding relies on the acquisition of knowledge from the past and the application of this knowledge to the future (via a model), it is subject to the same limitations and caveats as the applicability and validity of deductive reasoning versus inductive reasoning (see chapter 14, entitled "Deductive vs. Inductive Reasoning," for further discussion).

Importantly, it must be noted that no *algorithm*—regardless of its level of sophistication—can ever be the embodiment of understanding in and of itself. This is a bold statement and it is meant to be. Although it was the hope of many in the field of artificial intelligence that sets of *algorithms*—by means of their collective ability to define the precise processes for recasting preexisting information into different forms—could be all that is necessary to embody the phenomenon of understanding, this result has not been borne out by many decades of research. One obvious reason is that something outside of the algorithms themselves must view and interpret the results, so that a comparison can be made to actual events; this is because the concordance of predictions with subsequent observations is the sine qua non for concluding that a proper understanding exists.

It is now generally appreciated that the algorithmic approach to information processing represents a formalization that can often result in useful manipulations of preexisting data, but that it is intrinsically constrained. This is because algorithms represent sets of rules (or procedures) that embody only well-defined steps (i.e., a structure) for the execution of processes that are designed to manipulate information that is "fed into" them (see chapter 16, entitled "Computability: Algorithmically Definable Calculations," for further discussion). This may often result in the ability to gain additional perspectives and insights about preexisting information. However, by both definition and design, the execution of an algorithm must unfold rigidly and in accordance with sets of well-defined, prespecified rules.

Importantly, this is the case even if algorithmic calculations reach into domains that are chaotic (i.e., where the result could not have been predicted in advance of actually executing the algorithm), thereby unveiling something *new* that could not have been known before (see chapter 24, entitled "Chaos Theory: Implications for Macroscopic Predictability," for further discussion). Under these circumstances, algorithms must be regarded as the tools to arrive at the new findings, but they do not *themselves* understand anything by having cranked through the process to generate the previously unforeseen results. This is because the *outputs* of such *algorithmic processes* must still somehow be *appreciated* and *interpreted* by something outside of the rigid algorithmic framework that served as the basis for processing the information.

The conclusion concerning human understanding is this: it is *limited* to *directly accessible realms*—both in terms of the spaces that we know and can interrogate, as well as to times that have already occurred. It is not necessarily applicable to "other places" that we do not have access to or have not yet come across (i.e., inaccessible spaces and future times that have not yet occurred). If we try to extend our presumed understanding to these other realms, it constitutes nothing more than unfounded conjecture—a mere hope based on the presumption that what we already know will have applicability to other realms that we don't. Unfortunately, this assumption—no matter how universally applicable our understanding might be to other places and to times past—is always without an adequate foundation: the applicability of our knowledge and understanding can never be proven or guaranteed until those other places and times are actually reached. At that point, our prior understandings may be found to be applicable, and, if so, they may provide a shortcut to additional understandings, either directly or via *extension* or *analogy*. But, there is also the possibility that they may not be applicable to these other places and times at all, making them of no practical or theoretical value. Unfortunately, there is no way of knowing if our prior understandings will be useful in realms other than where they have already been tested until we actually get there to evaluate them.

CHAPTER 14
Deductive vs. Inductive Reasoning

The difference between analyses that involve past information and those that involve the future.

Deduction: Definition (Merriam-Webster Dictionary)

- The deriving of a conclusion by reasoning; *specifically*: inference in which the conclusion about particulars follows necessarily from general or universal premises
- A conclusion reached by logical deduction

Induction: Definition (Merriam-Webster Dictionary)

- Inference of a generalized conclusion from particular instances
- The act of bringing forward or adducing (as facts or particulars)
- A conclusion arrived at by induction

Deduction is a common type of reasoning that we employ routinely. It involves the construction and evaluation of arguments in an attempt to show that a *conclusion follows necessarily* from a *set* of (preexisting) *premises* or hypotheses (see chapter 11, entitled "Logic and Inference," for a further discussion). It is also referred to as *deductive logic.*

A *deductive argument* is based on information that is already available (i.e., concerning objects that are in existence and events that have already occurred). It is *valid* if its *conclusion follows properly* from its *premises.* When this occurs, its conclusion must be true if the premises are true. Thus, the validity of any argument ultimately depends on the relationships of its different elements, which is a reflection of its intrinsic *structure.*

An argument's structure determines if it conforms to certain defensible logical tenants. But the structure of an argument is not sufficient to assess the *truth value* of its *conclusions* in and of itself. A second element is also necessary to determine if the conclusion is true, which determines the argument's *soundness*: a deductive argument is *sound* only if it is (1) *valid* and (2) *all* of its *premises* are *true.* Then its conclusion must be true, because the argument is valid, and its conclusion issues from true premises. Thus, a deductive argument is classifiable firstly as either valid or invalid and then, only if it is valid, as either sound or unsound.

Deductive reasoning is considered by many to be a method of gaining knowledge. However from the construction of (valid) deductive arguments, it is obvious that *all* of the information needed to arrive at a sound conclusion is actually *imbedded* in the initial *premises* used to formulate the argument. This is because—aside from the use of the (presumably inert) logical connectives that combine, contrast, and/or equate the information contained in the premises—the premises themselves are the only *substrates* that have intrinsic *content* to form the basis for the conclusions derived from them. Thus, nothing new (in terms of additional information) can be gained as a result of this type of a deductive exercise, as the process simply takes the information that is contained within the original premises and *recasts* it (or *reformulates* it in an algorithmic way) into an *alternative format* that can then be *more readily interpreted* and *applied* to a particular situation (or question) at hand.

A classic example of a deductive argument is as follows:

a. All men are mortal

b. Socrates is a man
c. Therefore, Socrates is mortal.

The first two items constitute statements that are referred to as premises. Both are *self-contained* and neither is dependent upon the other for its truth or falsehood.

1. The first statement (i.e., premise) states that all objects that can be classified as *men* have the attribute of being *mortal* (i.e., that the concept of men necessarily contains—in all instances—a separate but universally imbedded concept as a part of its definition that is inescapable: that of mortality). Note that this association is based on preexisting observational evidence indicating that all known prior entities that were classified as men ultimately died. This, therefore, falls into the category of being a historical truth. It is not based upon either the observation of all men, nor is it necessarily predictive of what will be observed in the future in men who will subsequently exist (i.e., there may be men in the future who will be immortal—but because we are not able to evaluate them, we simply cannot know).
2. The second statement (another premise) states that Socrates—because of the collection of attributes that define him—is properly classifiable as a *man* (i.e., a member of the set of men).
3. The third item is the conclusion (i.e., inference), which states that Socrates must be mortal. This follows because Socrates inherits (or must embody) the attribute of mortality because he has been properly classified into the more general category of men.

Note that the key to reaching the conclusion of the argument is that a *bridge* can be drawn between the first and the second statements, which depends on a proper and consistent definition of the set of attributes that encompass the concept of a man.

Several features of deductive reasoning must be recognized to understand the scope of its utility. The first is that deduction deals with substrates (i.e., premises) that encompass the de facto totality of the information available about particular objects and events, and that this is then effectively organized into *classes*. Regardless of whether these relate to real (i.e., measured) or imaginary (i.e., mentally constructed) objects and events, they *embody* sets of properties that are then teased apart (rightly or wrongly) as if they are composed of effectively independent elements. These are then *reconstructed* to fit properly into some newly devised sets of categories.

Thus, the deductive process is akin to simply *reshuffling* the original information into other categories that are mutually consistent with what the original categories contained (i.e., the information is simply mapped from one set of categories into another). Internal consistency is presumed to occur because of the validity of the logic that is employed. With this type of a process—one that is entirely algorithmic in nature—nothing new is ever discovered or invented. The reshuffling of sets of individual elements means that the pool of information is either flat (i.e., it doesn't discard any of the initial information that was originally contained within the premises) or is more limited (i.e., it discards some of the original informational elements and *focuses in* on only a *subset*). Importantly, deductive logic may allow for the discarding of some information (which necessarily adversely affects the consistency of what remains—see chapter 11, entitled "Logic and Inference," for a further discussion), but it does not allow for any expansion of the fixed pool of information that was originally available from the starting premises. Because of this constraint, deductive logic is confined to being sound only for those objects and events that are already *known*. This means that deductive logic has applicability only for events and relationships that are either occurring *now* or that have occurred in the past (i.e., that *were*). Thus, deductive logic has *no direct applicability* to the *future*, which is necessarily *unknown* because it has not yet occurred.

In many ways, *inductive reasoning* represents a hope-filled extension of deductive logic, albeit one that is questionably founded. Instead of starting with specific (i.e., individual, well-circumscribed) premises and recasting that original pool of preexisting information into different but specific categories, it starts with *generalizations* (i.e., information about *patterns* that have been derived from past observations and cast into overarching *concepts*) and then tries to apply these concepts to specific (i.e., new and well-defined) circumstances. This process is also known as induction or *inductive logic*, and it represents a type of reasoning that attempts to construct or evaluate propositions that are abstractions—and ultimately extensions—of previous observations into realms where no direct information is available. One of these realms is different places than those that have already been observed; the other is the *future*.

Inductive logic is commonly construed as a form of reasoning that (A) first depends on generalizations based upon patterns and trends that have emerged from previously observed individual instances and then (B) applies these overarching concepts to as-yet-uninvestigated (or as-yet-unrealized) individual instances. By so doing, there is the hope of applying the same trends that have been gleaned from the past into the future but without the benefit of any direct observational evidence concerning their applicability. Therefore, although the methodology and structure of inductive reasoning is essentially identical to that used in deductive reasoning, the substrates are fundamentally different: in the case of deductive reasoning, they arise from specifics that have been observed and are well-investigated, but in the case of inductive reasoning, they are based on general concepts that have been derived from patterns gleaned from past observations. The utility of their application to hypothetical specifics about other places (which have not yet been observed) and the future (which has not yet occurred) is uncertain. In this sense, inductive and deductive reasoning are very different, and the soundness of inductive reasoning rests on much squishier ground.

To be fair, the formal philosophical definition of inductive reasoning is considerably more nuanced. Most logicians would submit that the premises of an inductive argument indicate some degree of support (i.e., inductive probability) for the conclusion, but do not demand it (i.e., that they suggest the truth, but do not ensure it). Using this type of an approach, it is possible to move from overarching generalizations assembled from past observations to the possibility of application to new individual instances. This line of reasoning is substantially less rigorous than for deductive logic and—with regard to the future—it depends on two additional beliefs concerning *like objects* and *like occurrences*:

- that those not yet observed will be *qualitatively* the *same* (or similar to) those of the past, and
- that they will behave in a *quantitatively similar* fashion to what was observed in the past.

Both of these assumptions are expected to be fulfilled to within a certain degree of likelihood or *probability*. And both depend on the idea of continuity (stability) in going from the past into the future (see chapter 17, entitled "Continuity (Smoothness) vs. Discontinuity (Roughness)," for further discussion).

This underlying assumption of stability pertains to essentially everything regarding inductive reasoning. It states essentially that, "If the universal platform upon which we operate is more or less the same in the future as it was in the past (i.e., there is "platform stability" that can be counted on despite ongoing changes in the universe), then we can presume that some types of objects and events that we observed in the past will be likely to exist or occur in the same or a similar way again in the future." This line of argument is effectively circular—we are doing nothing more than predicting the stability of events in the future by making an assumption of stability of the universe in the first instance. What is done differently is to place *error bounds* around the predictions, based on the level of security we have about our assumption of stability over time and the presumed *likelihood* that what we know about the universe will remain stable in the future. This is based upon past trends, but it represents nothing more than an (educated) guess about the future, which is yet unknown.

It is worth expanding on this point further: Although probabilistic (i.e., statistical) approaches to prediction can place (arbitrarily selected) *boundaries* around "most likely" expectations as they pertain to outcomes associated with particular sets of prior circumstances (i.e., how well they can be generalized to other circumstances of the past—see chapter 15, entitled "Generalizability: Internal vs. External Validity," for further discussion), they do not address the core issue that limits their utility regarding future predictions: the soundness of attempting to project previous experiences derived from the past into the future. Although probabilistic approaches can be used to place *confidence limits* around the expected outcomes derived from past observations, when they are used to predict the future they nevertheless remain deficient for the same reasons already cited: they attempt to predict the unfolding of future events only from past experience. Despite often being employed to do so, whenever statistical approaches are used to predict the probability of future events, their soundness is intrinsically limited due to the inductive nature of the process: the premises that are used are based only on past experience and not on any direct knowledge about the future.

These issues point out some of the difficulties regarding inductive logic.

Although it is based on the same structural rules as those for deduction, it presumes that the future will look a lot like the past, which is an assumption that must be accepted without proof; otherwise it is not defensible. In the final reckoning, the predictions made using inductive logic are predicated upon a belief in a well-defined, smooth, and stable "universal playing field", which may or may not be the case—or at least cannot be relied upon with any degree of certainty (see chapter 17, "Continuity (Smoothness) vs. Discontinuity (Roughness)," and chapter 18, entitled "Stability vs. Instability: System Inertia and Resiliency," for additional discussions concerning continuity and stability).

Thus, inductive logic does not provide very much in terms of insight or comfort when we attempt to use it to predict the circumstances of the future. At best, it can be used as a guide for us to be able to say, "Objects and events in the future will look something like this or that if they are anything like the way they were in the past" and "We can assume that if future objects and events look and behave a lot like those of the past, then they are likely to unfold with this or that type of a pattern with this degree of probability." Neither of these statements is very reassuring and neither provides much insight beyond what we already know based on projecting our past experiences into the future. Because of this, inductive reasoning reduces to something of an appeal to wisdom in attempting to project past trends into the future with some degree of confidence. But, unfortunately, just as with wise men making predictions that do not always come true, inductive reasoning is in no better position when it attempts to make predictions about the future.

CHAPTER 15
Generalizability: Internal vs. External Validity

The leap from specific instances to general cases requires assumptions about unknowns.

Generalization: Definition (Merriam-Webster Dictionary)

- To derive or induce (a general conception or principle) from particulars
- To draw a general conclusion from
- To give general applicability to
- To give a general form to
- A general statement, law, principle, or proposition
- The act or process of generalizing

Valid: Definition (Merriam-Webster Dictionary)

- Well-grounded or justifiable: being at once relevant and meaningful
- Logically correct
- Appropriate to the end in view: effective

Internal: Definition (Merriam-Webster Dictionary)

- Existing or situated within the limits or surface of something
- Intrinsic; inherent

External: Definition (Merriam-Webster Dictionary)

- Situated outside, apart, or beyond
- Of, relating to, or connected with the outside or an outer part
- Not intrinsic

Proving something about the universe necessarily entails *isolating* a portion of it for examination and explanation. This is because without isolation, whatever we wish to assess is connected to everything else, thereby making the required scope of evaluation effectively limitless and, therefore, impossible. Thus, a *sample* must be isolated to provide a tractable scope of investigation, with the hope that it will be representative of more than just the immediate portion of the universe that was subdivided off for inspection. If this is the case, it provides the potential to *generalize* the results to other *like systems*.*

By using a sample of something as the substrate for investigation, several important questions arise:

1. *How representative* is the sample to the whole *system* we are interested in learning about?
2. *How completely* has the sample been *separated* from everything else in its environment, so that we can be certain that the properties we measure about it refer only to it alone (i.e., how well has it been isolated)?

3. *How has isolating* the *sample* made it either exist or *behave differently* than it would have if it had been left *connected* to everything else in its native environment (i.e., prior to its isolation)?
4. *How representative* are the findings from sample to the entire *set* of other *like systems* that we may also be interested in also learning about (i.e., other systems that are separate and *similar*, but *not identical*)?

The answers to these questions are important to be able to understand the scope, limitations, veracity, and utility of what we have discovered about the *sample*—as well as its applicability to the *greater system* from which it was isolated and to *other systems* of *like type*. And they lead to two key ideas:

I. **Internal validity**: this refers to *how confident* we are that the *measurements* of the objects and events that we made in the *isolated sample* are *accurate, correct,* and *reproducible* (i.e., non-serendipitous) and that what has been demonstrated is *always true* within the sample itself
II. **External validity**: this refers to *how confident* we are that the *results* found for the *isolated sample*—the ones that have been measured, analyzed, categorized, and ultimately understood—are *generalizable* to both (a) the *greater system* from which it was taken and (b) to *other like systems*, despite these (i) having *not been measured directly* and (ii) being *still connected* to their *surrounding environments*.

Importantly, the term *validity* is used here in a different way than it was for deductive and inductive logic. There, the term was used to describe the "truthfulness" of the *structure* of arguments, irrespective of their contents. But in the present case of internal and external validity, the term refers to more than just structure; it refers to *both* structure and content, which makes it equivalent to the idea of *soundness* in deductive and inductive logic. This is a potentially confusing distinction in terminology that must be kept in mind.

Demonstrating internal and external validity is designed to provide us with some assurance that what we believe about what we know and understand is both (a) true and (b) potentially useful to us going forward. To do this, the following must be shown:

- First, it must be proven to our satisfaction that the beliefs we have are *internally valid* (i.e., accurate, precise, and reproducible) for the abstracted system that has been subjected to investigation (i.e., the sample).
- Second, the question must be addressed as to whether these beliefs are *externally valid* (i.e., if there is applicability of the results to other external objects and events—preferably directly, but at least by extension or analogy).

This latter idea represents the concept of *generalizability*, which can be thought of functionally as the *opposite* of *abstraction* or sampling: whereas sampling splits apart larger entities into smaller parts that are hoped to be representative of their larger wholes, generalization "extends" the applicability of the findings obtained from preexisting samples by applying them to other "like systems" that have not yet been examined, including those that are as yet unknown. (Note the analogy to what has already been discussed concerning the opposing ideas of dissection versus aggregation in analysis—see chapter 12, entitled "Analysis," for further discussion).

Although these ideas may seem simple, there are issues concerning both internal and external validity that are not trivial. The approaches used to assess the two may appear different, but they are actually quite similar.

Assessing *internal validity* relies on three elements:

1. Defining what constitutes the *system of interest*
2. *Isolating* the *system* from its surrounding environment
3. *Ensuring* that *measurements* of the system (a) are made *properly* (i.e., incorporate the necessary degree of accuracy and precision) and (b) are *reproducible* over repeated measurements.

Although the absolute number of consistent repeat measurements to ensure internal validity is not defined (i.e., an infinite number would be ideal, but not possible), the following is certain:

- The *larger* the *number* of *consistent repeat measurements*, the *more confidence* there can be regarding internal *reproducibility*, and
- The *more divisions* and subdivisions of original *system elements* that can be shown to *conform* to the *same results*—down to the level of

minimum size units—the *stronger* is the presumption of *internal consistency* and, therefore, *internal validity*.

It should be noted that both of these tests to assess internal validity can only be evaluated using information from the past. Unfortunately, there is no guarantee that these past results will persist into the future—although this is always the explicit hope (see chapter 14, entitled "Deductive vs. Inductive Reasoning," for further discussion).

In many ways, the idea of assessing external validity extends in the opposite direction as internal validity. To assess *external validity*, the schema is to:

- *Remove* (or at least *expand*) the *boundaries* of investigation to incorporate *additional domains* that contain *other* (*like*) *systems* that are *separate* from what was *originally* evaluated.
- *Investigate* the *applicability* of the findings that were shown to be *internally valid* in the original system by using *different sets* of *objects* and *events* that have *not yet been evaluated* to determine if the validity of the prior findings is maintained.

Using this as a basis, the overall approach to *testing* for external validity is in many ways analogous to that for internal validity. It can be summarized as follows:

1. *Define new like systems* of interest (i.e., those different from the original system that was used to test for and establish internal validity)
2. *Isolate* the *new like systems* in an analogous way to what was done for the first test system (i.e., the original one used to establish internal validity), and
3. *Obtain samples* from the *new like systems* and *test* them in the *same way* as the original sample from the first system, so as to assess their results for *consistency* compared to the original system.

If the *same results* are found for *samples* taken from multiple *unrelated systems* of *like type*, then there can be *increasing confidence* in the *external validity* of the original findings that were shown to be *internally valid* from the original (i.e., first) test system. This then provides greater *confidence* for *generalizing* the results to *additional* similar but *untested systems*.

Again, there is no rule as to the absolute number of unrelated systems that must have consistent findings to those of the primary test system to conclude that there is external validity. Although impossible, *consistent findings* for an *infinite number* of *unrelated like systems* would be ideal. Nevertheless, the larger the number of unrelated like systems that have results consistent with those for the primary test system, the more confidence there can be concerning the external applicability of the results, and the stronger is the presumption of external validity (i.e., the ideal being *universal validity*).

It should be noted that the test results for the multiple unrelated like systems can only be examined for times that have already occurred (i.e., that are in the past); thus, as is the case for internal validity, there is no guarantee that these will apply equally as well when similar tests are performed in the future (i.e., that they will be time invariant), although this is always the hope.

Overall, the goal of being able to generalize results is to *predict* what *outcomes* will be for like systems of interest when there are *no direct measurements* available for them. We would like to believe that an understanding of system *structure* and *function* would allow us to make predictions about these *untested* like systems without needing to make such measurements. If this is the case, then we would be able to do so not only for the like systems that exist and operate at the present time, but also for such systems that existed in the past (about which we have no direct knowledge) and for those that will exist in the future (for which measurements cannot yet be made).

Thus, *generalization* can be a very *powerful tool* if its limits are properly appreciated, and it is employed reasonably. However, as the preceding discussions concerning the assessment of both internal and external validity suggest regarding the reliability of such inferences, both are necessarily unprovable through repeat observation and testing alone; they are always prone to potential inaccuracies that have not yet been recognized. Thus, the accuracy and precision of all generalizations can only be guaranteed up through the present time (i.e., the boundary where it was possible to isolate and examine the last test system); they will not necessarily prove valid for the next test system that is examined in the future.

The conclusion must be that generalization is impossible to justify theoretically and that it is also prone to error in a practical sense. A good rule of thumb is: the *closer* an *untested system* is *to one* that has been *properly measured* and *well-characterized*—both in terms of its *design* and *size*, as well as its *energy* and *temporospatial proximity* to other systems that are known and tested—the *more likely* the *generalization* of known results to the untested system will *apply*. Thus, for those systems that are "very close" to the original type of test systems that have already been evaluated, the generalization of prior results is likely to apply best and is reasonable. However, for those like systems that are "far away" in terms of their design, size, energy, and temporospatial proximity to the ones that have already been tested, it is more likely that the generalization of known results to the untested systems will either not apply or be frankly misleading.

It can be concluded that the *ability* to *generalize* should be considered *most applicable* at only a *local level*. When objects and events are further away, generalization can be misleading (at best) and sometimes frankly incorrect (at worst). Under such circumstances, both the validity and the practical utility of the process of generalization must be questioned.

---

* The definition of a *like system* is necessarily subjective. In principle, like systems should have structures, functional components, and organizations that are analogous in all critical facets. They should also be of like size and energy, exist in the same or similar environment, and exist temporally close to the primary system to which they are being compared. However, the precise degree of similarity required in all these respects, as well as the precise limits of their necessary locality to the primary system in both time and space, is a judgment that is not rigorous. This results in such a determination of likeness being relative. The resulting uncertainty concerning *how like* is considered to be "*like-enough*" can cast doubt on the scope of like systems that might be believed to behave in the same way as the primary system that was tested.

CHAPTER 16

Computability: Algorithmically Definable Calculations

Computations require the quantification of data and a structure for their execution.

Compute: Definition (Merriam-Webster Dictionary)

- To make calculation: reckon
- To determine especially by mathematical means
- To determine or calculate by means of a computer

Calculate: Definition (Merriam-Webster Dictionary)

- To determine by mathematical processes
- To solve or probe the meaning of: figure out
- To forecast consequences
- To make a calculation

Algorithm: Definition (Merriam-Webster Dictionary)

- *Broadly*: a step-by-step procedure for solving a problem or accomplishing some end, especially by a computer
- A procedure for solving a mathematical problem in a finite number of steps that frequently involves repetition of an operation (as of finding the greatest common divisor)

The ideas of *computability* and *determinism* are *different*, but they are often confused.

The issue of *determinism* is framed by the question "Given the *current state* of the universe, is every *prior state* and every *future state* completely *determined*, such that it can be described exactly?" (See chapter 3, entitled "Agency: Free Will vs. Determinism," for further discussion.) If the answer is yes, then we live in a deterministic universe. This means that everything in the past, present, and future is completely determined and non-malleable, whether or not we know the precise set of rules that govern the progression of events from one set of circumstances to the next. If the answer is instead no, then we do not live in such a universe, and there is room for *variance* in the phenomena and outcomes that can occur from one well-defined juncture to the next.

This gives rise to the following question: if the universe operates in a deterministic fashion, does this necessarily mean that we then have the ability to *calculate* what its precise states are in remote places, were in the past, or will be in the future? This is the issue of *computability*, which is framed by the question, "Given the *current state* of the universe, is its precise *state at any future* or *past point* in time *calculable*?"

Underlying this question of calculability is another issue: Is it possible to reduce the universe (and its description) to something that is *algorithmic*? An algorithm is a *step-by-step procedure* that can be used to make a *calculation*, which can be expressed as a *finite list* of *well-defined instructions*. If the universe is algorithmic, this means that it is possible to write down a set of steps (i.e., procedures or equations) that can be used to (mechanically) "crank through" a process that will allow a precise description of any past or future state of the universe, starting from a description of only its present set of conditions (or its current *state*). If the answer to this question is yes—that the universe is algorithmically describable—then it may be computable, but this is still not certain. If the answer is no, then computability is not even a possibility.

If it is possible to write down a set of well-defined steps that can be used to describe any past or future states of the universe precisely, then an important question follows: Is the computation accomplishable within a *finite period* of time? If a result is theoretically calculable but cannot be delivered within a finite period, then the output of the computation will never be forthcoming. Thus, although a result may still be calculable from a technical standpoint, the result of the calculation would never be available, and it could serve no practical purpose.

Additionally, it is important to note that even if a calculation can be made within a finite period of time, another question arises: Is it accomplishable within *less time* than it will take for the *universe* to *get to that point* itself?

The first question addresses a fundamental issue associated with calculability: even if there is a well-defined set of steps (i.e., a prescriptive procedure) for arriving at an answer concerning the precise past or future state of the universe, is it possible to arrive at this answer within a finite period of time, or will it take more time to do so than even the whole lifetime of the universe? This is a seminal question, because even if there is a well-defined and sound procedure for arriving at such an answer by using an algorithm—but that answer cannot ever be known either now or in the future—then it is effectively as if it the result of the algorithmic process does not exist. In this case, it is functionally worthless and it makes the entire notion of calculability nothing more than a hollow, empty shell. This means that even if the results are theoretically calculable, if the procedure necessary to do so cannot be executed within a finitely definable time frame (even by using the fastest, state-of-the-art, light-speed technologies), then it *cannot be known in time* to do anything useful with the result, and it cannot be of any utility.

The second question relates to this first: even if there is an algorithmic set of operations that can be employed to arrive at a description of the universe's past and future states within a finite period of time, is it possible to obtain this result *before* the *universe gets to that point* itself? If the answer to this question is yes, then the results—as they pertain to future objects and events—are computable and (at least potentially) knowable before the events (and/or objects) occur, which makes them (potentially) useful and relevant in both a practical as well as a theoretical sense. If the answer is no, then—at least with regard to future objects and events—it will be *impossible* to *predict* them before they actually unfold in the universe. This latter circumstance undercuts the predictive value of these calculations—as their results would only be known after the events themselves occurred—and would make them valueless regarding the future in any practical or functional sense.

Therefore, with regard to the relationship between determinism and calculability, the following summary can be offered:

1. If the *universe* is *not deterministic*, then *past* and *future* events are *not calculable*.
2. If the *universe* is *deterministic*, then *past* and *future* events may *either* be *calculable* or *non-calculable*:

    A. If *past* and *future* events are *calculable*, then:

    i. If such calculations can be made within a *well-defined time span* that is *shorter* than the *lifetime* of the *universe*

    I. With regard to *past states*:

    a) The states are *theoretically calculable*

    b) The states *may* or *may not* be *practically calculable*, depending on *how long it takes* to arrive at a *result* (i.e., if they will only be available in a million years, then they will have very limited practical value, whereas if they are available in a week, they will likely have much higher practical value)

    II. *With regard to future states:*

    a) If the *calculation* can be made *faster* than the time necessary for the *universe itself* to *advance* to the *calculated state*, then it is *both theoretically calculable* and (at least potentially) *practically useful* (depending on how long it takes to arrive at the result), and it can have *utility* from the standpoint of *predictive value* (depending on how far in advance of the actual unfolding of the events it can be known)

b) If the calculation can only be made *more slowly* than the time required for the *universe itself* to *advance* to the *calculated state*, then it is *theoretically calculable* but *practically without value*, as it is *worthless* from the standpoint of having any *predictive utility* concerning the future

ii. If such calculations will *take longer* than the longest time period that is available (i.e., the *lifetime of* the *universe*)

I. Although the states *may* be *theoretically calculable*, they are *practically without value* from the perspective of having any type of *predictive utility* about the future, thereby making them *worthless* from a practical standpoint

B. If *past* and *future* states are *not amenable* to any type of *well-defined procedure* for *calculation* at all, this renders them *theoretically* (and, therefore, also *practically*) *non-calculable*.

It should be noted that the ability to perform calculations that pertain to the future falling under subpart (A) are dependent on the *speed* with which *calculations* can be *made* relative to the speed at which the *universe advances* from one state to the next. *Both* of these speeds may be defined (and *limited*) by the inviolable *speed of light* (see chapter 25, entitled "Absolutes vs. Relatives: Relativity Theory," for further discussion). If so, it may be that *no calculation* regarding the *future states* of the universe can be made at a *speed faster* than the *universe itself evolves* (since the former is *limited by* the *speed of light* and the latter *advances* from one state to another at *light speed*).

Advocates of *parallel processing* might argue that *multiple simultaneous calculations* at *sub-light speeds* can be made to avoid this limitation, so as to arrive at calculations regarding *future states* at *faster than light speed* (i.e., *more quickly* than the *universe itself evolves*). However, this type of strategy presents several difficulties:

- *Summing* the results of *multiple operations* that occur at *sub-light speeds* can *never exceed the speed of light* in their composite (i.e., the speed of light is an *inviolable* maximum speed for the progression of events for *all observers* that *cannot be exceeded*—see chapter 25, entitled "Absolutes vs. Relatives: Relativity Theory," for further discussion).
- Assuming that *sufficient resources* can be brought to bear to perform parallel calculations to arrive at a composite faster-than-light calculation *locally* (which is theoretically not possible), this approach cannot be universalized; this is because the additional resources required to perform such calculations in parallel for a specific calculation in *one particular venue* has the consequence of necessarily *limiting* the remaining *resources* that are available to perform other such calculations in other venues.

Therefore, even if it were possible to "win" by performing a *specific, local, faster-than-light calculation* to predict particular aspects of the future, the consumption of excess resources for the calculation would make it impossible to do so everywhere else simultaneously (i.e., there simply aren't enough "duplicate resources" in existence to calculate everything at faster than light speed everywhere). Therefore, the parallel computing strategy, even if it were implementable within particular local venues, *cannot be universalized*; this would make any such predictions about the future necessarily *incomplete* and, therefore, *inconsistent* (see chapter, 11 entitled "Logic and Inference," for further discussion).

It should also be noted that the issue of calculation, per se, is *not intrinsically* something that is *dependent on beings*. In order for a calculation to be made, the *rules* (i.e., procedures) for making it must be (1) *algorithmically definable* and (2) *executable* (in an automated fashion) by an *automaton* (i.e., a machine). This type of a formulation of the idea of calculation admittedly leaves out some other important issues, among these: How does the machine itself exist (i.e., who constructed it?); who (or what) programs the machine; who (or what) "provides" the necessary information (i.e., "feeds it into the machine") for the calculation to start; and who (or what) receives the output of the calculation and interprets and/or applies the results? All of these are important questions that are addressed in other chapters, but for the purpose of the current discussion, these will not be addressed further here.

Given the fundamental differences between the ideas of determinism and computability, it is entirely possible that the universe could be deterministic but that its future and past states might not be computable. From a practical perspective and from a functional standpoint, this would render the notion of determinism moot with regard to making predictions—the universe might be deterministic, but its precise set of past and future states would still, nevertheless, not be calculable (even in principle) and, therefore, not be knowable to anyone apart from those actually present at the stated time (i.e., those with the capability of taking direct [sensory] inventory of the particular state of affairs).

So, the question must now be asked "What would be the *utility* of *knowing* that the *universe* was *deterministic* if it were *non-computable*?" The answer is not much. Despite being deterministic, there would still be no way to access the information about its future (or past) states without actually *being there*—at that particular juncture in time—to take a precise empirical inventory of all the states of objects and events and their interactions. In effect, there would be *no shortcut* to obtaining that particular information at another time via calculative inference.

Based on the foregoing discussions, it is evident that it is impossible to consider issues of computability concerning the universe's states without first addressing the question of whether the universe is algorithmically definable. If it is, this at least provides a means by which such types of calculations might be accomplished; the reflex might be (in modern times) to appeal to the use of high-speed digital computers to perform the necessary calculations very quickly. The underlying principles according to which such calculations are permitted were first defined in a formal sense in 1936 by Alan Turing, the iconic British logician, mathematician, computer scientist, and code-breaker. It was then that he published his thoughts concerning what would subsequently become known as a *universal Turing machine*—an automaton for performing rule-based calculations. The advantages—and limitations—of universal Turing machines constitute the underpinnings of all modern digital computing and, through this, all modern (digital) information processing. Because of this, it is instructive to examine some of the possibilities and limitations of the processes associated with the types of calculations that can be performed using these types of universal calculating machines.

The issues outlined above concerning computability are, in principle, some of the same ones addressed by Dr. Turing via his universal calculators. These include:

- Is the answer to a particular question (or class of questions) something that is *calculable*? (Answer: If it is *algorithmically definable*, then there is a *chance* it *can be calculated*; but, if it is *not definable algorithmically*, then it *cannot be*.)
- How do you know when the *result* to a particular question (or class of questions) is arrived at? (Answer: When the *algorithmic program* entered into the universal calculating machine *stops its calculation* and *provides* an *output* that is the well-defined answer.)
- When will the *machine stop calculating* and provide an *answer*? (Answer: When it is *finished making* the *calculation*; however, the *number of steps* that will be necessary for it to do this—and the *associated time* it will take to do so—are *not calculable* by any auxiliary means *prior to* its *executing* the actual *calculation process* itself.)
- What if the *machine doesn't stop*? (Answer: This is what is referred to classically as the "halting problem" associated with calculations performed by universal Turing machines; it is *not knowable* in advance *if the machine will stop* at some time in the future and, therefore, whether the answer of interest is actually something that is calculable in finite time in advance of the answer being delivered). [Turing proved that the "halting problem" is undecidable (i.e., that in general, it is not possible to decide algorithmically if a calculation performed by a given Turing machine will ever halt).]

The answers to these questions mean that—even theoretically—there are *fundamental limits* to *what we can know* concerning the *calculability* of any *past* or *future state* of the *universe*. Some of these limitations are known but, unfortunately, the list is not necessarily exhaustive, meaning that there may be other limitations that are not yet known. The conclusion is that calculations may be able to provide some insights about future and past states of the universe under some well-defined circumstances, but the problems to which they can be applied are relatively specific and often constitute *narrow idealizations* (i.e., they may only *incompletely*, and therefore *improperly*, *reflect* the *true complexity* of the *universe* itself).

Often, events and circumstances that we would like to be able to calculate are simply not amenable to calculation. When this occurs, *approximations* can sometimes be made to make what is *incalculable* (even in principle) *similar to other events* and *circumstances* (from the past) that have already been shown to be calculable (as a result of prior experience). This represents an attempt to fit the problem (i.e., shoe-horn it) into a formulation that can then be approached *analytically* (i.e., in the current case, via appropriate *algorithmic* definition and subsequent *calculation*). For example, in order to permit analytical solutions to pressing practical problems, many engineering approaches to analyzing complex systems have done this for at least several centuries (i.e., many problems were *simplified* [by discarding higher-order terms] to *fit models* that could then be described by specific functions for which solutions were known—thereby generating *approximate solutions* when other, more exact solutions could not be found).

Frequently, the idea of *modeling* is used in both the hard sciences and the social sciences to try to *simplify complex issues* and make them *analytically approachable*, so that they are then calculable (see chapter 29, entitled "Modeling vs. Reality," for further discussion). But these circumstances are often akin to the approach taken by the owner of a hammer when he runs across a problem: he (or she) often evokes the proverbial adage: "If you have a hammer, everything looks like a nail." Even though a hammer is the wrong tool to use and its application is bound to produce a suboptimal result, it is used anyway because it is all that is available.

Despite these limitations, calculations can sometimes be made to provide insights that can be quite useful. But the calculation approach cannot be used universally. Very often, as is evidenced by the "halting problem," it is unclear when it can be used and when it cannot. Frequently, events and circumstances that appear to be potentially calculable really aren't. When this occurs, calculations are often made based on incomplete and/or inappropriate models, and these may sometimes be "forced" on us because of what we already know is calculable rather than trying to make the calculation reflect the circumstances that actually exist. This can result in calculated outputs that reflect incomplete views of reality, thereby making them imprecise, limited (in terms of their scope and applicability), and (potentially) misleading. Thus, they may sometimes be regarded as "good enough for government work" (with this often being very good, as evidenced by successes in sending astronauts to the moon, building reliable bridges, etc.), but this belies the fact that they are actually intrinsically flawed—and sometimes fatally so.

The type of approach that uses calculation as its basis—although sometimes quite practical—provides us with little assistance in predicting the future in ways that we would like and expect: with a high degree of certainty and with the ability to manipulate current circumstances in a manner that will result in future outcomes being changed to better comport with our wishes, hopes, desires, and dreams.

CHAPTER 17
Continuity (Smoothness) vs. Discontinuity (Roughness)

Flows through space-time can either be smooth and continuous or turbulent and rough.

Continuity: Definition (Merriam-Webster Dictionary)

- Uninterrupted connection, succession, or union
- Uninterrupted duration or continuation especially without essential change
- The property of being mathematically continuous

Smooth: Definition (Merriam-Webster Dictionary)

- Not sharp or harsh
- Free from lumps
- Having a continuous even surface
- *Of a curve*: being the representation of a function with a continuous first derivative

Discontinuity: Definition (Merriam-Webster Dictionary)

- Lack of continuity or cohesion
- Gap
- The property of being not mathematically continuous
- An instance of being not mathematically continuous; *especially*: a value of an independent variable at which a function is not continuous

Rough: Definition (Merriam-Webster Dictionary)

- Marked by inequalities, ridges, or projections on the surface: coarse
- Having a broken, uneven, or bumpy surface
- Coarse or rugged in character or appearance
- Turbulent, tempestuous
- Characterized by harshness, violence, or force

Some objects appear to be smooth and others do not. For example, we might characterize a silk scarf as feeling *smooth*, but a sheet of sandpaper as feeling *rough*. We also might characterize ocean waves as having smooth contours (at least until they break), while the coastline upon which they land can often be rocky and jagged (rough).

We all have an intrinsic idea of the difference between smoothness (i.e., something conveying *continuity*) and roughness (i.e., something manifesting *discontinuities*) based on our personal experiences with different objects and events in the environment (see figure 6 for examples). Interestingly, however, despite this common familiarity with the idea of roughness, most of us choose to believe that the universe typically behaves in a smooth fashion. What's more, if we find examples where it behaves in a discontinuous manner, we tend to think of these as being transient and anomalous deviations from smoothness, rather than as endemic and recurrent.

Smooth surface   *Rough surface*

Figure 6: Smooth versus rough surfaces

The image on the left depicts stones that have smooth, continuous surfaces; on the right is an object with a rough, craggy, jagged, and discontinuous surface.

Two implications arise from this underlying supposition of universal smoothness. By making this assumption, we have chosen to characterize our universe in a way that allows it to

- react to perturbations in predictable ways, and
- have reactions (*outputs*) to incremental changes (*inputs*) that are both commensurate and scalable (i.e., perturbations of progressively greater magnitude result in smoothly increasing effect sizes of larger magnitude).

In defense of this assumption, our everyday experience typically reinforces our impression that the universe is smooth and predictable. As a result, we generally expect that small changes in inputs will result in small changes in outputs when dealing with virtually all the systems we interact with—whether they are mechanical, social, economic, personal, or otherwise. However, it is often the (unspoken) case that the local systems we commonly interact with are not free to evolve spontaneously in many of the domains in which we operate (i.e., behave in an unconstrained way). Often, they are specifically designed (by us) to incorporate *restraints* that make them behave in a smooth and stable manner, even though they would not necessarily do so if they were left to evolve and develop freely by themselves.

An example helps to illustrate this point. Consider an indoor ice-skating rink where the local air temperature is well above freezing: in this case, the ice represents a forced, localized *pseudo-stable state* that occurs only because of the continuing expenditure of (external) energy resources to provide ongoing cooling of the water. But, there is nothing intrinsically stable about the ice in the rink. Because of the high ambient temperature around it, if the cooling mechanism were shut off, the ice would melt and become a pool of water. Thus, without the continued expenditure of external energy to cool the rink, the ice would undergo a transition from a solid to a liquid via an inherently *discontinuous* change (an abrupt *change in state* known as a *phase transition*). Thus, the ice in the rink depends for its sustenance and (pseudo) stability (i.e., remaining frozen) on the continuing expenditure of external energy resources to *force* the system toward a stable-appearing operating point (i.e., ice). However, the ice would not stay that way by itself; if left alone, it would melt. To extend the example, if the ambient temperature were even higher and the water were to heat up further to its boiling point, it would make another (abrupt) phase transition to a gaseous state of water vapor, which would again represent a discontinuity from the preexisting state of liquid water.

Interestingly, despite the lack of continuity associated with the behavior of many real systems, we generally believe that even when such kinds of abrupt transitions (i.e., discontinuities) occur, the *changes* associated with the evolution of systems are still *predictable*. If this were the case, then the issue of the intrinsic smoothness or roughness of the universe would make no difference with respect to our ability to predict the future. But, fortunately or not, the occurrence of discontinuities has a major impact on the predictability of events.

Based on widely accepted observations, discontinuities occur often in our universe, and, when they do, the results are not predictable in any precise sort of way. These can range from shattered glass, to erupting volcanoes, to earthquakes, to buildings destroyed by tornados, to the disjointed actions of unstable governments, to collapsing financial markets, to exploding supernovas, to people who die from one moment to the next. All of these events represent abrupt discontinuities that are irreversible. (Note: even though some—but not all—of these occurrences may be fixable [i.e., repaired], the idea of repair is different from reversibility; reversibility involves the step-by-step retracing of events in reverse order, while reparability invokes different pathways to arrive back at a desired preexisting state, which requires the expenditure of external energy; see chapter 20, entitled "Thermodynamics: Laws Prohibiting the Spontaneous Reversibility of Physical Events," for further discussion).

There are many known cases where small changes in system inputs can precipitate much larger outputs, some of which can be cataclysmic. An obvious example is when an object breaks. Typically, this is not because of the application of an unexpected and overwhelming force (such as when a glass inadvertently tips off a table and smashes on the floor), but because of a subtle excess load placed on it that pushes it beyond its normal operating limits (e.g., as in the proverbial case of the *straw that broke the camel's back*). An instance of the latter is when a previously reliable roof fails under the stress of an incremental but critical excess load that creates intolerable strain (e.g., the weight of accumulated snow—unfortunately there are many well-documented examples of this). Another example is when system resonances amplify externally applied forces until they exceed the capacity of materials and structures to withstand them (e.g., an example of this is shown in the iconic photo from 1940 of the collapse of the Tacoma Narrows Suspension Bridge, figure 7).

Figure 7: Collapse of a suspension bridge

Photo of the suspension bridge at Tacoma Narrows, Washington, at the time of its collapse (United States, 1940). The bridge collapsed in 40 mile per hour (64 km/h) winds. The precipitating cause was aeroelastic flutter. This was the result of forced resonance from the wind, which had an external periodic frequency that matched the bridge's natural structural frequency. The energy input per cycle by the aerodynamic excitation was larger than could be dissipated by the damping within the bridge, causing the amplitude of the vibrations to increase. This process resulted in self-exciting oscillations of increasing excursion, which ultimately resulted in intolerable stress and strain that caused the bridge to structurally fail. [Public domain photo obtained from Cflhd.gov]

The reason all of this is important is that *smoothness (continuity)* and *roughness (discontinuity)* have different implications with respect to predictability. *Continuity* is associated with the idea of *stability* and a particular associated notion: that any imposed *change* will result in an *incremental effect* of similar magnitude. In contrast, *discontinuity* is associated with system *instability* and endemic potential for *rapid change, divergences,* and *non-predictability,* as well as the risk of ultimate *chaos* (see chapter 24, entitled "Chaos Theory: Implications for Macroscopic Predictability," for further discussion). These differences raise a key question: Which of these two alternatives represents the natural predisposition of the universe? If it is the former, then we can count on events unfolding in generally predictable ways. But if it is the latter, then the pockets of stability that we identify are really only *pseudo-stable* over certain limited domains of space and time. Beyond those defined limits, instability (and possibly chaos) may very well reign.

Another important implication arises: if different portions of the universe are not completely isolatable from each other in space and in time (i.e., if the universe is intrinsically connected in all facets, such that no portion of it is truly isolated from anything else), then the requirement of smoothness (i.e., continuity) for the successful prediction of future events would be elevated to the status of a universal imperative (see chapter 22, entitled "Entanglement vs. Separability: The Locality Issue," for a discussion of separability). If so, this would mean that the universe needs to be predictable everywhere (i.e., in its entirety) in order for it to be predictable anywhere; this is because if it were not predictable in any one domain, then the non-predictability of events in even a small domain would *spill over* into every other domain, thereby making them all unpredictable.

Thus, the question of *interconnection*—whether different portions of the universe are isolatable and *separable*—represents a key determinant of whether an *all-or-none* phenomenon exists concerning its predictability everywhere (or lack thereof), or if it is possible for the universe to be predictable in some domains while not being so in others. If everything is intrinsically interconnected, it would not be possible for one portion of the universe to be predictable while other portions of it were not. A corollary of this is that even if only a single example of non-predictability is discovered, then the universe cannot be predictable in any precise way anywhere. This is a key consideration, because as has been outlined previously, without predictability there cannot be understanding in any type of a functional or operational sense (which is the *sine qua non* for believing that we have a proper understanding—see chapter 13, entitled "Understanding," for further discussion).

An important discovery regarding the smoothness of the universe was made during the latter part of the nineteenth century by the influential French mathematician Jules-Henri Poincaré. Poincaré was interested in knowing if all the mathematical functions used to describe the evolution of classical dynamical systems (i.e., those arising from Newtonian mechanics) are integrable (i.e., if the area under the curve that describes the evolution of the system can be uniquely defined). To accomplish this, he investigated standard Newtonian models of interacting bodies, where the kinetic and potential energies of each are well defined. Famously, in 1887 he showed that such systems involving three or more bodies (the so-called *three-body problem*) are non-integrable. (Interestingly, this issue was first raised by Isaac Newton in 1687 in his landmark work *Philosophiae Naturalis Principia Mathematica* in reference to celestial mechanics). Poincaré concluded that a general solution cannot be expressed in terms of unambiguous coordinates and velocities of the bodies (i.e., algebraic expressions and integrals). He also noted that *discontinuities* (i.e., places where the next value of a function is not connected to the preceding ones—see figure 8 for an example) can make functions *non-integrable* (although this is not always the case*), thereby causing them to be *unpredictable* in any precise sense (i.e., one that is mathematically definable).

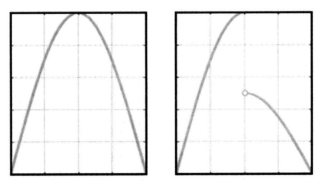

Continuous Function (left) vs Discontinuous Function (right)

Figure 8: Continuous versus discontinuous functions

An example of the difference between continuous and discontinuous functions is shown graphically in two dimensions (the concept is equally applicable to functions in any dimensional space). Functions that are continuous (left) are smooth without any jumps or breaks. In the case of discontinuous functions (right), there is a jump from one point to another without any connection between the two (i.e., it ends abruptly near the top of the graph and then starts again with its next well-defined point after the "jump" to a new value following the open circle). In general, a function is continuous if it can be drawn without lifting a pen from paper.

Poincaré concluded that the *non-integrability* of the mathematical functions describing Newtonian mechanics is quite generalized, affecting a *large proportion* of *ordinary dynamical systems*. This implies that their future trajectories through space and time are not predictable in any precise sense (i.e., that there are discrepancies between the predictions that can be made by using measurements of their current state and what is subsequently observed, with the extent of divergence being generally unpredictable). This was a major discovery, but—surprisingly—it was largely overlooked until the second part of the twentieth century.

Not only did Poincaré arrive at this conclusion concerning the *non-integrability* of the mathematical functions that describe common dynamical systems, but he also discovered the reason for it: *system resonances*. Resonance is a phenomenon that arises from the superposition of oscillations of different frequencies. This is not an esoteric concept: a common example is what occurs routinely in the realm of music. When harmonic superpositions occur, unique qualities of sound emerge from the integration of different resonant frequencies into a composite whole. None of the individual frequencies can provide the unique sound that arises from their integration; their superposition imparts a rich quality and a unique timbre to the composite sound that is absent from all of the underlying frequencies individually.

Thus, it is the interactions that occur among different components of an entire system that create resonance. Resonances are fundamentally *non-local*, because they do not arise from any single system element alone. This means that the description of any system at the level of single elements (e.g., individual component trajectories) is ultimately deficient, because it does not account for the so-called *emergent phenomena* that result from—and then provide local feedback to—the entire ensemble of system components. These emergent phenomena provide feedback that influences the individual system elements that created the resonances that fostered the overall system changes in the first place.

Poincaré's discovery that functions describing real systems are *non-integrable* suggests that *roughness (discontinuity) abounds* in our universe. This implies that natural systems are fundamentally *unpredictable* in terms of their *future states* (i.e., behaviors) in any precise sort of way. By extension, if the universe is intrinsically interconnected in its overall structure, this suggests that (precise) prediction of future events (by us) is not possible. Thus, our expectations regarding predictability are generated by nothing more than hope, historical associations, and precedent (arising from the perceived successes of past predictions). Because of the presence of discontinuities, there can be nothing more that underpins our predictions in any well-defined or reproducible analytical sense.

What follows in the next chapters are more comprehensive descriptions of how the effects of discontinuity impact dynamical certainty, what we are able to actually know about the present, and how all of this affects our ability to predict the future.

---

* Although some discontinuous functions are non-integrable, this is not the case for all of them. An example of a discontinuous function that is integrable is the function f(x) = 0 for x ≤ 0 and f(x) = 1 for x > 0. Although it is not smooth (i.e., it is discontinuous at x = 0), it still has a well-defined integral. What can be concluded is: if a function is non-integrable, then it cannot be smooth and must have discontinuities; however, if it is integrable, it at least has a chance of being continuous and smooth, but it does not necessarily need to be so.

CHAPTER 18
Stability vs. Instability: System Inertia and Resiliency

Systems move between states either in a smooth (stable) or jerky (unstable) fashion.

Stable: Definition (Merriam-Webster Dictionary)

- Not changing or fluctuating: unvarying
- Firmly established: fixed, steadfast
- Permanent, enduring
- Designed so as to develop forces that restore the original condition when disturbed from a condition of equilibrium or steady motion
- Placed so as to resist forces tending to cause motion or change of motion
- The property of a body that causes it when disturbed from a condition of equilibrium or steady motion to develop forces or moments that restore the original condition
- Not readily altering in chemical makeup or physical state

- Resistance to chemical change or to physical disintegration

Unstable: Definition (Merriam-Webster Dictionary)

- Not stable
- Not firm or fixed
- Not constant
- Not steady in action or movement; irregular
- Vacillating
- Lacking steadiness: apt to move, sway, or fall
- Liable to change or alteration
- Readily changing (as by decomposing) in chemical or physical composition or in biological activity

System: Definition (Merriam-Webster Dictionary)

- A regularly interacting or interdependent group of items forming a unified whole
- A body considered as a functional unit
- A group of interacting bodies under the influence of related forces
- A group of related natural objects or forces
- A group of devices or artificial objects or an organization forming a network especially for distributing something or serving a common purpose

Inertia: Definition (Merriam-Webster Dictionary)

- Indisposition to motion, exertion, or change; inertness
- A property of matter by which it remains at rest or in uniform motion in the same straight line unless acted upon by some external force

Resilient: Definition (Merriam-Webster Dictionary)

- Capable of withstanding shock without permanent deformation or rupture
- Tending to recover from or adjust easily to change or misfortune

Stable systems are those where *perturbations* may *disturb* the *organization* and *dynamics* of the system *temporarily*, but where the *tendency* is to *return* to their *original state* over time. By contrast, *unstable systems* are those for which *small perturbations* tend to *result* in ongoing and even *larger changes*, such that the *final state* of these systems will be *different* from where they began.

It is easy to illustrate the difference between a stable and an unstable system. Consider the following example: two marbles under the influence of a gravitational field, one at the bottom of a concave bowl and one perched on the top of a hill (or, as an alternative to the latter, a pencil balanced upright on its tip—see figure 9). All of these systems are at *equilibrium* (i.e., they are motionless). The difference in the case of the two marbles is that if the one at the bottom of the bowl is perturbed slightly from its resting position by an outside force, it will *oscillate* back and forth around the basin temporarily but will ultimately come to rest again at the bottom of the bowl. This is the hallmark of a *stable* system: when perturbed by a small amount, it *deviates* from its *original state transiently* but *comes back* to regain its original state over time. However, this is not the case for either the marble at the top of a hill or the pencil balanced on its tip. If anything perturbs them even slightly, they will begin to accelerate away from their original positions and fall down. Thus, the marble will come to rest at the bottom of the hill and the pencil will end up horizontal in a very different state from where it began. The hilltop marble and the upright pencil are both in equilibrium initially, but even the slightest change to their positions starts them careening along a path away from their starting points, such that they wind up in different states (i.e., ones of lower potential energy). This is the hallmark of an *unstable system*: compared to its initial state, the change in its final position shows that it had a lack of *inertia*, as evidenced by its lack of *resiliency* with regard to change.

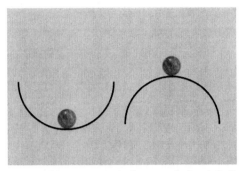

Two marbles—one at the bottom of a bowl (left) and the other on the top of a hill (right)

A pencil balanced on its tip

Figure 9: Stable versus unstable positioning of a marble and a pencil balanced on its tip

The marble on the left side of the diagram is at rest at the bottom of a bowl, while the marble on the right is perched precariously at rest atop a hill. In both cases, gravity exerts a downward force on the marble. If the marble on the left is perturbed by an (outside) force away from its resting position, it will oscillate back and forth until it dissipates the newly imparted energy (via friction, etc.) and comes to rest again. The potential energy of the marble will be the same at the end of this process as at the beginning. This marble is in a stable equilibrium. However, if the marble at the top of the hill is perturbed even slightly from its resting position, it will continue to accelerate downward away from its starting position until it comes to rest at the bottom (after dissipating its newly acquired kinetic energy via friction). Its final state will be different from where it began, and its potential energy will be diminished at the end compared with the beginning. This indicates that it was initially in an unstable equilibrium. The situation for a pencil balanced on its tip (far right) is analogous to the marble at the top of the hill. Here, if a force is exerted on the pencil, it will accelerate in the direction of the perturbation (due to gravitational force) and fall down. The upright pencil is also in an unstable equilibrium that lacks resiliency with respect to change.

As mentioned in the preceding chapter, Jules-Henri Poincaré discovered in the nineteenth century that many mathematical functions that describe the evolution of classical dynamical systems (i.e., those defined by Newtonian mechanics) are *non-integrable*. This indicates that many *natural systems* evolve in a fundamentally *unpredictable* way regarding their *future states* (see chapter 17, entitled "Continuity (Smoothness) vs. Discontinuity (Roughness)," for further discussion). This finding was subsequently expanded upon by twentieth-century investigators who developed new theories that categorized the trajectories of systems (i.e., their evolution over time) as being either *nice* (i.e., *integrable* and *deterministic*) or *random* (i.e., *non-integrable—irregular, wandering,* and *unpredictable*). However, the use of the term "random" in this context is a misnomer: their behavior is deterministic, but it is nonetheless unpredictable due to overall system *resonances* that feed back on all of the system elements. These resonances result in effects that constitute the hallmarks of system *complexity* (see chapter 17, entitled "Continuity (Smoothness) vs. Discontinuity (Roughness)," for further discussion).

When the energy within a dynamical system is increased, the total number of potential resonances also increases. This occurs because the denominator of the term describing the number of resonances approaches zero, making the ratio tend toward infinity. Under such circumstances, Poincaré indicated that they become "dangerous" due to their propensity to explode into very large numbers. As a consequence of this increasing density of system resonances, the probability that immediately neighboring trajectories will diverge also increases. Using these findings as a starting point, Poincaré demonstrated that the issue of system resonances is a general one that underlies all of Newtonian dynamics (except for the very simplest of systems, which are artificially constrained). Because of this, he concluded that the various components of overall system energy are predisposed to diverging in unpredictable ways. In its fully developed form, rapid divergences of immediately adjacent trajectories give rise to unpredictable paths forward, resulting in *chaotic dynamics* (see chapter 24, entitled "Chaos Theory: Implications for Macroscopic Predictability," for further discussion).

As a practical example of a chaotic behavior involving real systems, there is the long-appreciated scientific phenomenon of the *random walk*. This occurs when the *precise path* taken by a system cannot be known prior to its direct observation (or explicit calculation), even when the overall direction of change is predictable more generally. In these instances, the net result of the future system trajectory can be thought of as targeting a zone—i.e., a *zone of probability*—rather than any particular point. This description of system behavior is applicable to many types of *diffusion* processes, as well as to many other types of natural phenomena. (Note: in the parlance of *chaos theory*, the analogous zone of probability—or target—is referred to as an *attractor*).

Importantly, virtually all *natural systems* (i.e., those that are not artificially constrained) are *complex*. Even when such systems appear to be simple, they cannot be if (1) "everything-is-connected-to-everything-else" and (2) complexity exists anywhere (i.e., in a completely interconnected universe, it would take only one complex subsystem to make everything in existence complex—see chapter 17, entitled "Continuity (Smoothness) vs. Discontinuity (Roughness)," and chapter 22, entitled "Entanglement vs. Separability: The Locality Issue," for further discussion).

The issues arising from these insights are twofold.

The first pertains to the question:

- What can we know with certainty about dynamical systems in general?

And the second is:

- How can we use this information to predict what will happen in the future?

In answer to the first question, the work of Poincaré and subsequent researchers has shown that attempting to analyze the multiple trajectories of interacting dynamical systems as isolated *subset trajectories* is, in general, bound to failure. This is because the composite of the elemental interactions gives rise to *resonances*, which constitute an overall system phenomenon. Because these resonances are fundamentally *non-local* in nature, they provide *feedback* at the level of all of the individual system trajectories that contributed to their origination. Accordingly, this feedback has local effects that place a fundamental limit on the precision of what can be known about the position and momentum of any individual system element in isolation at any particular time.

With regard to the second question regarding our ability to predict the future, sometimes the effect of system resonances is minor and essentially inconsequential, leaving individual trajectories continuous and integrable. However, often the effects are more major, resulting in *discontinuities* that direct the evolution of the overall system in ways that are *non-integrable* and, thus, fundamentally *unpredictable*. The question is *where* does the dividing line exist between a small input that has only a minor effect as opposed to one having a disproportionate major effect that fosters discontinuities?

Unfortunately, because the precise boundaries between continuous to discontinuous domains are unknown even in principle, the transition points between them are not predictable. The only insight that can be offered is a rule of thumb: because it is unknown where the dividing lines exist between continuous and discontinuous domains, if systems are operating within stable domains, it is *more likely* that *small changes* will *stay within* the *smooth boundaries* of *continuity* than if large changes are introduced (which entail more major system excursions). When larger perturbations occur, larger numbers of intervening states are crossed, meaning that there is a greater chance that one of them will be within a discontinuous domain. (Note: The assumption with this type of reasoning is that macroscopic systems cannot just "jump" over discontinuities from one stable domain to another.) But even when only small perturbations are introduced, continued stability is only a question of likelihood, which depends on the density of discontinuities in the surroundings; there is not any guarantee that a discontinuous domain does not exist immediately adjacent to a continuous one and will not be encountered.

Thus, it can be concluded that *stable systems* are at least *potentially predictable* with a reasonable degree of accuracy while *unstable systems* are *not*. Furthermore, unstable systems are not a rarity in our universe—they appear to be the norm. Lastly, it is not immediately obvious where seemingly stable systems will make the (potential) transition to becoming unstable.

All of these factors place fundamental limits on the degree of confidence we can have in making *predictions* about the *time-dependent behaviors* of *natural systems*. The biggest challenges in this regard are when we attempt to make assessments of (a) whether apparently stable systems will remain so and (b) whether the outcomes of current trajectories will remain predictable when they are projected into the future.

The final conclusion to be reached is that with *stability*, there is at least a *chance* that the *evolution* of events can be *predicted* with some degree of confidence. But *without stability*, there is *no reliable way* to *predict* what will occur elsewhere or in the future.

CHAPTER 19
Dynamical Certainty vs. Uncertainty: Trajectories

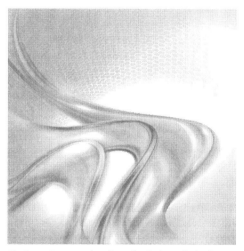

Trajectories can be described, but their future directions are not definable unerringly.

Dynamics: Definition (Merriam-Webster Dictionary)

- A branch of mechanics that deals with forces and their relation primarily to the motion of bodies but sometimes also to equilibrium

Certain: Definition (Merriam-Webster Dictionary)

- Known or proved to be true: indisputable
- Fixed, settled
- Dependable, reliable
- Inevitable
- Assured in mind or action

Uncertain: Definition (Merriam-Webster Dictionary)

- Indefinite, indeterminate
- Not clearly identified or defined
- Not known beyond doubt: dubious
- Not certain to occur: problematical
- Not reliable: untrustworthy
- Not having certain knowledge: doubtful
- Not constant: variable, fitful

Trajectory: Definition (Merriam-Webster Dictionary)

- The curve that a body describes in space (as a planet or comet in its orbit or a rocket)

Dynamics is the branch of classical (i.e., Newtonian) mechanics used to describe the *evolution* of *physical systems* over *time*. It requires knowledge of the *positions* of *objects*, as well as the *forces* acting upon them. By using it, *trajectories* (which describe the positions of physical entities as they change over time) can be *predicted* based on the application of *physical laws* (i.e., universal rules) to *physical bodies*. Dynamics has its roots in the classical *laws of motion*, which were first formulated by the Italian scientist Galileo Galilei in the seventeenth century. These were subsequently refined by the iconic English mathematician and physicist Sir Isaac Newton.

Classical dynamics represents an example of a *deterministic model* for describing *system evolution*. Remarkably, the formulations of classical dynamics have no preferred direction in time, which means that they can be used to describe (i.e., calculate) the past states of any system of interacting physical bodies just as readily as any future states. This is a critically important aspect of dynamical theory: it is not directionally time dependent, and, because of this, its predictions are entirely *reversible*. However, this is only the case in theory; in reality, when a system and its surrounding environment are examined together, it is only under very special circumstances (i.e., artificial ones) that the evolution of a system is completely reversible.

Consider this: if all real events were perfectly time-reversible, there would be no forward direction to evolution (i.e., there would be no *arrow of time*). In fact, it would be just as likely that events could *run backward* as they would forward. For instance, it would be just as likely that a shattered glass would spontaneously reassemble itself immediately after shattering as it would to stay broken. Although this type of time reversibility would effectively make *all directions possible* (which might sound egalitarian and possibly even favorable), it would violate a cardinal tenant of our collective belief that particular objects and events serve as the cause(s) of others (i.e., their consequences), and not that consequences are responsible for precipitating the objects and events that caused them to occur in the first place (see chapter 4, entitled "Causality: Linking Events Separated by Time and Space," for further discussion).

Tellingly, no one has ever observed the spontaneous occurrence of precisely the same set of real events in reverse order (at least not without the addition of outside energy to do so—which, by definition, would make them non-spontaneous). This is not to state that there cannot be the reestablishment of preexisting states for many of the systems we deal with; in fact, we often design systems and orchestrate events specifically to make this happen (e.g., as occurs with any cyclically-designed physical process—such as with a reciprocating gasoline engine). Another example is illustrated by what we do when we clean our house after a party. In this case, we reestablish the initial cleanliness of the house, but not via the reversal of each and every prior event that caused it to become dirty in the first place. We return it to its initial state of cleanliness, but via a different path—by using brooms, mops, vacuums, garbage disposals, etc.—and we expend (externally derived) energy to do so (i.e., energy from outside of the house itself—such as our own biological energy reserves, electricity produced externally, etc.). Thus, the return of the house to its preexisting state of cleanliness is *not* the result of the *precise reversal* of the *paths* that got it from being clean to dirty originally. If this were possible, then the party itself would be a completely reversible event that could be *erased* (i.e., made simply to never have occurred) by running events in reverse order. As suggested by this example, this would mean that all events would be reversible, thereby implying that there would be nothing to propel events in a forward direction (i.e., such that they could occur without the possibility of being erased). If this were so, then what would exist to cause events to progress in a forward direction in time? Would it simply be chance or something else?

There have been attempts to reconcile the intrinsic lack of time directionality of classical dynamics by invoking notions of *unavoidable energy losses* that would prevent systems from returning to their prior states spontaneously (e.g., such as the friction between physical bodies). But even these types of losses could be avoided if the evolution of physical systems were advanced through time sufficiently slowly (i.e., in a *non-dissipative* sort of way). Therefore, this limitation would still not provide an ironclad guarantee that sequences of events could not run backward. A corollary is that a necessary constraint for the evolution of physical states in a directly reversible way is that they would need to evolve in a continuous (i.e., smooth) manner that was not disjointed, otherwise they would not be non-dissipative. (Note: this assumption is inconsistent with observations that have been made concerning the existence of discontinuities in the universe; see chapter 17, entitled "Continuity (Smoothness) vs. Discontinuity (Roughness)," for further discussion.)

Fortunately, there is also another explanation for why time's arrow progresses spontaneously—and monotonically—in a forward direction. It arises because some of the assumptions made in classical dynamical theory are merely *idealizations*, meaning that they are not properly reflective of the universe's true nature.

In the previous chapter, it was noted that there is a fundamental difference between the description of *single trajectories* as they pertain to individual system components (when they are examined in isolation) and *multiple trajectories* (as they relate to different system elements) when there are numerous overlapping components within any real system (which is the case for virtually all natural systems that are not artificially constrained). This means that to describe the evolution of events in any real system, instead of appealing to single, isolated trajectories as the starting points for analysis, there must also be an accounting of the *higher-level* (i.e., *non-local*) *effects* that result from the unavoidable *interactions* of *ensembles* of *trajectories*. As mentioned in the previous two chapters, these interactions give rise to system *resonances* that have global (non-local) effects on the greater (overall) system. These effects then feed back on the (contributing) individual system elements, thereby giving rise to (*modulating* or *modifying*) local effects (i.e., local feedback).

Therefore, in any real (complex) system there are non-local effects that *entangle* every system component with every other. These effects are system-wide and constitute *emergent phenomena* that arise from the *entire system*, not from any one portion of it.

What we can conclude is that the following pattern is applicable to all real systems: (1) Single (i.e., intrinsic) component trajectories combine with (2) other system component trajectories to create (3) resonant effects that influence the whole system to provide (4) individualized feedback for all the contributing system elements (5) which were themselves responsible for originating the overarching system-wide resonant effects in the first place.

This process results in the generation of emergent, non-local effects in all real systems (i.e., ones that are complex). These emergent effects then generate temporal asymmetry and time directionality in a natural way. This process imparts a forward direction to the evolution of real systems and makes them *irreversible* (i.e., non-erasable).

Fortunately, the principle involved here is entirely consistent with analogous concepts that arise in *thermodynamics* (i.e., the second law, which incorporates the macroscopic concept of *entropy*) as well as in *statistical mechanics* (i.e., which involves the description of populations of particles at the submicroscopic level).

In thermodynamics, the concept is that *irreversible processes*—those represented by virtually all naturally-occurring events—cause an increase in overall entropy that precludes a system's ability to spontaneously return to its previous state (see chapter 20, entitled "Thermodynamics: Laws Prohibiting the Spontaneous Reversibility of Physical Events," for further discussion). *Entropy* can be thought of as a measure of system *disorder* and—from the standpoint of statistical mechanics—it is a reflection of the total number of possible *microstates* (i.e., system states involving submicroscopic objects) that all give rise to a single indistinguishable *macroscopic state* (i.e., a state of the *large-scale* objects that we all generally recognize [typically our human scale plus or minus several orders of magnitude]). The *increases* in *entropy* that occur as a result of all spontaneous processes—together with the associated implications they have for *time irreversibility*—evolve at the level of the *sum* of *all system interactions* (i.e., those involving the "greater system" comprised of the local system of interest plus the entire *surrounding environment*). Therefore, time symmetry is routinely broken as a result of the evolution of real systems that have real-body interactions.

Imbedded in this line of reasoning is the idea of so-called *thermodynamic isolation*, which presupposes that objects and events can be isolated from all interactions with their surrounding environment. Although attempts can be made to isolate systems from one another on a large scale, this is only an idealization at a more fundamental level. This is due to the non-uniformity of the temperature in different regions of the universe (i.e., the temperature difference between any real system and the surrounding environment in which it is imbedded). Because of this, the *complete* thermodynamic *isolation* of any real system *cannot* be *accomplished* due to the *obligatory exchange* of *radiant energy* between regions of the universe at different temperatures. These differences in the *absolute temperature* of objects result in the exchange of so-called *black body radiation* (see chapter 25, entitled "Absolutes vs. Relatives: Relativity Theory," for further discussion). Accordingly, it is not possible for any real object or event to exist or to occur in complete isolation; to assume otherwise is merely an idealization that is incorrect.

In addition to this limitation, there are also other factors that result in time asymmetry that arise from other types of idealizations that are assumed in classical dynamics. The most important among these are that (1) *bodies* can be represented as mere *points*, (2) their *masses* and the *forces* that act upon them are definable with *absolute certainty* (i.e., with *absolute accuracy* and *precision*), and (3) *energy* is a *continuously variable* quantity (i.e., something that is non-quantized). Unfortunately, none of these assumptions reflects the universe's true nature; they likewise constitute only conveniences.

Collectively, these idealizations result in significant limitations for classical dynamics. Although dynamics provides a very valuable description of physical interactions at the *macroscopic* level (i.e., for building bridges, earthquake-proofing buildings, sending astronauts to the moon, etc.), it *breaks down* when applied to interacting particles at the *submicroscopic level*.

As outlined in the previous chapter (see chapter 18, entitled "Stability vs. Instability: System Inertia and Resiliency"), stable dynamical systems are those in which slight changes in their initial conditions produce correspondingly small downstream effects over time. For these systems, descriptions based on (A) *individual trajectories* (i.e., using classical dynamics) and (B) *probabilities* (i.e., using statistical mechanics) are equivalent. But, *instability destroys* the *equivalence* between the descriptions at the *individual (trajectory) level* and the *statistical (probability) level*. As a result, probabilities acquire an additional and intrinsic meaning that cannot be accounted for at the descriptive level of individual trajectories. This is because for unstable systems, *individual trajectories* quickly become *inaccurate* due to their *extreme sensitivity* to *initial conditions*. If these initial conditions cannot be described with infinite accuracy and precision (which they cannot—see chapter 9, entitled "Measurement: How Circumstance and Change are Assessed," for further discussion), then this can (and often does) result in *divergences* in individual submicroscopic trajectories away from what had been expected (on average) based on the precise specification of the initial conditions.

Observation has shown that there are a proportion of dynamical systems where *small perturbations* in *initial conditions* are *amplified* over time. *Chaotic systems* represent an extreme example of this type of behavior that ultimately results in unpredictability (in any sense other than providing very general targets—see chapter 24, entitled "Chaos Theory: Implications for Macroscopic Predictability," for further discussion). In these cases, the trajectories identified by distinct initial conditions—no matter how close they are to each other—diverge over time. This type of *extreme sensitivity* to *initial conditions* can result in what has been termed the fabled *butterfly effect*, whereby a single butterfly flight over China can be amplified and have a progressive downstream effect that eventually results in major influences over the entire subsequent weather patterns of the Northern Hemisphere.

What this all means is that the idea in classical dynamics of *single trajectories* is a mere *idealization*. To claim that there is a single unique trajectory arising from a set of initial conditions would require infinite accuracy and precision in the specification of both the starting conditions for all objects as well as the forces acting upon them. For stable systems, this has no practical significance, because all such trajectories parallel each other and can be computed; in these cases, even though they may be not precisely equivalent, the trajectories are related to each other in well-defined and calculable ways. But for unstable systems, the trajectories diverge—often exponentially—making the best possible description a probability distribution of all possible sets of trajectories, some of which are far-flung. This means that when dynamical systems are unstable and the initial conditions are imprecisely known (which is always the case), the idea of a single well-defined system trajectory becomes untenable. This is a far-reaching and profound conclusion, but it has a benefit: the probability distributions that arise for these unstable systems contain additional information that was lacking in the more simple descriptions of the original (idealized) single trajectories. It is from these ensembles of trajectories that the rules applying to chaotic systems arise.

To be clear, unstable dynamical systems still have trajectories, but they result from processes that ultimately fall into the realm of probabilities, not certainties. This occurs because no human measurement can define the initial conditions for any system—or the forces that act upon it—with absolute accuracy and precision, which would necessarily need to be infinite. Ultimately, this sends us back to issues pertaining to the accuracy and precision of measurements, as well as the related topic of quantum uncertainty (see chapter 9, entitled "Measurement: How Circumstance and Change are Assessed," and chapter 21, entitled "Quantum Theory: Uncertainties of the Very Small," for further discussions). Here, it is sufficient to note what the Nobel prize-winning twentieth century physicist Werner Heisenberg wrote with regard to his fabled uncertainty principle:*

> One can never know with perfect accuracy both of those two important factors which determine the movement of one of the smallest particles—its position and its velocity. It is impossible to determine accurately *both* the position and the direction and speed of a particle *at the same instant*. (italics added)

The implication is that no matter how precisely two matched sets of initial conditions may appear to be, there is no way to guarantee that they are precisely identical. As has been emphasized, for stable systems this is of little practical import, because all adjacent trajectories merge to a mean value that is central, predictable, and stable. But for unstable systems, these non-identical conditions result in divergent sets of future trajectories that are markedly different. This combination of (a) the non-duplicability of initial conditions and (b) the increasing divergence of the sets of trajectories arising from initial small differences has the effect of breaking the reversibility of the dynamical processes, thereby breaking time symmetry and imparting a *natural direction* to the *arrow of time*.

Other factors also make classical dynamical systems imprecisely predictable. One of these was outlined earlier (see chapter 17, entitled "Continuity (Smoothness) vs. Discontinuity (Roughness)"): it is that the state of systems of particles (i.e., the sum of their kinetic and potential energies) must be an *integrable function* of *time* if their *future* (and *past*) *states* are to be *uniquely definable* from their present state. If this is not the case, then both their future and their past states are not uniquely knowable based on conditions that are (presently) measurable.

Advances during the latter part of the twentieth century, especially in the field of non-equilibrium thermodynamics by the Nobel prize-winning chemist Ilya Prigogine, have helped to shed additional light on these issues. But for now, it is sufficient to appreciate that classical dynamics is based on idealizations that are not properly reflective of the actual characteristics of the universe in which we live. Because of this, its formulation is freely time-reversible, which does not comport with the *arrow of time* that we routinely observe in the spontaneous unfolding of events. Therefore, the description of the universe at the level of *individual trajectories* is *deficient* and, as such, it is *prone to errors* when it attempts to *predict* the *future*. Approaching the issue from both the macroscopic and the submicroscopic perspectives (i.e., via thermodynamics on the one hand and statistical mechanics on the other) confirms this conclusion. Thus, *classical dynamics*—although useful for many practical applications at the local level—represents an incomplete approximation that is *not capable* of *predicting future events* with the *level of certainty* we would like.

---

* Werner Heisenberg, *Die Physik der Atomkerne* (*The Physics of the Atomic Nucleus*) (3. Aufl., Braunschweig: Vieweg, 1949).

PART 3
FUNDAMENTAL QUANTITIES, RELATIONSHIPS, AND LIMITATIONS

CHAPTER 20
Thermodynamics: Laws Prohibiting the Spontaneous Reversibility of Physical Events

Thermodynamics describes energy exchange and the evolution of energetic systems.

Thermodynamics: Definition (Merriam-Webster Dictionary)

- Physics that deals with the mechanical action or relations of heat
- Thermodynamic processes and phenomena
    - o Being or relating to a system of atoms, molecules, colloidal particles, or larger bodies considered as an isolated group in the study of thermodynamic processes

Spontaneous: Definition (Merriam-Webster Dictionary)

- Developing or occurring without apparent external influence, force, cause, or treatment
- Controlled and directed internally: self-acting
- Not apparently contrived or manipulated: natural
- Proceeding from natural feeling or native tendency without external constraint

Reversible: Definition (Merriam-Webster Dictionary)

- Capable of being reversed or of reversing
    - As in capable of going through a series of actions (as changes) either backward or forward

Thermodynamics is often perceived as an imposing subject, but it deals with something very simple: the *transfer* of *heat* between physical objects. The discipline had its modern-day beginnings in the nineteenth century, when it was first employed to quantify the relationship between the amount of the *heat exchanged* between *physical objects* and the resulting ability of the systems containing such objects to perform *useful work* (i.e., work external to the system where the heat exchange occurs).

As we have all experienced, the transfer of heat occurs spontaneously between physical bodies that are not of equal temperature (if you don't believe it, try putting your hand on a hot stove—heat will be transferred to it quickly enough that you will withdraw your hand immediately!) The process of heat transfer often results in the liberation of *free energy* (i.e., energy that is not bound up in any other form), so that it is available to be transferred to other systems. This energy can then be utilized to perform *useful work* on the outside environment (external to the system where it was derived), so as to *drive* sequences of *events* in a direction that would not otherwise occur (i.e., in a way that would not occur spontaneously). Thermodynamics provides a method for quantifying the relationship between heat transfer (a form of energy exchange) and the amount of useful work that can be performed by any real system.

All of thermodynamics is based on one premise and three *laws* (i.e., rules that are considered so obvious that they are promulgated without proof). The premise is that bodies at equal temperature do not exchange heat (this is often referred to as the zeroth law of thermodynamics). The subsequent three laws address the issue of how much *energy* can be *extracted* from self-contained (i.e., isolated) *physical systems* so that it can be delivered to the surrounding environment. The liberated energy is then available to be harnessed in a fashion that would make it useful (at least potentially). In addition, these laws address how much *external heat* (i.e., heat delivered to a system) can be *converted* by any real process into a form that can perform *useful work* on the system's surroundings (i.e., the environment outside of the system itself).

The three *laws of thermodynamics* can be summarized as follows (for readers interested in the mathematical formulations of the first and second laws, please see the Appendix at the end of this book):

Statement of the first law:

> The *increase* in *internal energy* of a closed system is equal to the *difference* of the *heat supplied* to the system and the *work done* by it.

Common formulation: **You can't win**

> What it means: *It isn't possible to get something for nothing.* No physical system can deliver more *useful energy* to perform work on its environment than (1) the amount of energy delivered to it by the addition of external *heat* plus (2) any decrease that occurs in the *internal energy* of the system itself.

> Corollary: It is *not possible* to *create energy* from nothing (i.e., energy can be *converted* from one form to another, but it *cannot* be *created* de novo).

Statement of the second law:

> The amount of *heat delivered* to a system divided by its *absolute temperature* is less than or equal to the *increase* in *system entropy*.

Common formulation: **You can't break even**

What it means: In the case of all *real* physical systems, they *cannot deliver* even the *same amount* of *energy* to their environment (in any useful form) as what is *provided* to them plus the amount that the *internal energy* of the system is *diminished* (i.e., what the first law defines as the maximum possible energy output).

Corollary: Energy conversion can never be 100 percent efficient, regardless of the process used for its conversion. This is due to *unavoidable energy losses* and is where the thermodynamic concept of *entropy* arises.

Statement of the third law:

As the temperature approaches *absolute zero*, the *entropy* of a system approaches a *minimum*, constant value.

Common formulation: **You can't get out of the game**

What it means: For any system operating at a temperature above absolute zero (i.e., above 0° Kelvin [−273.15° Celsius]—as all real systems do), *entropy production* is *unavoidable*; thus, there is no way to circumvent the restrictions imposed by the first and the second laws.

Corollary: Unless the temperature of a hot object (i.e., the "higher temperature reservoir") from which heat is being transferred is *infinitely high* or the cold object (i.e., the "lower temperature reservoir") to which heat is being transferred is at *absolute zero* (neither of which is possible), *complete efficiency* in the *conversion* of *energy* to a useful form is *impossible*.

(Note: a perfect crystal's entropy is zero at a temperature of absolute zero [0° Kelvin], which provides an absolute point of reference; however, it is not possible for any real system to reach a temperature of absolute zero.)

Remarkably, these three laws of heat transfer and their relationship to energy conversion constitute the entire basis of thermodynamics. They give rise to a powerful implication: real *events* that *spontaneously change* the *state* of any system do so precisely because they are *energetically favored* (i.e., result in lower energy states) over other (past and present) states. By so doing, they cause the *unavoidable production* of *higher overall entropy* (i.e., the total entropy encompassing *both* the *system* of interest plus the *environment* in which it is imbedded) with advancing time (i.e., in the *forward* time direction).

The concept of entropy that arises as a result of the second law is extremely important. It can be likened to a measure of system disorder. In principle, it arises because there are many more ways for the components of any real system to be disordered than there are for them to be ordered (i.e., organized). From a statistical standpoint, ordered states are much rarer than disordered ones. They also embody more potential energy, which is routinely liberated when they become disorganized. Ordered states are energetically more difficult to create and to maintain (because there are fewer of them) compared with those that are disordered (of which there are considerably more). And because order is associated with a higher degree of organization, it means that ordered systems contain more potentially convertible energy compared with those that are more disordered.

A common example illustrates this point. A house is something that can be considered a relatively well-ordered structure. It has a foundation, a frame, a roof, walls, plumbing, electrical wiring, a heating system, etc. Such structures take many man-hours to construct, and they have a multitude of well-organized components that themselves require time and energy to produce. As such, the components of a house and their structural relationships are intrinsically well-ordered. However, if a tornado were to rumble through and deliver enough external energy to destroy the house, its different components would typically survive, but they would be fragmented and highly disordered in their subsequent configuration. For instance, pieces of pipe and wiring might be flung as far as miles away from the frame and the roof of the house.

If something like this were to happen, there are an exceedingly large number of ways that the components of the house might be strewn about the landscape. All of these would represent different states of disorder. But, the original ordered way in which the house began—as an intact and highly integrated structure—had only a much more limited number of ways that it could be properly assembled and maintained in order to be regarded as a house. The difference between the large number of ways that the components of the house could be fragmented and disordered compared with the relatively few ways that they could be ordered and functional (i.e., constituting what we regard as a house) is analogous to what entropy is measuring in physical systems; it can be thought of as a measure of the *probability* of finding a set of *system* components in an *ordered state* as compared to the other states, which are intrinsically more disordered.

An important additional implication is that it is typically easy to make a collection of components (i.e., a system) go from a state of order to one of disorder. It takes *work* (i.e., the expenditure of *energy*) to order them, with the amount of work being a reflection of what is contained in the sum of the potential and internal energy of an ordered system. What's more, real systems almost never go from being disordered to being ordered spontaneously in any systematically sustainable way (unless they create even more disorder in their surrounding environments). Once again, this is because the probability of any set of system components being disordered is much higher than it is for them to be ordered. Therefore, energy must be expended to make something become ordered from an intrinsic starting point of disorder.

So, the idea of *entropy* in thermodynamics can be regarded as a *measure* of *system disorder*. As spontaneously occurring events unfold, the total amount of entropy in the universe increases (i.e., the entropy associated with *all* the systems in the universe collectively) and the amount of total free energy decreases. Because the total amount of entropy in the universe increases as events evolve in a forward direction, there is no way for the universe to return to prior states spontaneously by simply reversing the direction of those processes—which collectively constitute the evolution of all spontaneous events. Hence, it is not possible to run events backward and make them occur in a reverse time sequence. This is because it would require doing active work on all of the systems in the universe at the same time to return them to their prior states. But, if by the term universe we are referring to all that is (i.e., everything—seen and unseen, known and unknown, etc.), then there is not any external source of energy outside of the universe to allow this to happen. This means that any additional individual system changes within the universe to return them to their prior states would necessarily create even further entropy increases in the overall universe to get the systems back to their initial states—all of which would collectively embody a lower amount of entropy. This presents a dilemma (i.e., inconsistency) that cannot be reconciled. Due to this intrinsic limitation, there is no way back to making everything just the way it was in the past; something must always be different. Thus, the monotonic increase in the overall entropy of the universe dictates that there is only a single direction for time evolution: forward!

The conclusion is that all future states of the universe (when it is considered in its entirety) must be different than its past states. From a thermodynamic (i.e., energetic) standpoint, there is simply no "external energy source" to drive everything back to the previous collective set of states of all the universe's systems concurrently.

So the key limitation imposed by the laws of thermodynamics is that *all spontaneous processes* evolve according to a single maxim—they result in *increases* in the *overall entropy* of the *universe* and are, therefore, *irreversible* from a universal standpoint. This results in higher (overall) levels of physical disorder (again, with regard to the sum of the entropy for any isolated thermodynamic system of interest plus its surrounding environment, which includes the entire universe—see chapter 26, entitled "Energy," for further discussion). In conjunction with this type of spontaneous time evolution, there is also a move toward universal states with a lower quantities of overall free energy compared with past states.

In summary, the second law of thermodynamics—which defines and quantifies the concept of *entropy*—*prohibits spontaneous reversibility* (i.e., *reverse causality*) from ever being a possibility from a purely energetic standpoint. This arises exclusively from energetic considerations—i.e., those embodied by unavoidable increases in entropy that are due to the spontaneous transfer of heat (i.e., energy) between physical bodies. This is comforting: it means that our fundamental concept of time directionality, as it pertains to the unidirectional evolution of events must remain intact. This allows us to continue believing in the notion of causality, which we otherwise could not.

CHAPTER 21
Quantum Theory: Uncertainties of the Very Small

The behavior of matter and energy at extremely small scales involves quantum uncertainty.

Quantum: Definition (Merriam-Webster Dictionary)

- Any of the very small increments or parcels into which many forms of energy are subdivided
- Any of the small subdivisions of a quantized physical magnitude (as magnetic moment)
- Quantity, amount
- Portion, part

Quantum Theory: Definition (Merriam-Webster Dictionary)

- A theory in physics based on the concept of the subdivision of radiant energy into finite quanta and applied to numerous processes involving transference or transformation of energy in an atomic or molecular scale
- *Quantum mechanics*
  - A theory of matter that is based on the concept of the possession of wave properties by elementary particles, that affords a mathematical interpretation of the structure and interactions of matter on the basis of these properties, and that incorporates within it quantum theory and the uncertainty principle—also called *wave mechanics.*

Uncertainty Principle: Definition (Merriam-Webster Dictionary)

- A principle in quantum mechanics: it is impossible to discern simultaneously and with high accuracy both the position and the momentum of a particle—also called *Heisenberg uncertainty principle*

The idea of a *quantum* is simple: it is that physical quantities come in minimally sized units or *packets* that are discrete and not further divisible. The idea is that there is a lower limit to how small objects and other physical quantities can become. The alternative would be that the smallest objects and events would still be divisible into tinier and tinier parts in a continuous way (i.e., that they would remain smooth and non-disjointed to progressively smaller levels ad infinitum).

The question of how small physical substances can be subdivided before they are no longer divisible is not new. For millennia, the idea has circulated that discrete units exist that cannot be further divided. The concept took root in the Western world in the fifth century BC when the Greek philosopher Democritus coined the term átomos to refer to the smallest possible physical objects, which means "uncuttable" or "the smallest indivisible particle of matter." In 1661, the Anglo-Irish philosopher Robert Boyle argued that physical substances were composed of various combinations of different "corpuscles" or *atoms*. In 1789, the French scientist Antoine

Lavoisier discovered the law of conservation of mass and defined an element as a basic substance that could not be further broken down by chemical methods. In 1805, the English natural philosopher John Dalton used the concept of discrete atoms to explain why elements always react in ratios of small whole numbers, which is referred to as the law of multiple proportions. As the basis for his theory, he proposed that each element consists of atoms of a single, unique type. However, in 1897 the British physicist Sir J. J. Thomson discovered electrons and concluded that they are components of every atom. Thus, he overturned the belief that atoms are the indivisible, ultimate particles of all physical substances. But, the question of how far the division of substances could continue was still left open.

Near the turn of the twentieth century, a new theory emerged to address the issue of the minimum size of substances. This was in response to the need to reconcile inconsistencies between classical predictions of the intensity of light that radiated from dark, hot bodies (so-called *black body radiation*) and the spectrum of what was observed. Subsequent experiments showed that the *packet sizes* of energy (i.e., *quanta*) are incredibly small—many orders of magnitude tinier than the smallest quantities that we normally encounter in our everyday lives. Further investigations showed that the idea of *quanta* applies equally to dimensions, times, etc. Just how small? With regard to length, to dimensions on the order of subnuclear size, which are measured in fractions of angstroms (less than one ten thousandth of a millionth of an inch!).

The incredible tininess of these quantities is the reason we don't routinely notice that the objects and events we deal with at a macroscopic level are not continuous (i.e., that they jump from one discrete state to another). The minimum size of the transitions we are able to detect using our senses is much larger than any individual quantum leap, meaning that the very small sizes of quanta make the underlying jumps between these values too small to notice at our usual macroscopic levels of interrogation (i.e., using our eyes, ears, etc.). So, at the larger scales at which we generally operate, quantum transitions are inapparent—they are simply below our ability to resolve and, therefore, beneath our level of detectability. The result is that everything *looks* and *feels continuous* at the scales we are familiar with, even though the underlying changes that give rise to the macroscopic objects and events that we interact with are not.

Nevertheless, *quantum jumps* from one state to another are detectable using scientific instruments that are more sensitive than our biological senses. What has been discovered is that very small objects and energies are quantized and that they exist only in very specific, discrete, and well-defined amounts—or in the next available *step* that is either above or below that level—and nothing in between. They are, therefore, *jerky* in terms of both their quantities and their transitions from one value or amount to another, because they must somehow jump from one value to the next. Accordingly, they can only take on values that are *separated* from each other (in terms of quantity) by some sort of an *intervening gap* (i.e., in space, time, energy, etc.). A reasonable analogy might be that "quantum is to continuous" what "digital is to analog": in both cases, the former is *discrete* with a distinct boundary to define its full extent, whereas the latter is *continuous* and varies in a flowing, non-disjointed, and smoothly subdividable sort of way.

The question is: Even if quanta exist, why should we be concerned about them? If we can't even notice them, why should we care?

The idea that physical quantities are quantized is important for two reasons:

1. The very smallest amounts of everything in existence (i.e., energy, length, mass, time, etc.) operate according to rules that apply to *quanta* (i.e., *quantum mechanics*)
2. Our overarching presumption is that everything that is big is made up of smaller components.

If these two premises are correct, then shouldn't all physical quantities—those that are big as well as small—behave according to the same underlying *quantum rules*? This would seem only reasonable. The alternative would be that small objects behave according to quantum rules, but that the larger objects that they make up do not. Although this latter proposition may sound unreasonable, it should not be dismissed out of hand—it actually serves as the basis for one of the major interpretations of quantum theory.

Perhaps not so strangely, many properties of physical objects that exist at the usual scales of our everyday experience cannot be understood without appealing to quantum theory. Many principles and phenomena that are familiar to scientists working with macroscopic objects and events—such as those involving semiconductors, superconductivity, and nuclear reactions—cannot be explained using classical (i.e., Newtonian) mechanics. But, they can be explained using quantum theory. In fact, despite generating often baffling paradoxes, quantum mechanics is the most consistently correct theory ever to be developed: to date, none of its predictions has ever been proven wrong. Because of this, it is a powerful tool for describing the behavior of very small objects and, like it or not, its implications are not in the realm of everyday experience. Since we exist at a much larger scale than where the fundamental rules of quantum mechanics dominate to govern the evolution of events, quantum effects are not obvious to us.

This brings up an even larger issue: while all of our ordinary human experience is based on conditions that we perceive in our immediate environment, these experiences don't necessarily tell us very much about what goes on in other domains beyond the *borders* of the local realm where we exist. This is the case both with regard to the very small objects that quantum theory helps us describe, as well as with very large-scale objects—such as our galaxy—where the theory of general relativity provides us with an operating framework. We, and our local environment, are at a size that is intermediate between these other two domains. Nevertheless, because these other realms rest to either side of our own, we generally assume that they must have some connection to what happens in our immediate environment. This is because we believe—via our notion of causality—that all events have effects on other events (or at least that local events are somehow *contiguous* or connected with others nearby—see chapter 4, entitled "Causality: Linking Events Separated by Time and Space," for further discussion).

Despite this, something obvious is often ignored: we have extremely limited direct access to objects and events in either submicroscopic domains or at stellar dimensions. This means that by using our senses alone, we are often restricted (and sometimes functionally blind) in our abilities to appreciate the types of interactions that occur among the basic building blocks that comprise what we are (on the small side) and that make up the greater environment in which we live (on the large side). Most all the information we have about these other realms is obtained via proxy, extension, and inference (i.e., by using scientific instruments to measure what we can't ourselves see, feel, touch, hear, etc., and via analogy to what we have direct information about). When this information does not conform to our expectations, we invent new theories to explain the phenomena as they appear to exist elsewhere. This is where quantum theory comes in:

it describes the rules of interactions among extremely small objects and quantities that border the scale where we exist—those that are inapparent to us within our macroscopic environment.

So what is it about these very small objects and energies that make them different from our ordinary experience? Many experimental clues arose in the latter part of the nineteenth century to suggest the need for a new theory to describe very small quantities and dimensions.* To satisfy this need, in 1900 the Nobel prize-winning physicist Max Planck introduced the idea that energy (see chapter 26, entitled "Energy," for further definition) is packaged—in its smallest quantities—in discrete bundles called *quanta*. This was a major break from classical physics, where energy could take on a full range of continuous values without restriction. By postulating *quantized jumps* in energy from one value to the next among very small quantities, he was able to derive a formula for the distribution of energy intensities over the frequency range emitted by opaque substances (i.e., those that absorb all varieties of radiant energy—so-called *black bodies*). The formula is referred to as Planck's law, and it incorporates a new fundamental physical constant (subsequently named Planck's constant). This approach yielded extremely successful predictions of the measured values of *black body radiation* as a function of temperature in a way that classical Newtonian methods could not (see chapter 25, entitled "Absolutes vs. Relatives: Relativity Theory," for further discussion).

Albert Einstein extended this insight by advancing a theory as to why incident light falling on some materials could eject electrons (the photoelectric effect). He posited that electromagnetic radiation, including light, could be divided into a finite number of *energy quanta* that are localized at points in space. Einstein won the Nobel Prize in physics for this work. In his seminal 1905 paper on the subject, he stated:[†]

> The energy of a light ray spreading out from a point source is not continuously distributed over an increasing space but consists of a finite number of *energy quanta* which are localized at points in space, which move without dividing, and which can only be produced and absorbed as complete units. (italics added)

This idea was revolutionary. Until then, standard electromagnetic theory (as developed in the 1860s by the Scottish physicist James Clerk Maxwell), regarded light as simply a wave and not as energy-containing particles. By changing this paradigm, Einstein was the first to ascribe to light a wave-particle duality. This was ultimately ironic, because Einstein was never able to fully accept the unavoidable implications of his discovery (i.e., the idea of an intrinsic uncertainty in quantum theory that was not resolvable).

Although all these theories involving quanta were very successful, there was still no rigorous theoretical justification for the idea of quantized packets of energy until 1924. It was then that the French physicist Louis de Broglie promulgated a new theory of matter by hypothesizing that, just as light could manifest as particles, matter could exhibit the characteristics of waves. This fundamental insight—that all physical objects could be described as waves as well as particles—resulted in the inception soon thereafter of modern quantum mechanics. In 1929, de Broglie was awarded a Nobel Prize for his work.

In 1925, the German physicists Werner Heisenberg and Max Born developed what was called *matrix mechanics*, while the Austrian physicist Erwin Schrödinger invented *wave mechanics* (all received Nobel Prizes for their work). Schrödinger's famous equation provides a description of the *time evolution* of *physical systems* via a mathematical construct called the *wave function*, which describes the probability that a system will be found in a given state at a given time. Schrödinger subsequently showed that his wave description of quantum mechanics was equivalent to the descriptions of matrix mechanics.

In 1927, Heisenberg promulgated what became known as his famous *uncertainty principle*. This stated that there is a fundamental limit to the accuracy with which certain pairs of physical properties—such as the position and momentum of a particle—can be known simultaneously (i.e., that the more precisely one of the properties is measured, the less precisely the other could be known, determined, or controlled).

For decades there was a highly polarized debate over whether this *uncertainty* is a fundamental limit of actual *things-in-themselves* (as Kant would have referred to them) or merely a manifestation of our inability to make measurements without perturbing them. The first of these possibilities resulted in the so-called "Copenhagen interpretation" of quantum uncertainty (referring to the school of thought promulgated by the two Nobel prize-winning physicists Neils Bohr and Werner Heisenberg of Denmark), while the second assumed that these limits constituted an artifact that arises from the perturbation of systems due to measuring processes themselves. Einstein was an ardent advocate of the latter interpretation—that the particle properties exist in a well-defined (i.e., absolutely precise) way, but that the process of measurement causes them to change.

To support his position, Einstein—together with his post-doctoral fellow Boris Podolsky and his assistant Nathan Rosen—published a paper in 1935 outlining a measurement paradox to challenge the Copenhagen interpretation of what could be measured and known simultaneously.[8] This is often referred to as the *EPR thought experiment* (see chapter 22, entitled "Entanglement vs. Separability: The Locality Issue," for further discussion).

Fortunately, regardless of the correctness of the differing interpretations, the underlying cause of quantum uncertainty is not relevant with regard to the issue of predictability. This is because irrespective of whether the uncertainty regarding paired physical properties is an *intrinsic property* of nature or merely a manifestation of a knowledge deficit that we are faced with due to the unintended but unavoidable effects of having to use physical *probes* to try to discover information about real systems, there is still intrinsic *uncertainty* for *us* in the knowledge that we can have about them.

So the significance of quantum theory with regard to what we can know can be summarized as follows: quantum mechanics is a well-developed and widely tested theory of very small quantities that has resulted in fantastically accurate agreement in predicting otherwise inexplicable experimental results that involve objects and events at the submicroscopic level. One of its key results is that there is a fundamental limit to which physical quantities can be measured beyond which the certainty of paired physical quantities cannot be further defined or better known (e.g., the simultaneous position and momentum of a submicroscopic object). This sets limits on the certainty with which we can ever know the complete set of *initial conditions* for any system, as well as the precise magnitude and direction of the forces acting upon it. And these critical uncertainties impact the precision with which we can ever know the trajectories of objects and events as they move forward in time (or outward in space) and into the future.

Although it is not something encompassed by quantum theory itself, this intrinsic uncertainty in the position and momentum of objects provides an explanation for the natural and intrinsic dynamical uncertainty that was discussed previously (see chapter 19, entitled "Dynamical Certainty vs. Uncertainty: Trajectories," for further discussion). Because of the intrinsic uncertainty associated with all starting positions and energies, as well as well as to the external forces applied to all systems, this provides the necessary theoretical basis for the widespread dynamical uncertainty that is so commonplace in nature. As a result, it provides a basis for the intrinsic irreversibility of most natural processes. The best way to think of this is as follows: if there is uncertainty in the forward trajectory of events, and there is similar uncertainty that would occur for any process operating in the backward direction (i.e., if one would try to reverse the process in a step-by-step fashion), then the *probability* that the forward and backward trajectories would overlap precisely to reestablish the initial conditions (which, due to the Heisenberg uncertainty principle, cannot be precisely defined anyway) would be *extremely low*. The point is that there are many more non-overlapping forward-and-reverse trajectories than the one perfect set that would overlap precisely. This provides another explanation for why it is not possible to reverse real events without adding external energy to a system (i.e., to constrain the reverse trajectory to a particular path rather than to all others that are available) and why this makes changes over time (i.e., *time's arrow*) move consistently forward. By doing so, it explains why the future is always different than the past.

The important guiding principles that can be gleaned from quantum theory as they apply to the idea of future predictability can be summarized as follows:

I. All fundamental quantities ultimately reach a limit below which they can no longer be divided and where they are represented as *quanta*.
II. The submicroscopic scale of the quantum realm operates in ways that are not generally noticeable at the macroscopic level where we have direct access to information.
III. Nothing at submicroscopic scales ever remains static from one instant to the next—everything is always in flux.
IV. Quantum theory (i.e., Heisenberg's uncertainty principle) tells us that our knowledge about (A) all starting positions and (B) the magnitude and direction of external forces acting on all real systems is intrinsically imprecise (uncertain).

V. Since trajectories cannot be predicted to within limits that are more precise than the knowledge about any system's (a) starting conditions and (b) the magnitude and direction of the external forces acting upon them, predictions about the future are unavoidably unpredictable; this is the case in the short run, but these uncertainties are further compounded by the increasing passage of time and by increasing distance, making long-range predictions even less reliable.

Quantum theory, which is the most accurate scientific theory devised to date, adversely affects our ability to predict events in the future as well as those that occur at a distance (i.e., all events that occur in other realms). This occurs because of the uncertainty it introduces into the precision of what we can know by making measurements. In addition, the fundamental limits that it sets in this regard compromise our ability to intervene to influence future events in any particular or predictable way. Because large-scale structures arise from smaller ones that underlie them, this unpredictability applies not only at the inciting submicroscopic level, but also at the larger (i.e., macroscopic) scales to which these smaller quantities and structures ultimately give rise.

---

*e.g., the discovery of radioactivity by Becquerel in 1896 and the splitting effect observed by passing the light emitted by hydrogen through a magnetic field in 1899 (by Zeeman), the discovery of alpha and beta rays as distinct types of emitted radiation by Rutherford, etc.

† Albert Einstein, "Über einen die Erzeugung und Verwandlung des Lichtes betreffenden heuristischen Gesichtspunkt" ("Concerning an Heuristic Point of View Toward the Emission and Transformation of Light"), *Annalen der Physik* (ser. 4), 17, 132–148 (Leipzig: J.A. Barth, 1905) (Translated into English by the *American Journal of Physics*, 33, no. 5, May 1965, Woodbury, NY).

δ Albert Einstein, Boris Podolsky, Nathan Rosen, "Can quantum-mechanical description of physical reality be considered complete?", *Physical Review*, 47, 777-780 (Princeton: Institute for Advanced Study, May 15, 1935).

CHAPTER 22
Entanglement vs. Separability: The Locality Issue

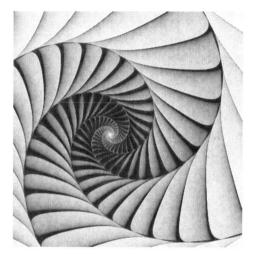

The fundamental entanglement of objects and events makes them inseparable.

Entanglement: Definition (Merriam-Webster Dictionary)

- The condition of being deeply involved
- Something that entangles, confuses, or ensnares
- The action of entangling: the state of being entangled

Separability: Definition (Merriam-Webster Dictionary)

- Capable of being separated or dissociated into parts

Locality: Definition (Merriam-Webster Dictionary)

- The fact or condition of having a location in space or time
- A particular place, situation, or location

When are objects (or events) truly *separate*? Or alternatively, the question can be asked: Where does one object (or event) end and another begin? Although this might seem like a simple question, the answer may not be as easy.

In general, we like to believe in *boundaries* or limits to objects (and events), both in space and in time. For instance, we typically judge that a car is a separate entity from the road that it rolls on, that a tree is separate from the soil that it grows in, that a parent is separate from his or her children, etc. These distinctions might seem obvious and even trivial. But when they are scrutinized, they may become less clear than they first appear.

For example, what if we consider the case of a car more closely? Such a vehicle may have thousands of parts, all of which can be considered separate items, many of which are obtained from different suppliers. These can have many different shapes and functions, and they are often made up of different substances. As an example, in the case of the tires, they often have multiple parts that include inner belts made of metal, an outer layer made of rubber, a valve, etc. So was our characterization of a car being a single item separate from the road that it travels along right or wrong?

Using this type of reasoning, one might choose to invoke a more restrictive definition for allowing objects (or events) to be regarded as single entities. For instance, one might choose to specify that all objects (or events) must be considered separate unless they are contiguous. But then the question arises: Contiguous in what sense and at what scale? For instance, would it be sufficient to say that if two metals comprising a bimetal rod were fused together that they would comprise a single entity (a single bimetal rod), or would they still be two different metals fused together in a rather arbitrary (but purposeful) fashion with many rough points of contact (at a microscopic level)?

To obviate these types of concerns, we might become even more restrictive in our definition and say that for something to be considered a single entity, it needs to be *pure* (i.e., comprised of only a single chemical *substance*). But, what if we were to admit that pure substances are themselves comprised of a large number of component parts (i.e., *atoms*)? And what if these component parts were internally *inhomogeneous* (i.e., *non-contiguous*), because they had additional component parts themselves (i.e., subatomic particles, such as *protons, neutrons, electrons*, etc.), many of which are separated by comparatively vast amounts of intervening space (as is the case for atomic nuclei that are surrounded by electrons)? And what if those subatomic particles were comprised of even smaller elements (such as combinations of different types of *quarks*)? Where would it all end? What would then be considered either *pure* (i.e., homogeneous) enough or *contiguous* enough to be categorized as a *single entity* (or a single *event*), and what would not?

These considerations are not just theoretical. The categorization of objects (and events) as being discrete entities as opposed to (potentially) separable into component parts can also be very challenging at a practical level. In chapter 21 (entitled "Quantum Theory: Uncertainties of the Very Small"), the 1935 EPR publication by Einstein, Podolsky, and Rosen was mentioned. In their article, the authors suggested that by performing different measurements on physically distant particles of their position and momentum—the properties of an *entangled partner* at a distance could be discovered without disturbing it in any way. This assertion puts a new wrinkle into the question of the separability of objects and events: aside from the prior examples of purity and contiguousness, it would appear that *quantum entanglement* must also be considered.

The argument made by Einstein and his colleagues in the EPR thought experiment is that when two particles have properties that are completely predictable based on particular properties that are manifest in the other, if one property were to be measured in one particle (with an arbitrarily high degree of accuracy and precision) and a second property were measured in the other particle (again with arbitrarily high accuracy and precision), then both properties could be known exactly and simultaneously for both particles. If this were possible, then each particle would necessarily possess well-defined (i.e., "exact") values of both position and momentum that could both be measured and known precisely. This type of an approach would yield a level of precision in the two measurements that would violate the Heisenberg uncertainty principle. As such, it constitutes the crux of Einstein's argument that the uncertainty principle inherent to quantum theory arises due to issues that pertain to its incompleteness as a theory, and not to any real physical uncertainty in the natural universe. Thus, his contention was that quantum theory is overlooking and failing to account for critical variables that exist but that are not known.

It is important to understand why these difficulties arose: in quantum mechanics, predictions are formulated in terms of probabilities (as implied by the wave function of Schrödinger's equation). This type of probabilistic thought gives rise to many paradoxes (perhaps the most famous of which is referred to as *Schrödinger's cat*), which fostered the philosophical objection that Einstein had to quantum theory. Einstein summed up his objection as follows:*

> I think that a particle must have a separate reality independent of the measurements. That is: An electron has spin, location and so forth even when it is not being measured. I like to think that the moon is there even if I am not looking at it.

Schrödinger and Einstein exchanged letters about Einstein's EPR article, and Einstein pointed out a host of paradoxes if quantum theory were to be taken at face value. One of these was that the quantum mechanical state of an unstable keg of gunpowder would, after a suitable period of time, necessarily be represented by a superposition of both exploded and unexploded states. This *overlapping state* would then *reduce* to one state or the other when the keg was actually observed (i.e., a measurement was made). The precise method for this *reduction* was not defined, but it appeared to depend on external factors that would instantaneously force the system into one or the other of the two states. This seemed completely absurd to Einstein, who did not think it reasonable that the universe could be a place where *multiple states* could be reality *simultaneously*, with objective reality being wholly dependent (ultimately) on somebody (or something) making an observation.

To further illustrate the apparent incompleteness of quantum mechanics, Schrödinger also proposed his now famous hypothetical cat scenario: a cat is sealed in a box, where its life (or death) depends on the state of a subatomic particle (figure 10). According to Schrödinger, the Copenhagen school interpreted quantum mechanics to imply that the cat is *both alive and dead* (to the universe outside the box) until the box is opened (i.e., until the cat is actually observed by virtue of some measurement of it taking place). How can this be?

Schrödinger wrote:[†]

> One can even set up quite ridiculous cases. A cat is penned up in a steel chamber, along with the following device (which must be secured against direct interference by the cat): In a Geiger counter, there is a tiny bit of radioactive substance, so small that perhaps in the course of the hour, one of the atoms decays, but also, with equal probability, perhaps none; if it happens, the counter tube discharges, and through a relay releases a hammer that shatters a small flask of hydrocyanic acid. If one has left this entire system to itself for an hour, one would say that the cat still lives if meanwhile no atom has decayed. The psi-function of the entire system would express this by having in it the living and dead cat (pardon the expression) mixed or smeared out in equal parts. It is typical of these cases that an indeterminacy originally restricted to the atomic domain becomes transformed into macroscopic indeterminacy, which can then be resolved by direct observation. That prevents us from so naively accepting as valid a "blurred model" for representing reality. In itself, it would not embody anything unclear or contradictory. There is a difference between a shaky or out-of-focus photograph and a snapshot of clouds and fog banks.

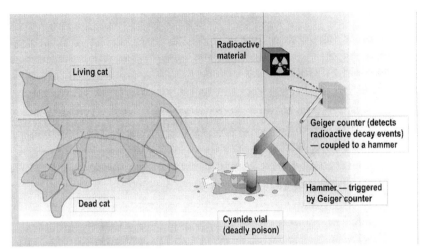

Figure 10: Schrödinger's cat

The figure portrays quantum uncertainty as it relates to the macroscopic condition of the cat in the box being alive or dead. Within the box, there is a source of radioactive material that has a probability of decaying within a certain period of time. But, the actual time that needs to elapse before the decay event occurs is uncertain. When the decay occurs, it is registered by a Geiger counter that triggers the motion of a hammer to break open a vial of cyanide poison, which immediately kills the cat. Because the decay of the radioactive material can only be described in probabilistic terms, there is an associated probability that the cat will be alive (or dead) at any particular time. The Schrödinger wave equation accounts for this probability by superimposing the wavefunctions associated with the alive and dead states of the cat simultaneously. The state only becomes one or the other (i.e., the cat actually being either alive or dead) upon the reduction of the wavefunction, which is triggered by an observation of the cat (e.g., the opening of the box by someone—or something—to look inside and see the cat). Before this occurs, the wavefunction is consistent with the cat being both alive and dead simultaneously. [Adapted from diagram of Schrödinger's cat theory authored by Dhatfield 26 June 2008; Source http://en.wikipedia.org/wiki/File:Schrodingers_cat.svg with permission granted to copy, distribute and/or modify the document under the terms of the GNU Free Documentation License, Version 1.2 or any later version published by the Free Software Foundation].

The paradoxes outlined by Einstein and Schrödinger fall into the classic realm of *reductio ad absurdum*, because they fly in the face of what we think of as objective reality within the macroscopic environment that we all perceive and experience. Einstein dismissed quantum mechanics' description of the universe as unreasonable, instead choosing to champion reality as being both well-defined and definite. Quantum mechanics' intrinsic weakness was viewed as its inability to make predictions definitively in the macroscopic world, which led to the contention by Einstein and others that it was an incomplete theory (and therefore, inconsistent—see chapter 11, entitled "Logic and Inference," for further discussion).

The counterproposal was that there might be some unknown theory (often referred to as a *hidden variables theory*), that could predict the quantities that quantum mechanics was incapable of predicting exactly, while at the same time being in precise agreement with the probabilities predicted by quantum mechanics. If such hidden variables were to exist (encompassing the types of properties that Einstein posited when he lodged his repeated objection to quantum mechanics that "God does not play dice with the universe"γ), then because they are not accounted for by quantum mechanics, it would make quantum theory incomplete.

Following the publication of the EPR article, quantum theory's credibility fell into serious jeopardy. The two possibilities were either that: (a) quantum mechanics suffers from a profound limitation due to its intrinsic incompleteness (in the sense that it fails to account for key elements of physical reality), or (b) *instantaneous signaling* between distant particles was possible, such that they could somehow *know* that the other had been interrogated (thereby making the proposed measurements of the EPR experiment non-independent). If the latter were the case, it would need to occur instantaneously, which would violate the primary sacrosanct principle of relativity theory—that signals carrying information could not travel faster than the speed of light.

To address this issue, Irish physicist John S. Bell published a manuscript in 1964 entitled On the *Einstein Podolsky Rosen Paradox*.§ In it, he derived what is known as Bell's theorem beginning with the same two basic assumptions as EPR, namely that:

1. *Reality exists* (i.e., that microscopic objects have a *definite state* that determines the values of all real properties determining the outcomes of quantum mechanical measurements that is independent of their being observed).
2. *Objects exist locally* (i.e., that reality is not influenced by measurements performed simultaneously at large distances; if observers are

sufficiently far apart, a measurement made by one can have no effect on a measurement made by the other, meaning that they are *separate*).

Bell's theorem depends on the idea that if the degree of correlation between the properties of particles at a distance stems from local random variables, then there is a limit to how much correlation can exist between them unless they somehow continue to interact. Its derivation relies on the following two premises:

a) Each quantum-level object has a *well-defined state* accounting for all its measurable properties, and
b) Distant objects *do not exchange information faster* than the *speed of light*.

Quantum theory regards pairs of particles that have interacted with each other and then separated as *entangled*. But the constraints imposed by local realism—which is governed by the relativistic principle that precludes any type of a signal from transiting the speed of light—should constrain the subsequent degree of correlation between the properties of the two particles once they have separated. This approach is sufficiently broad to encompass all potentially hidden variables (i.e., all variables that are either unknown or inapparent). Furthermore, its great strength is that it is experimentally testable.

Remarkably, modern experimental results have violated the threshold of the inequality arising from Bell's theorem in favor of quantum mechanical theory.[8] Thus, Einstein's position in his EPR paper concerning the concreteness of physical reality could not be maintained.

The implication of this finding is profound: at least one of the two assumptions underlying Bell's theorem is not correct. This means either (or both) of the following:

1. quantum-level objects do not have intrinsically *well-defined states* that account for all of their measurable properties, meaning that reality is somehow *observer dependent* (i.e., the physically measurable properties of objects are not intrinsic to them, but they are somehow dependent on being *observed*), and/or
2. objects (and events) are *not separable* and can *exchange information faster* than the *speed of light* (i.e., all objects—and events—are somehow *connected*).

Another way of characterizing the experimental violation of Bell's inequality is that either quantum theory is correct or the notion of local realism is wrong—or both.

To most of us, this should be a very disturbing conclusion. It means that

A. *objective reality does not exist* independent of its being observed (by something else—as the now standard interpretation of quantum theory posits), and/or
B. *everything is connected to everything else* (somehow—and in a way that is not completely known or understood).

Because of quantum mechanics' consistent accuracy in predicting the results of experiments involving physical interactions of submicroscopic particles, most modern physicists interpret the experimental results that violate Bell's inequality as supporting quantum mechanics. But, the additional possibility is that *everything is influenced by everything else*—regardless of *where* it is (i.e., no matter how far away it is in terms of distance) and *when* it is (no matter how far distant it is in the past—or in the future). This latter result seems at odds with what we experience directly via our senses in the macroscopic world regarding the typical scope of influence of our actions. But it is also not too surprising: from a functional standpoint, it means that everything in the universe would be a part of a *single, inseparable*, and *non-subdividable* system that encompasses all that exists (i.e., all objects and events) in all directions of both space and time.

Thus, the results of tests of Bell's theorem have demonstrated that even though a complete set of particle properties may not be entirely known, they are still correlated with those of other particles due to *quantum entanglement.* Bell himself concluded that "no local deterministic hidden-variable theory can reproduce all the experimental predictions of quantum mechanics."[e]

What Bell's conclusion suggests is that there may be an intrinsic connectedness to all objects (and events). Even when objects and events appear not to be contiguous (in terms of their extents and boundaries), they may nevertheless still be *connected* to everything else that is beyond their immediate limits (i.e., due to quantum entanglement). This suggests that there may be no such entity as a *separate object* (or a *separate event*) at all.

The implications stemming from this conclusion are profound: in a universe bound together by quantum entanglement, *everything* that occurs has an *inescapable effect* on *everything else*, thereby making everything part of a single and inseparable *total system*. If this is the case, then attempting to investigate any particular part of the system in isolation with the hope of drawing conclusions about any *local* reality would be only a local approximation—essentially an artificially truncated, *incomplete*, and (ultimately) *inconsistent* view of reality. And, if this is the case, then any such investigation to try to arrive at generalizable principles that would then increase what we actually know about the universe is bound to failure (see chapter 11, entitled "Logic and Inference," and chapter 15, entitled "Generalizability: Internal vs. External Validity," for further discussions).

Thus, what we can know is fundamentally limited by the fact that it may not be possible to investigate (or even interrogate) subdomains of reality without changing everything else that exists. This would necessarily (a) change the very tools we use to perform our measurements (i.e., those that we use for our interrogations, which undergird the information that we can obtain about objects and events) and (b) mean that the *facts* we discover change immediately (and irrevocably) from what we think we have determined, directly as a result of the interrogations themselves. This type of universal interconnectedness places a limit on what we can know about objects and events of the present—as well as about the past, the future, and ourselves.

---

*Carl Seelig, *Albert Einstein: A Documentary Biography* (London: Staples Press, 1956).

†Erwin Schrödinger, *Die Naturwissenschaften* (*The Natural Sciences*) (Berlin; New York: Springer-Verlag, 1935). [From a translation of the article that appeared in 1935.]

ʸDavid A Shiang, *God Does Not Play Dice: The Fulfillment of Einstein's Quest for Law and Order in Nature* (Lexington, Mass.: Open Sesame Productions, 2007). [Einstein is quoted from a letter he wrote to Max Born in 1944: "You believe in a God who plays dice, and I in complete law and order in a world which objectively exists... Even the great initial success of the quantum theory does not make me believe in the fundamental dice-game."]

§John S Bell, *On the Einstein Podolsky Rosen Paradox, Physics* 1, 3, 195–200 (1964) δe.g., beginning with the results of an initial experiment performed in 1969 to test if Bell's inequality could be violated (i.e., that the degree of correlation between measurements would be different than predicted by its starting premises), as well as several more definitive experiments starting with those of Aspect *et al* in 1981.

εM. Bell, K. Gottfried, M. Veltman, eds., *John S. Bell on the Foundations of Quantum Mechanics* (Singapore; New Jersey: World Scientific, 2001).

CHAPTER 23

Many Worlds: Parallel Universes as an Explanation for Quantum Paradoxes

Parallel universes have no connection, which precludes them from exchanging mass, energy, or information.

Universe: Definition (Merriam-Webster Dictionary)

- The whole body of things and phenomena observed or postulated: cosmos

Parallel: Definition (Merriam-Webster Dictionary)

- Extending in the same direction, everywhere equidistant, and not meeting
- Everywhere equally distant (as in concentric spheres)
- Similar, analogous, or interdependent in tendency or development
- Readily compared: companion
- Having identical syntactical elements in corresponding positions

Paradox: Definition (Merriam-Webster Dictionary)

- An argument that apparently derives self-contradictory conclusions by valid deduction from acceptable premises
- A self-contradictory statement that at first seems true
- A statement that is seemingly contradictory or opposed to common sense and yet is perhaps true
- One (as a person, situation, or action) having seemingly contradictory qualities or phases

The idea of the universe is that it encompasses *all that is*—everything, everywhere (over all spaces and all dimensions), for all time. However, what if other objects, places, times, and events exist that are completely separate from the universe that we are part of, such that nothing can *get there from here* (and vice versa)? If this were the case—with absolutely no connection or capability of communicating with these other places (i.e., the objects and events in other space-times)—then they could be considered both outside of our universe and completely immaterial, precisely because of their total inability to influence anything in our universe. This idea raises the possibility of the existence of *parallel universes*—places that exist entirely apart from each other, with absolutely no way of exchanging any matter, energy, or information between them.

The so-called *many worlds* interpretation of quantum theory hypothesizes that many other universes exist in addition to our own. These different universes are posited to be separate and non-communicating, each with a history that evolves in divergent ways due to the *alternative unfoldings* of possible events. These alternatives result from the decoherence of the superposition of the different solutions to the universal wavefunction (i.e., the Schrödinger equation) at each point in time (see chapter 21, entitled "Quantum Theory: Uncertainties of the Very Small," and chapter 22, entitled "Entanglement vs. Separability: The Locality Issue," for further discussions).

The many worlds theory asserts that the universe we know is an objective and real consequence of the *universal wavefunction* that arises from quantum mechanics. However, it avoids the collapse of the wavefunction into any single reality from the different superimposed states that are possible. Instead, it accepts that *all possible realities* (i.e., all alternative histories, presents, and futures) are *real*, and that each of them is embodied in an actual universe (i.e., a *world*) that exists objectively, but entirely separately. The set of these universes constitutes a fantastically large number of all the possible permutations of the solutions to the Schrödinger wavefunction over time. Thus, each universe embodies an objective reality that is different and *just as real* as every other—they simply exist in parallel and are non-communicating.

The many worlds explanation for the "spontaneous reduction" of the *superposition* of *quantum states* eliminates the difficulty that physics has had in explaining the collapse of the wavefunction into a single reality. It was first proposed by Hugh Everett in 1957 and was originally termed the *relative state formulation*. It was subsequently renamed the "many worlds" theory and popularized in the 1960s by Bryce Seligman DeWitt. It falls into a class of so-called decoherence theories for the interpretation of quantum events, which has given rise to many multiverse hypotheses in physics and philosophy. The theory is now regarded as a mainstream interpretation of quantum mechanics along with other decoherence interpretations and the longstanding Copenhagen interpretation (see chapter 21, entitled "Quantum Theory: Uncertainties of the Very Small," for further discussion).

There is a distinct advantage to the multiverse interpretation of reality: it provides a ready explanation for the outcomes that ultimately result from the superposition of quantum states, making it possible to remove both (1) chance and (2) observer-dependence as explanations for the reduction of the wavefunction into a single outcome (i.e., a *single reality*). In particular, for every quantum event with a non-zero probability of being an alternative outcome, *all* of these outcomes *actually occur*, with each in a *different parallel universe*. However, despite this occurrence of all possible outcomes, we are only aware of the one that occurs in our universe, because it is the one that we can observe. The overriding idea is that there are a myriad of universes besides the one that we are part of and know about—all very real, but all with different states and histories, and completely separate.

Several versions of the many worlds theory have been proposed, but they all maintain that there is no necessity for observation-triggered collapse of the wave function, as the Copenhagen interpretation of quantum theory proposes. The exact form of the modeled quantum dynamics—whether it involves the non-relativistic Schrödinger equation, relativistic quantum field theory, quantum gravity, string theory, or some other yet-to-be-discovered theory—does not alter the validity of the interpretation. This is because the many worlds interpretation represents a meta-theory that is applicable to all linear quantum theories (to date, there is no experimental evidence for any nonlinearity of the wavefunction). The theory's main conclusion is that the universe (or more properly, the multiverse) is composed of a superposition of very many—possibly an infinite number of—increasingly divergent, non-communicating universes or quantum worlds.

Before the many worlds theory, reality had always been viewed as a single history (i.e., a single past), a single present, and a single (but uncertain) future. However, with the many worlds interpretation, reality can be thought of as a branching tree, where every possible quantum outcome has actually been realized (in the past), is realized (in the present), and will be realized (in the future). Thus, the theory has the potential to reconcile the observation of non-deterministic events, such as the probabilistically-based occurrence of spontaneous radioactive decay, with the fully deterministic equations of quantum physics—and all without the necessity of employing any notion of chance (which would have made Albert Einstein happy!). Instead, the collapse of the universal wavefunction is explained by quantum decoherence, which results in *every possible outcome* at every juncture of reality actually *existing* in its own universe (i.e., world), thereby resolving the potential paradoxes that would otherwise arise from quantum theory.

A potential challenge arising from the idea of parallel universes pertains to the conservation of mass-energy. Because the events that occur in each of the alternative universes unfold differently, the energetic potential associated with each of the resulting states must also vary, making them energetically non-equivalent (see chapter 20, entitled "Thermodynamics: Laws Prohibiting the Spontaneous Reversibility of Physical Events," for further discussion). However, this can be reconciled by positing either that (a) conservation of mass-energy must be maintained within each of the individual parallel universes (which would be consistent with what we observe in our own universe) or, alternatively, that (b) the total mass-energy for the entire set of universes (i.e., the multiverse) must be preserved overall.

The many worlds hypothesis proposes that there are a very large number of universes that exist in parallel and that everything that could possibly have happened in our past but did not (in our universe), has occurred in the past of some other parallel universe (or universes). Likewise, everything that could possibly happen in our present but has not, is occurring in another parallel universe (or universes). Finally, everything that could possibly happen in our universe in the future but will not, will nevertheless occur in some other parallel universe. This makes all possible pasts, presents, and futures an actual reality—somewhere, but not anywhere that we can ever know about.

CHAPTER 24
Chaos Theory: Implications for Macroscopic Predictability

Chaotic systems are imprecisely predictable without making explicit calculations of their future states.

Chaos: Definition (Merriam-Webster Dictionary)

- The inherent unpredictability in the behavior of a complex natural system (as the atmosphere, boiling water, or the beating heart)
- A confused mass or mixture

Macroscopic: Definition (Merriam-Webster Dictionary)

- Observable by the naked eye
- Involving large units or elements

Predict: Definition (Merriam-Webster Dictionary)

- To declare or indicate in advance; *especially*: foretell on the basis of observation, experience, or scientific reason

Chaos theory is a relatively new discovery of the twentieth century. It addresses the idea that *very small changes* to the *inputs* of a system can *drastically change* its *outputs* (i.e., its *behavior*). The phenomenon was first discovered in 1961 the meteorologist Edward Lorenz, but its implications are wide-ranging, such that it pertains to the majority of real systems.

Lorenz first encountered chaotic behavior accidentally while investigating weather prediction using a digital computer. He was trying to make a duplicate printout of an interesting sequence he found while calculating the evolution of weather patterns using a set of equations. He started at the point in the sequence that interested him the most and entered the numbers specifying the conditions at that particular time from his hard copy of the data. But to his surprise, the weather pattern that emerged in his new printout was very different from the original. Instead of evolving in an identical way, it started in the same place but then diverged, becoming wildly different as time progressed.

This result seemed impossible. Computers are designed to execute algorithms that are both deterministic and calculable (see chapter 16, entitled "Computability: Algorithmically Definable Calculations," for further discussion). No matter how many times a computer runs its calculations with the same inputs for the same equations it was programmed to execute, it should generate the same results. To have different outputs after entering the same starting parameters didn't make any sense. But Lorenz found there was a reason for it: he discovered that the computer's internal registers had originally stored the numbers of his calculations to a precision of six decimal places. But when he reentered the numbers manually to begin his calculations for the second time, he entered them to only three decimal places. For instance, in the original sequence the number for one of the initial conditions was .506127. But, the precision that he specified in the printout of his original hard copy of the results was only to three significant figures. So, when he reentered the number, he used only the first three digits of .506. The difference in these starting numbers between the first and second runs of the same program was 0.0251 percent (less than 3 parts in 10,000). This extremely small difference was enough to generate a widely divergent weather pattern as time marched forward in his calculations.

What Lorenz discovered is now regarded as a hallmark of *unstable dynamical systems* (see chapter 18, entitled "Stability vs. Instability: System Inertia and Resiliency," and chapter 19, entitled "Dynamic Certainty vs. Uncertainty: Trajectories," for further discussion). In contrast to *stable dynamical systems* where *slight changes* in the *initial conditions* produce correspondingly *small downstream effects* over time, *unstable dynamical systems* are those where *small perturbations* in the *initial conditions* become *amplified* over time. *Chaotic dynamics* represents an *extreme example* of this type of system *instability*, because the *trajectories* identified by distinct initial conditions—no matter how close they are to each other—*diverge* over time (see chapter 19, entitled "Dynamic Certainty vs. Uncertainty: Trajectories," for further discussion).

This type of *extreme sensitivity* to *initial conditions* can result in changes akin to the fabled *butterfly effect* that was discovered by Lorenz: because of the extreme sensitivity of his weather model to exquisitely small changes in starting conditions, it implied that a single butterfly flying over China could cause a major downstream effect that would influence the weather patterns of the entire Northern Hemisphere for decades—and likely for all time. Not all butterflies will have such an effect, and it cannot be known in advance which ones will and which will not (see chapter 16, entitled "Computability: Algorithmically Definable Calculations," for further discussion). But given the proper conditions, there is a possibility that this will occur. And we now know that these types of effects happen in real systems all the time.

Something very interesting about *dynamical chaos* is that it does *not* result from either *random inputs* or *random variations* that are either unpredictable or unknown. In fact, everything about these dynamical systems can be accounted for (at least to within the physically allowable limits of accuracy and precision—see chapter 9, entitled "Measurement: How Circumstance and Change are Assessed," and chapter 21, entitled "Quantum Theory: Uncertainties of the Very Small," for further discussion), and the systems are completely deterministic. Rather, dynamical chaos results from the *exquisite sensitivity* of these *systems* to *small changes* in initial conditions (or inputs). Whereas these types of very small changes might be expected (by most of us) to produce commensurately small changes in downstream effects (via a causal chain of events), the effect in chaotic systems is very often larger and not predictable (at least short of calculating the result explicitly).

One way of explaining this type of an outcome is this: some *threshold* is exceeded in the specification of the initial conditions, such that the newly entered domain is different than the one that preceded it on the other side of the *small difference*. For example, on one side of the threshold, everything is *stable* and operates *smoothly* and *predictably*, in the sense that *small changes* in system inputs result in *small differences* in *outputs*. But on the other side of the threshold, a *chaotic domain* is entered where the *effect sizes* associated with the small changes are *unsmooth* and *greater*, making the *outputs* and behaviors *fluctuate unpredictably* from one time point to another—but still always in a deterministic way. Thus, the chaos arising in these types of dynamical systems is referred to as *deterministic chaos*, which distinguishes it from the common definition that is often implied by the term in colloquial usage (where it connotes a state of randomness or utter confusion).

Importantly, there is nothing confused about chaotic dynamical systems. It is simply that long-term predictions are impossible (except in the most general terms), with only broad targets available for their behaviors that are referred to as *attractors*. This is despite the fact that these systems are completely deterministic, as their future behavior is fully determined by their starting conditions, without the injection of any random elements. In other words, even though they are deterministic, this does not make them predictable in any precise sense (at least not short of completing an actual calculation to predict what they will evolve into at a particular time of interest).

Weather prediction provides a good example of a *complex system* (i.e., one with multiple nonlinear interactions among numerous system components), which predisposes it to behave chaotically. With the advent of high-speed digital computing, the hope was that changes in the weather would become a tractable issue and that long-term weather prediction would become possible. Until the 1960s, it was assumed that accurate weather prediction was simply an exercise in data acquisition and raw number-crunching: if enough information could be obtained at any one time about the temperature, pressure, humidity, wind speed, etc. of the earth's atmosphere with sufficient granularity (i.e., over small enough volumes), then a computer program could crank through the appropriate algorithms to calculate the weather at each location above the earth's surface as a function of time—not just for days, but for weeks, months, and years.

Unfortunately—as evidenced by the frequently erroneous weather predictions of modern-day meteorologists—this degree of predictive accuracy has never been realized. This is despite the availability of voluminous data concerning the earth's weather conditions at any given moment, excellent weather modeling algorithms, and high-speed digital computers of ever greater power.

This predictive failure occurs for two reasons: (1) the granularity of weather parameter information is still too coarse to allow for long-range modeling to be accurate, and (2) the elements that constitute the atmosphere's weather comprise a *complex system* that incorporates *chaotic domains*. The first of these involves the known limitations associated with the accuracy and precision of measurement (see chapter 9, entitled "Measurement: How Circumstance and Change are Assessed," and chapter 21, entitled "Quantum Theory: Uncertainties of the Very Small," for further discussion), and the second reflects the fact that changes in weather patterns are *not* always smooth; they can (and often do) change abruptly, such that turbulent entities (like hurricanes and tornados) have the potential to result in erratic disruptions that are only predictable in terms of *probabilities*, not certainties.

Despite this, we all routinely rely on the macroscopic trends we have previously observed in weather patterns: that the temperatures are typically colder in the winter than during the summer, that if it snows it will more likely be during the winter than in the spring, etc. These are examples of seasonally-determined historical benchmarks that we define empirically as *attractors* regarding the weather, although they are always imprecise (i.e., it is still possible to have warm days in the winter and cold ones in the summer). Ultimately, this means that the different features about the weather are not cast in certainties, but instead in terms of *relative likelihoods*.

In chaos theory, these types of overarching generalities—which can also be thought of as *expectations*—are known as *attractors*. In the previous example, the attractors that were mentioned for temperature, precipitation, etc. were based on historical experience, but the size, shape, and distribution of such attractors can also be calculated prospectively from defining algorithms. Thus, attractors can be thought of as *targets* about which future conditions (or outcomes) will most likely be *around*; however, exactly where the actual system of interest will wind up at any given moment is not any more predictable until a calculation is completed or a direct observation is made.

This type of description seems inconsistent with the many known successes of physical science. For many centuries, scientific investigations have yielded well-defined and predictable results, with these arising from systematic investigations and the application of well-honed scientific theories. So where does chaos enter the picture? The answer is: *everywhere*. The reason for the apparent inconsistency is that for centuries, rightly or wrongly, empirical scientists, logicians, theoreticians, mathematicians, etc. selectively chose—quite deliberately—to investigate stable systems that were tractable and that could be modeled in precise and predictable terms. This is because to be able to explain them, they must be capable of yielding both predictable and reproducible results. Thus, there was a selective pressure on investigators to limit their realms of investigation to those that were tractable from the standpoint of predictability (given the tools available at the time). But these selections were systematically artificial and unrepresentative of the full set of all the natural systems that exist; in fact, they encompassed only a small—and poorly generalizable—minority of them.

In fact, influences on scientific experiments that made them behave unpredictably were considered nuisances that were often characterized as background *noise, fluctuations,* or *random interferences*. The response was to systematically *control* and *eliminate* these "interferences" and to constrain local experimental conditions so they would not occur. Experiments were often designed to hold a myriad of conditions constant while investigating the effects of a single (or single group) of well-defined and reproducible interventions. Almost always, this was with the hope of subsequently being able to generalize the results to a wider set of interventions, conditions, and domains. In analytical realms, analogous instabilities that crept into models were also systematically squelched and eliminated in favor of ones that were more stable and predictable.

In general, this approach of seeking stable investigational models has allowed the energies of many excellent researchers to be focused on realms that could be successfully modeled and understood—so that the results could be rationalized, conceptualized, and locally generalized to wider spheres than originally tested, with many useful results. But, in the case of complex systems that have the propensity to migrate into chaotic domains without warning, this approach has been perennially unsuccessful. In fact, it has been so unsuccessful that such domains have been essentially ignored until recent times.

The triumph of modern chaos theory is that it has made room for understanding complex systems that are inherently unstable, which constitute the majority of natural systems in the universe. The more simple systems explained by classical mechanics, for example, are both deterministic and predictable. This is why this approach has been so successful, but also why it is so limited: the predictions are reliable, but typically only over very restricted (and artificial) realms, with their applicability resting almost entirely within the limited domains over which they have been tested. With respect to other domains that fall beyond where (and when) the original investigations were conducted, they are typically applicable only in a much more limited and qualified way—if at all (see chapter 15, entitled "Generalizability: Internal vs. External Validity," for further discussion).

If we wish to predict the behavior of chaotic systems, some guidelines can be applied to estimate how they will evolve into the future. But without actually cranking through the calculations to establish exactly where such systems will be at any particular time, these only represent *weighted probabilities* of where they are most likely to be. These distributions constitute a macroscopic analogue of what quantum mechanical probability densities represent on submicroscopic scales. In direct analogy to what occurs on quantum scales (due to fundamental quantum uncertainties), the degree to which we can glean information and project it either forward or backward in the macroscopic world is limited by the occurrence of chaotic domains (where the divergences of closely positioned single trajectories occur), which makes the smoothness assumption about reality break down (see chapter 17, entitled "Continuity (Smoothness) vs. Discontinuity (Roughness)," for further discussion). What's more, these chaotic domains occur commonly, making inputs and outputs lose their one-to-one correspondence with regard to their magnitudes of change. The result is that small changes in starting conditions can generate markedly disproportionate downstream effects within such systems.

Thus, we can conclude that *chaotic domains* are *widespread* in our universe, significantly affecting the behavior of most real (i.e., *complex*) systems. This poses a fundamental limit to what we can predict about the trajectories of objects and events at the macroscopic level, which reduces our knowledge about their behavior to only generalities and trends. This is instead of anything approaching the tractable level of certainty that most of us would hope to have and that we routinely seek in our lives.

CHAPTER 25

Absolutes vs. Relatives: Relativity Theory

Relativity posits that the speed of light is absolute and that space-time is warped.

Absolute: Definition (Merriam-Webster Dictionary)

- Being self-sufficient and free of external references or relationships
- Fundamental, ultimate
- Having no restriction, exception, or qualification
- Perfectly embodying the nature of a thing
- Independent of arbitrary standards of measurement
- Relating to or derived in the simplest manner from the fundamental units of length, mass, and time
- Free from imperfection: perfect

Relativity: Definition (Merriam-Webster Dictionary)

- The state of being dependent for existence on or determined in nature, value, or quality by relation to something else
- The quality or state of being relative

- A theory which is based on the two postulates (1) that the speed of light in a vacuum is constant and independent of the source or observer and (2) that the mathematical forms of the laws of physics are invariant in all inertial systems and which leads to the assertion of the equivalence of mass and energy and of change in mass, dimension, and time with increased velocity—called also *special relativity, special theory of relativity*
- An extension of the theory to include gravitation and related acceleration phenomena—called also *general relativity, general theory of relativity*
- Something that is relative: relativism

Relativity theory constitutes one of the major scientific breakthroughs of the twentieth century. Its emergence was foreshadowed by the discovery of numerous theoretical and experimental inconsistencies in physics during the nineteenth century, but it took explicit form with Albert Einstein's theory of *special relativity* in 1905 (being advanced in a scientific paper with the unlikely and seemingly narrow title of "On the Electrodynamics of Moving Bodies"*). This was expanded and enhanced by Einstein into a universal theory with the more all-encompassing formulation of *general relativity* in 1915.

Although Einstein is credited with discovering the idea of relativity, the underpinnings of special relativity were established by many other scientists and theoreticians who contributed to the foundations of the theory during the nineteenth century. Among the most prominent of these figures were the great French mathematician Jules Henri Poincaré and the visionary Dutch Nobel prize-winning physicist Hendrik Lorentz.

Why did this idea of relativity represent a breakthrough? Because, it provided a universal framework for consistency by positing that there is only one inviolable metric against which all events can be compared: the *speed of light*. This universal metric was theorized to be the same for all observers, regardless of their inertial frame of reference (i.e., irrespective of their own velocity or acceleration).

At first, this seemed a very strange idea that was at odds with many assumptions that had previously been thought to be self-evident based on common-sense experience. Until then, the velocities and accelerations of objects within any given frame of reference were considered to be additive. This was the standard view of Newtonian mechanics. For instance, if a train was moving at a speed of 30 miles per hour relative to the surrounding countryside and if a passenger walked forward through the train at a speed of 2 miles per hour (i.e., in a collinear fashion with the motion of the train), then the speed of the passenger relative to the countryside would be 30 + 2 = 32 miles per hour. In this example, the countryside would be considered as the *fixed frame of reference* against which both the train and the passenger were moving.

However, this perspective concerning the motions of the train and passenger relative to the countryside ignores something fairly obvious: the countryside itself is anything but fixed! That is because it is connected to the Earth, the surface of which is spinning (about its own axis) at an average of ~1,040 miles per hour (at the equator). In addition, the Earth moves about the sun (at a radius of ~93 million miles): given that the Earth rotates around the sun once per year, its average orbital speed is ~66,700 miles per hour. And then there is the matter of the velocity of the sun (and its surrounding solar system—of which the Earth is part) as it rotates around the center of the galaxy (the Milky Way) every 230 million years (or so) at a radius of ~25,000 light-years; this results in an orbital speed of ~490,000 miles per hour. And last but not least, there is the velocity at which the Milky Way galaxy itself moves through the known universe, which is at somewhere between 1.3 and 2.2 million miles per hour (depending on the frame of reference that is chosen!). So, it should be evident that the countryside over which a train passes is anything but fixed. By adding and subtracting these relative motions, the Earth is moving relative to the center of gravity of the universe at something between ~0.8 and 2.7 million miles per hour. And this is the case for everything on Earth, including all of us—even if we happen to be just sitting in a chair. The question is: What effect (if any) does all this have on the notion of adding velocities together locally?

This may seem like an esoteric question given the differences in the scales involved (i.e., lengths of inches to miles [locally] versus thousands of light-years [on a galactic scale] and times that are measured in seconds [locally] versus hundreds of millions of years [again on a galactic scale]). But, it is not. There are many potential contradictions in our local environment that cannot be accounted for or reconciled unless the issues concerning the relative motions of objects are properly addressed. The consequences of not doing so simply become bigger and more dramatic as the time-distance scales and the relative velocities and accelerations between objects and events increase.

One of the most important consequences of the choice of the speed of light as the universal, invariable metric for all observers in relativity theory—regardless of their frame of reference—is that other measures that were previously presumed to be constant must become unfixed and malleable (i.e., lengths, times, etc.), so as to provide a single and consistent view of the same events for everyone from all points of view. Otherwise, there would be observers in some reference frames where events would appear to be different and inconsistent compared to the viewpoints of others. A glaring example would be that, unless there were a proper reconciliation of the varying perspectives from different inertial frames, some causally-related events could be observed to occur in reverse order (i.e., meaning that consequences could precede causes, which would violate our fundamental notion of temporal causality—the idea that event A must precede a subsequent event B if A is presumed to be the cause of B, etc. [see chapter 4, entitled "Causality: Linking Events Separated by Time and Space," for further discussion]). Quite counterintuitively, the other measures that must be made malleable are the notions of time on the one hand, which can be either dilated or contracted, and length on the other, which can be either stretched or foreshortened.

Thus, the key change in the framework that underlies the theory of relativity is that space and time—which were both thought previously to provide a firm and immobile stage for the occurrence of events—are both really malleable, interrelated quantities that depend for their size and pace on the perspective of observers. The theory maintains that neither space nor time is any longer sacrosanct and that they are—in some very predictable and calculable ways—interconvertible. This emerges as a direct consequence of the speed of light being a constant for all observers.

Many excellent and comprehensive treatises have been written about the marvelous and bizarre implications of relativity theory. Numerous experimental measurements of space and time have tested the predictive accuracy of the theory to date; all have confirmed it to an astounding degree of accuracy and no significant violations have been uncovered. But the purpose of discussing relativity theory in this book is to point out two of its profound implications that impact our ability to make predictions:

1. The scope of information that any observer can ever have access to from his or her vantage point is *truncated*, such that there are large regions of information in the universe that cannot be accessed; and

2. Very dense bodies generate extremely strong gravitational fields that create *event horizons* beyond which information exists, but where it is shielded and inaccessible to any observer residing in the ordinary universe outside.

These two consequences of relativity theory have significant implications regarding the scope of information about the universe that we can access and, hence, what we can know about it.

The first of the two implications can be explained using the idea of *light cones* (figure 11) and the second by the idea of ultra-dense *singularities* (i.e., so-called *black holes*, which *bend light waves* so strongly with their immense *gravitational fields* that *electromagnetic radiation cannot escape* beyond a certain radius from their center) (figure 12). These two consequences of general relativity impinge on our ability to make predictions about the future, as they bear upon the scope of the information we can have access to about the universe—i.e., by demonstrating that there is information we have no hope of gaining access to at all.

With regard to the first issue of the *truncated vantage points* that exist for all observers, two very different domains are conveniently summarized in (Minkowski) *light cone* diagrams (figure 11). The idea is simple: since the speed of light is both finite and absolute, if we exist at a certain point in space-time, then there is a limited spatial field of information from the past that can "get to where we are" via the fastest route possible—the speed of light; anything farther away cannot catch up to get to where we are within the time allotted. For the same reason, there is a limited *sphere of influence* that our current actions can have on objects and events that occur in different spatial domains going forward into the future—which is again limited to distances (domains) that can be reached by the speed of light within the allotted time.

This idea requires additional explanation. In the first case, if something in the past occurred at a distance that is farther away from us than light can travel over the time that has elapsed since the event, then the information has no way to reach us. And in the second case, if there is a spatial region that is far enough from us that it cannot be reached by a light-speed signal emitted locally, it has no way to ever get there and to have any influence upon any local events that occur. Thus, the speed of light serves as a barrier to communication between different areas of the universe that are simply too far-flung in terms of their spatial distance from each other (at least within the confines of the four-dimensional space-time that we know and routinely operate within).

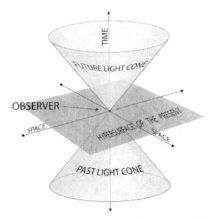

Figure 11: Light cone (depiction in two spatial dimensions plus a time dimension)

A light cone depicts the path that a flash of light, emanating in all directions from a single event (a single point in space at a single moment in time), would take through space-time. If we imagine that the light is confined to a two-dimensional plane, it spreads out in a circle after the flash occurs. We can then graph the growing circle of light along the vertical axis that represents time, resulting in a cone. The cone that points upward in the diagram into the future is known as the future light cone. The cone pointing downward into the past is the past light cone. The latter behaves like the future light cone but in reverse: the circle of light away from the flash contracts at the speed of light until it converges to a point at the exact position and time of the event. (Note: in three spatial dimensions, the light would form an expanding or contracting sphere in three-dimensional space rather than a circle in two-dimensional space, making the actual light cone a four-dimensional version of a cone whose cross-sections form three dimensions, but this is too hard to visualize and even harder to draw!) Because signals cannot travel faster than light, the light cone plays an essential role in defining the limits of causality: for a given event, the set of events that lie on or inside the past light cone would also be the set of all events that could emit a signal that would have time to reach the current event and influence it in some way. For example, any point on or inside the cone could send a signal moving at the speed of light that would have time to influence the event, while points outside of the cone could not send a signal to reach it and would not be able to exert any causal influence. Likewise, the set of events that lie on or inside the future light cone of the event would also be the set of events that could receive a signal sent out from the position and time of the event, so the future light cone contains all the events that could potentially be causally influenced by the event (i.e., a flash of light). Events that lie neither in the past nor the future light cone of the event (i.e., in hyperspace) can neither influence nor be influenced by the event. [Note: permission is granted to copy, distribute and/or modify this figure under the terms of the GNU Free Documentation License, Version 1.2 or any later version published by the Free Software Foundation].

The separation of information into mutually inaccessible realms would appear to be in conflict with the idea of universal connectivity that arises from the experimentally verified violation of Bell's inequality (see chapter 22, entitled "Entanglement vs. Separability: The Locality Issue," for further discussion). However, this contradiction can be resolved—at least potentially—by positing that even if silos of non-communicating information exist in our four-dimensional space-time, that these nonetheless have access to each other (i.e., are in communication) via paths in higher dimensional spaces to which we as humans have no direct access. In support of this hypothesis, recent attempts to unify the four fundamental forces of nature (i.e., the strong force, weak force, electromagnetism, and gravity) via a single grand unified theory have concluded that additional dimensions are required to do so beyond those that we recognize in our ordinary experience (currently believed to be a total of at least eleven). These additional dimensions may create "shortcuts" between times and distances as they appear in our four-dimensional space-time, thereby creating adjacencies between objects and events that would otherwise be far-flung; this would allow for their direct communication "behind the scenes" of the ordinary space-time that we are aware of. If this is the case, it provides a means to reconcile the apparent conflict between universal connectivity on the one hand and information silos (in our four-dimensional space-time) on the other.

A second idea that emerges from relativity theory is that of so-called *singularities* (i.e., *black holes*). These are regions of the universe where matter is so dense that the resulting *gravitational field* created by them is *so strong* that it *precludes* the *escape* of anything *beyond* their *event horizons*—even the emission of light (i.e., the *escape velocity* to get beyond their gravitational field is larger than that of light, which is ~186,000 miles per second). This serves as an effective barrier to the outward egress of any useful information about what exists behind the event horizons, meaning that whatever information there is cannot ever be known to anything or anyone on the other side (i.e., anything that exists in our ordinary universe's four-dimensional space-time). In effect, black holes act as one-way trap doors for energy, mass, and information from our universe; these can be pulled into them from the ordinary space-time that surrounds them (thereby being lost to the rest of the universe), and once they are inside, nothing about what happens to them subsequently can be known to the rest of the surrounding universe in which they are imbedded. Thus, black holes serve as another limitation to the scope of information that is available to observers residing in our universe (figure 12).

Static Black Hole

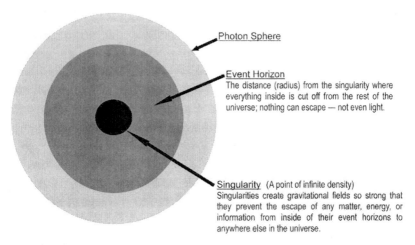

Figure 12: Static black hole (two-dimensional depiction)

Black holes are regions of space-time that prevent anything, including light, from escaping past their event horizons. General relativity theory predicts that a sufficiently dense (i.e., compact) mass will deform space-time to form a black hole. Around a black hole is a mathematically defined surface called an event horizon that marks the point of no return to the rest of the universe for anything within the black hole. The hole is called black because it absorbs all the light that hits its horizon and reflects nothing, as would a perfect thermodynamic black body. Quantum field theory predicts that the event horizons of black holes emit radiation in curved space-time like a black body with finite temperature. Another surface beyond the event horizon where gravity is strong enough to force photons to travel in orbits around the black hole is called the photon sphere. Although black holes are invisible, their presence can be inferred by the effects of their immense gravitational fields on surrounding matter. Many black holes have been identified by astronomical observations—as of mid-2013, there were at least twenty-six black hole candidates identified in the nearby Andromeda galaxy alone.

Thus, with the advent of relativity theory and the wide body of scientific evidence supporting its predictions, universal perspectives that were previously based on absolute measures have now taken a back seat to the idea of relativism. This is all except for the single absolute metric of the speed of light (in a vacuum), which is posited to be the only invariant for observers in all frames of reference. As such, the speed of light represents the equivalent of proverbial glue that cements together the way that objects and events appear throughout the universe, such that they all maintain their consistency from every point of view.

Although it may seem that some of the quantities that were previously presumed to be fixed within the framework of Newtonian mechanics have been somehow corrupted by the new structure of relativity theory (such as the pace of time flow and the physical lengths of objects), this prior presumption must be regarded as merely a historically quaint local illusion of convenience. In the grand scheme, these always represented mere approximations that were applicable over limited domains at a local level—and they were very good for most common purposes. The problem is that these local assumptions do not apply over very large (or very small) dimensions, when very large forces are involved, or very high energies, or over very long time frames. Although these general approximations may be good ones in the local realms where we usually operate, we have somehow become complacent enough to presume (albeit wrongly!) that these would apply over other non-local domains. Fortunately or not, this is not the case. Nevertheless, it should be noted that there is no intrinsic inconsistency between modern relativity theory and classical mechanics; Newtonian mechanics is merely an adequate local approximation that becomes practically applicable when relativistic effects become very small. Thus, classical mechanical theory is subsumed by the greater theory that arises from relativity theory, not negated by it.

At its core, the difference in perspective between viewing objects and events in absolute versus relative terms abuts directly with another issue that has already been addressed in an earlier chapter (see chapter 22, entitled "Entanglement vs. Separability: The Locality Issue," for further discussion): Do the objects and events that we regard as *discrete entities* really have *separate* existences in and of themselves, or are they definable only in relationship to, and within the context of, other objects and events? The answer from the standpoint of relativity theory is, once again, that the notion of absolutes is only a quaint approximation at a local level but that the correct view must be one of relativistic perspectives and universal interactions to ensure consistency overall. This means that nothing can be considered in isolation, which serves to both complicate (at a functional level) and simplify (at a conceptual level) the way in which we must view the universe. The implication is that everything, everywhere in the universe, must be considered in order to properly appreciate, know, and understand any particular object or event. Anything short of this type of a comprehensive view is (by definition) truncated and incomplete, with the resultant generation of inconsistencies and paradoxes that are not resolvable (see chapter 11, entitled "Logic and Inference," for further discussion).

Thus, the conclusion we must draw from relativity theory is that any local view of reality is myopic and prone to error because (1) no object or event is ever truly definable in a local context (i.e., without connection to the greater framework of the universe) and (2) everything else that exists and occurs in the universe has an impact on what is local (i.e., what occurs locally does not occur in isolation and is materially affected by everything else that exists elsewhere). (Note: Gravity, as well as other forces, play key roles in exerting these types of long-range influences). Furthermore, additional dimensions may exist beyond our ordinary four-dimensional space-time that permit access to the information from hyperspace and from beyond the event horizons of singularities.

This means that what we observe locally is the end result of all the influences in the universe as they act locally but that the mechanisms by which these local effects occur are so widespread and diffuse that we cannot possibly know about and account for all of them. What's more, the information about relevant contributions from far-flung distances (i.e., hyperspaces that are beyond the light cone that would permit the possibility of communication) and other shielded portions of the universe (i.e., what exists beyond the event horizons of black holes) is inaccessible to *us* even in principle (at least as long as we are bound by the limitations of our ordinary four-dimensional space-time), making the specter of complete knowledge of all the universal contributions to reality a specious hope that we can never realize.

Thus, in the end we are guided by only what we can observe and experience locally, which encourages us to infer that the local associations we identify between objects and events are causally related, when in fact they may not be (see chapter 10, entitled "Associations vs. Causality," for further discussion). This is simply because we do not have the ability to access all the information regarding the panoply of factors that bear upon our particular local situations. Without it, there is no hope of attaining a *complete* view of the universe, and, without that, there cannot be *consistency* (see chapter 11, entitled "Logic and Inference," for further discussion). But, completeness and consistency must both be the hallmarks of the universe as a whole because, by definition, anything short of this cannot be "all that is" (meaning that a portion of the universe's information would necessarily be omitted).

Because of the implications of relativity theory, we are once again hamstrung by the inability to access all of the information contained in the universe as well as by the underlying connectivity of the universe in its entirety. These factors make local perspectives only approximations that cannot provide any degree of certainty regarding the predictability of future events. For this, we would need to know about everything that exists everywhere in the universe, which relativity theory proclaims that we cannot. Unfortunately, without this complete set of information, we remain stymied in our attempt to attain the level of clarity that we would need to predict the future with certainty in any absolute sense.

---

* Albert Einstein, "Zur Elektrodynamik bewegter Körper" ("On the Electrodynamics of Moving Bodies"), *Annalen der Physik* (ser. 4), 17, 891–921 (Leipzig: J.A. Barth, 1905).

CHAPTER 26
Energy

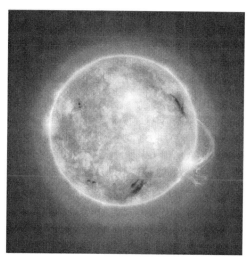

The sun provides nearly all of the energy that is required to sustain us locally.

Energy: Definition (Merriam-Webster Dictionary)

- A fundamental entity of nature that is transferred between parts of a system in the production of physical change within the system and usually regarded as the capacity for doing work

What is *energy* and how does it relate to the issue of what we can know? The energy available in any system represents a measure of its ability to do *work* (i.e., to move something). It is relevant to what we can know because energy and information are inextricably linked (see chapter 28, entitled "Energy and Information: Maxwell's Hypothetical Demon," for further discussion). This chapter examines the nature of energy and the constraints that it imposes on what types of occurrences are possible in the universe.

Energy must be defined with reference to a *system*. The idea of a system is simple: it is any entity that can have a boundary drawn around it to separate it from its surrounding environment (at least imaginarily). For instance, a system can be a rock, a cell, a mouse, a lake, a house, the Empire State Building, the ocean, the earth, the solar system, or even our galaxy—anything that we care to define as included within a circumscribable volume of interest. As such, systems can contain many different components.

When a system is defined in this way—no matter how simple or complex it is—it also contains something that is referred to as *internal energy*. In the low-energy extreme—one that represents a system that is completely homogeneous at a temperature of absolute zero (i.e., 0º Kelvin, which is a temperature that has only been approached—no laboratory has yet been able to make anything that cold)—the internal energy of the system (it's so-called quantum mechanical *zero-point energy*) is at its lowest level, and no external work can be done by it on anything in its surrounding environment (see chapter 20, entitled "Thermodynamics: Laws Prohibiting the Spontaneous Reversibility of Physical Events," for further discussion). For all other systems at non-zero temperature, there is a quantitatively definable amount of energy contained within the system that is in excess of its minimum zero-point energy. Although this energy may be dauntingly difficult to calculate from first principles, it is measureable (at least in principle) with the proper equipment. However, this latter possibility is typically not feasible for very large systems (e.g., those approaching the size of a mountain). And, as always, there arises an issue regarding the limits of accuracy and precision for such measurements (see chapter 9, entitled "Measurement: How Circumstance and Change are Assessed," for further discussion). But for our current purposes, these last two issues can be considered as mere inconveniences.

Some fraction of the internal energy of systems that exist at temperatures above absolute zero is integrally *tied up* as an essential part of the system itself. This is related to the non-equilibrium nature of the system's components, the relationship of these component parts to one another, and the associated non-zero temperature of the system—the latter being a reflection of the internal motion of its constituents. This inaccessible portion of the system's energy is not retrievable under ordinary circumstances (i.e., in the absence of the degradation of the system to a state of complete randomness). But another fraction of this energy is referred to as *free energy* (according to a variety of definitions), and this can be retrieved (or extracted) from the system to do *useful work* on the outside environment.

We all have our own notions about what *work* is, but it has a formal definition. In classic Newtonian physics, work is defined as a force exerted over a particular distance. Fortunately, both force and distance also have very specific definitions: force is the change in momentum (i.e., [mass] x [velocity]) of an object over time. These quantities and the distance over which the force acts can be measured rather precisely (ignoring the inherent limitations arising from quantum uncertainty). The amount of energy expended by a system is exactly equal to the amount of work done by the system on its external environment (this being ideally true, barring dissipative losses). Thus, energy is a defined quantity for any physical system.

There is another feature about energy that is held to be inviolable: it can be *interconverted* from one form to another or *transferred* from one place to another, but (on average) it can *never* be either *created* (from nothingness) or *destroyed* (erased without a trace). This fundamental principle is referred to as the *conservation of energy*, and it constitutes one of the most basic pillars of physics, applying equally well to classical Newtonian mechanics and to relativistic formulations. As such, it is a fundamental concept with a gravitas equal to that of causality; virtually every known relationship in our physical universe relies on it.

The idea of *conservation of energy* amounts to something very profound: since all objects depend on the presence of (internal) energy for their *meaning* (in terms of having a non-equilibrium physical existence that therefore contains some [potentially retrievable] information—see chapter 27, entitled "Information," for further discussion), this amounts to a fundamental prohibition against creating "something of meaning from nothingness." Here the term *meaning* refers to cogent (i.e., non-random) information, not necessarily information that is semantically interpretable. This is an important constraint that is based on everything we know about the universe; otherwise we would all be able to construct *new* items from nothing at whim, effectively like genies conjuring up anything they wanted.

If we accept the idea of conservation of energy, then to provide consistency, our universe must have *started out* with a *certain amount* of *energy* and that's *all there is* (the term universe includes *everything in existence—everywhere*, whether accessible or inaccessible, known or unknown, including energy residing behind the event horizons of black holes, in hyperspace, and in potential extra dimensionalities that may exist in addition to the ordinary four-dimensional space-time to which we routinely have access). This means that from the outset of the universe, energy has only been interconverted from one form to another and transferred from one place to another, but that none has ever been created or destroyed.

An example that illustrates why this must be the case is the historically notable idea of a *perpetual motion machine*. This is something that, if it could be made, would do useful work (ordinary physical machines fit this description) but would not require any external energy to operate. In effect, such a machine would be able to perform useful work on its surroundings in the absence of any expenditure (i.e., consumption) of energy from another source. If it were possible to design such a machine (and many have attempted to do so!), then the newly created energy delivered to the surrounding environment would be able to perform useful work on other systems. This process could then be duplicated ad infinitum, thereby permitting the generation of newly created energy at will. A consequence of this would be that the extra energy would systematically increase the mean energy content (and temperature) of the universe. Sadly or not, no observational or experimental evidence supports the contention that spontaneous energy generation is possible. In fact, there is good theoretical evidence to suggest it is not. So, as wonderful as this idea might seem, it is a violation of everything that has been observed to date about the way the physical universe operates. And if it occurred, it would result in contradictions that would be irreconcilable.

This conclusion is important for many practical as well as theoretical reasons, including the implications it has with regard to the limitations associated with finite energy resources—all of which are exhaustible (i.e., fossil fuels, fissionable materials, etc.). But for the purposes of our present discussion about predicting the future, one of its most important implications pertains to the total amount of information contained in the universe. To define this quantity as a function of the energy contained in the universe would require identifying the relationship between energy and information. The following chapters serve to both clarify the nature of information and to investigate its relationship to energy—in order to demonstrate that they are manifestations of one and the same phenomenon.

CHAPTER 27
Information

Information permeates the universe and provides the substrate for all knowledge.

Information: Definition (Merriam-Webster Dictionary)

- Facts, data
- A signal or character (as in a communication system or computer) representing data
- Something (as a message, experimental data, or a picture) that justifies change in a construct (as a plan or theory) that represents physical or mental experience or another construct
- The attribute inherent in and communicated by one of two or more alternative sequences or arrangements of something (as nucleotides in DNA or binary digits in a computer program) that produce specific effects
- Intelligence, news

Information has been discussed throughout this book but, curiously, it has not been defined until now. This is because we all have an intuitive notion of what information is, and in many ways we are right. As already discussed, the information we obtain about the universe constitutes the *primary substrate of all human knowledge*. But, in order to advance arguments about information's relationship to energy (see chapter 26, entitled "Energy," for further discussion), the nature of information needs to be more rigorously defined.

First, it is important to recognize that information that originates outside of us comes from a variety of sources but that it always represents a "code" that is *intrinsically organized*. We can gain access to it only because it has a *physical representation* that permits us to interact with it (via receptive apparatuses) and then perceive it (see chapter 5, entitled "Perception," for further discussion). Thus, it exists only because it has a *representation* in some kind of *physical medium*. Because of this, information is neither *free-floating* nor *amorphous*. Additionally, the types of physical media that information employs for its embodiment are themselves *organized non-equilibrium structures* that cannot exist in a uniformly homogeneous universe (i.e., one that is *maximally disorganized* with *maximum entropy*). Thus, without a physical platform for its embodiment, information cannot be physically represented, and it *cannot exist*.

To put this into perspective, it is useful to consider circumstances where there is *no* information. One of these would be in a *uniformly homogeneous universe* (i.e., one in *complete thermal equilibrium* at a temperature of *absolute zero* [0° Kelvin]). In such a universe, there would be *no energetic difference* among its *different regions*, either in space or in time. Therefore, there would be *no free energy* available to accomplish any *useful work* (i.e., change). In addition, since the universe constitutes everything that exists, no useful work could be performed on it by anything outside (since there is nothing else). In such a uniform universe, *no organization* is possible (either spontaneously or externally driven) and, therefore, the existence of non-equilibrium (i.e., organized) structures that embody intrinsic informational content would be precluded—including beings of any type.*

Currently, available astronomical evidence suggests that our universe is expanding. If a non-equilibrium universe of the type we live in continues to expand indefinitely with no further energy added to it from the outside (which would be impossible, since the universe incorporates everything that exists), its mean *kinetic energy* (per unit volume) would diminish, and its temperature would eventually approach *absolute zero*. At that point, all regions of the universe would become progressively more homogeneous and, eventually, the physical motion associated with heat would slow down. These are the hallmarks of an *ultra-low energy density* universe. If the universe were to actually reach a temperature of absolute zero (which would be impossible, as it would violate the principle of *conservation of energy* if it were to occur everywhere—see chapter 26, entitled "Energy," for further discussion), all of the thermal motion of matter would cease (except for the fluctuations due to quantum mechanical zero-point energy that are persistent even when matter is in its lowest energy ground state). Then, there would be complete uniformity of the (maximally disorganized) universe, and there would be no means for representing, storing, or transferring (i.e., communicating) information from one place to another. All regions of the then maximally cold universe would be precisely the same: motionless and lifeless. This type of a uniform universe has been referred to as succumbing to *thermal death*.

The conclusion to be drawn from this is that *information cannot exist* in a system at *complete equilibrium*. This is because in a completely isotropic environment (where everything is homogeneous), there are no energy (or mass) differences among any of the internal system constituents (on average). Since no meaningful difference exists anywhere, there isn't any way for something with intrinsic meaning to be *physically represented* or stored. Thus, for the simplest representation of information (i.e., some physical entity that either *is* or *isn't*, which can be represented by any fundamentally *dichotomous physical state*, such as *charged* vs. *not charged*, *up* vs. *down*, etc.) there is no way to establish such a difference within such a system. Because this is the most basic way that information can be represented and stored, the consequence is that there can be *no useful* (i.e., *retrievable*) *information* associated with any *system* that is entirely *homogeneous*.

Despite this conclusion that information cannot be represented in a completely homogeneous universe, one might still argue that there could be quantum fluctuations that would transiently increase the energy density of one region of the universe compared with others. This would create differences in potential energy that might permit the performance of useful work (with the associated potential of allowing the creation of organized structures), but these differences would only be transient and could not be sustained long enough to be significant in any physically meaningful way. This is consistent with our knowledge that nothing (permanent) can be created from nothingness (i.e., that *energy* is *conserved*, making *perpetual motion machines impossible*) and that it is *not permissible* to (spontaneously) *create* persistent regional *energy differences* from a starting circumstance of uniformity (see chapter 26, entitled "Energy," for further discussion).

The implications stemming from this are numerous, with three of them pertaining directly to the relationship between information and energy:

1. Even if information could exist in a uniform universe (which it cannot), *information transfer* from one region to another would not be possible. As will be outlined in the next chapter, this is equivalent to stating that there can be no transfer of energy from one region to another in a uniform universe, which is a natural consequence of its homogeneity.
2. *Knowledge* is *impossible* within a *uniform universe*, because (a) no information exists and (b) the existence of *sentient* platforms (i.e., *beings*) capable of *appreciating* it would violate the underlying assumption of the universe's homogeneity, making their presence impossible (i.e., they could not exist because they are organized, non-equilibrium structures with non-uniform internal states—see chapter 6, entitled "Consciousness," and chapter 8, entitled "Knowledge," for further discussions).
3. *Self-organization* is *precluded* in a uniform universe at a temperature of absolute zero. Not only is such a universe static (in terms of its homogeneity), but—as has already been mentioned—it has *maximum entropy* and *no free energy*. There is also nothing external that can provide any additional energy to it or where a change in entropy can be created (i.e., since the universe represents all that exists, there is nothing external to it). Thus, there is no ability for such a universe to undergo any transformation to change its state (either self-induced or externally driven—see chapter 20, entitled "Thermodynamics: Laws Prohibiting the Spontaneous Reversibility of Physical Events," for further discussion).

These main points can be further summarized. Because of the thermal (energetic) homogeneity underlying a uniform universe, there is:

I. Complete disorder (a complete lack of system organization with maximum entropy)
II. No ability to represent differences
III. No free energy
IV. No ability to perform any useful work, and
V. No ability to self-organize.

As a result, it would be impossible to physically represent information in such a universe, meaning that *useful information cannot exist*. Accordingly, such a homogeneous universe would not only be static and changeless, but also *contentless* (from an informational standpoint).

We can gain additional insight by also examining the opposite circumstance: a universe of *ultra-high energy density* (one that is extremely hot!). This is very likely what the universe was like during the earliest stages after its creation. Under such conditions, electromagnetic energy is converted from one type to another, but there is very limited ability for mass to congeal into stable structures at such high temperatures. In addition, the *lifetime* of any particular state at any specific location of the universe is extraordinarily short, such that information can only be stored and maintained in any region for a very brief period before it is *drowned out* by ambient *thermal noise*.

Therefore, in such an ultra-high energy density universe, there is the opposite problem from what has been described for one of ultra-low energy density regarding the representation, storage, transmission, and processing of information. In the case of an *ultra-high energy density universe*, matter is not stable enough to serve as the building blocks for the creation of physical systems. Furthermore, even if it were possible for such systems to exist for anything but the briefest period of time, the *half-life* of *information* before its transformation (due to the ambient high temperature) would be so brief as to make all information *transient* and elusory in nature. In essence, by the time that any such information could be *recognized* by a sentient being—assuming that one could exist under such hostile conditions, which is very unlikely, as the conditions would preclude the long-term maintenance of its structure and homeostasis—it would be *transformed* or *relocated*, such that it would have no local accessibility or utility.

Thus, we have two different types of problems with regard to information as we reach the extremes of energy density. In the case of an *ultra-low energy density* universe that is approaching *thermal equilibrium* near *absolute zero*, there is more than sufficient stability over time to store information, but there is *insufficient free energy* to create and maintain the necessary physical media for its representation, as well as to transfer and process the information to make it of any practical use. Additionally, the presence of *sentient systems* (i.e., beings) in such an ultra-low energy density universe is precluded by the fact that there is *not enough free energy* to *assemble*, *maintain*, and *operate* them. In the case of an *ultra-high energy density* universe, the problems are different, but they result in the same limitations: again there is uniformity, but at a *very high temperature*, which results in *tremendous time-dependent instability* of information. Thus, even though information permeates the universe, it has such a *short time constant* (before local *erasure* by thermal fluctuations) that it is functionally worthless. In essence, by the time that information could be recognized by a sentient system—which also could not exist because of the lack of sufficient stability to create sustainable structures—it is already gone and a part of history (i.e., it is no longer applicable to the [new] current state of the universe).

Given these considerations, it can be concluded that information is *intrinsically organized*, requiring *representation* in a *stable*, *(non-equilibrium) physical medium* to exist. Therefore, *useful information* (i.e., *information* that is *persistent* and *stable* enough to be both *recognizable* and *analyzable*) can only exist when conditions are somewhere in the middle ground between the two extremes of an *ultra-low energy density* universe on the one hand and an *ultra-high energy density* universe on the other. Thankfully, our universe exists near the midrange of this energy density spectrum. This makes its conditions relatively ideal for the maintenance, storage, retrieval, transmission, and processing of information. This is fortunate, because without such appropriate conditions, (a) physical media (i.e., platforms) for the representation of information would not exist, (b) sentient beings (like us) would not be possible, and (c) there would be no useful information in the universe for us to know about.

---

* This pertains to everything, including living organisms and any other potentially sentient systems.

CHAPTER 28
Energy and Information: Maxwell's Hypothetical Demon

Maxwell's hypothetical demon affords the linkage between energy and information.

One result of Albert Einstein's special theory of relativity is familiar to nearly everyone: $E = mc^2$ (Energy = [mass] x [velocity of light] squared). The meaning of this seemingly simple equation is that mass can be converted into an energy equivalent (in principle) and that the opposite is also true, i.e., that energy and mass are *interconvertible*. This makes mass and energy essentially two sides of the same coin—different representations of the same fundamental entity (often referred to as mass-energy).

Something that is not so well appreciated is that energy and information are also interchangeable in an equally fundamental way. This was first hinted at by a paradox formulated by the famous nineteenth century English physicist James Clerk Maxwell (who was also responsible for unifying the theories of electricity and magnetism into a single theory of electromagnetism). The paradox involves a hypothetical agent known as the *Maxwellian demon* and can be summarized as follows: consider two homogenous gases in separate containers (distinguishable say, by one being comprised of circular and the other of triangular molecules). If these two containers are placed side by side, and if the barrier between them is removed such that the two gases are allowed to mix completely to arrive to an equilibrium state of complete homogeneity, then the result will be a uniform gas mixture of circular and triangular molecules that is the same throughout the container (on average). The act of mixing the gases results in the liberation of energy from the two previously pure gas systems (i.e., the so-called *energy of mixing*). This liberated *free energy* can then be captured (using a suitable machine) and harnessed to do useful work on the surrounding environment.

When the two gases are mixed completely to make a homogeneous system and free energy is liberated, there is no longer any of the excess energy that was previously associated with the unmixed states of the two (pure) gases. If we then want to separate the gases again, we would need to *do work* on the new mixed gas system to return it to the two original pure gases This might be accomplished by means of some ingeniously designed separation procedure that depends on a small difference in physical attributes between the two types of gas molecules. This would be an energy consuming process (i.e., it would require harnessing energy from the outside environment) to operate some type of machine to separate the mixed gas again into its two constituent parts. The amount of energy necessary to re-separate the two components of the mixed gas into their pure circular and triangular molecular states would be equivalent to (1) the amount of energy that was previously liberated by their mixing plus (2) whatever extra amounts of energy would be necessary due to (a) the design and construction of the "separation machine" and (b) other dissipative and conversion energy losses (i.e., inefficiencies) that might occur as a result of the machine's operation. In the idealized case, the dissipative and energy conversion losses could be minimized (i.e., if the machine were efficient enough, operated slowly enough, etc.), but the total energy consumption required to restore the mixed gas to its original premixed state would always be more than was liberated by the original mixing.

Now instead of going through this process of designing, constructing, and operating a machine to accomplish the separation of the mixed gas at the cost of supplying the necessary (outside) energy to accomplish the task, imagine that we simply replace the previous barrier that existed between the two original gas chambers. Because the mixture is now homogeneous, there is no difference between the uniform mixture of the circular-plus-triangular gas on the right and left sides of the barrier. However, imagine also that a tiny frictionless gate is incorporated into the barrier, such that its dimensions are just large enough—when opened—to allow for the passage of a single gas molecule. Then, if there were some sort of a tiny creature—referred to fondly as the *Maxwellian demon*—that could discern exactly when a circular molecule was coming at the gate from left to right, and similarly when a triangular molecule was coming at the gate from right to left, then he could open the (frictionless) gate at just the right time to separate the gas into its original pure circular and pure triangular components (figure 13). But this would create a problem—of the perpetual motion machine variety!

If a frictionless gate were used together with enough forewarning, then the demon could potentially open and close it exceedingly slowly, effectively expending no energy in the process (at least ideally). If this were possible, then the demon would be able to re-separate the homogeneous gas mixture into its original pure circular and triangular components. But, as has already been stated, the separated pure gases have a potential energy that is higher than that of the uniformly mixed gas (which gave rise to the liberation of the *energy of mixing* when the two were allowed to mingle together). Thus, the demon's action provides a pathway back to a higher energy state than for the mixed gas—all without the expenditure of energy! If this were possible, then the gases could be remixed and separated time and again, thereby providing an endless source of energy created from nothingness. This would clearly be a violation of the conservation of energy rule and the result would be a perpetual motion machine!

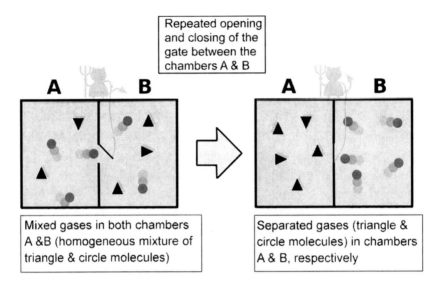

Figure 13: Maxwell's demon

The famous English physicist James Clerk Maxwell wrote the following with regard to his hypothetical demon's ability to separate fast and slow-moving molecules (which is directly analogous to separating circular and triangular molecules): "If we conceive of a being whose faculties are so sharpened that he can follow every molecule in its course, such a being, whose attributes are as essentially finite as our own, would be able to do what is at present impossible to us. For we have seen that molecules in a vessel full of air at uniform temperature are moving with velocities by no means uniform, though the mean velocity of any great number of them, arbitrarily selected, is almost exactly uniform. Now let us suppose that such a vessel is divided into two portions, A and B, by a division in which there is a small hole, and that a being, who can see the individual molecules, opens and closes this hole, so as to allow only the swifter molecules to pass from A to B, and only the slower ones to pass from B to A. He will thus, without expenditure of work, raise the temperature of B and lower that of A, in contradiction to the second law of thermodynamics."* [Schematic figure of Maxwell's demon from 2 February 2007 by Htkym; Source http://commons.wikimedia.org/wiki/File:Maxwell's_demon.svg with permission granted to copy, distribute, and/or modify this document under the terms of the GNU Free Documentation License, Version 1.2 or any later version published by the Free Software Foundation]

So how can we reconcile this quandary? Tiny demons do not exist, of course. But, the question is: what is it that such a demon would need to allow it to open and shut the frictionless gate at just the right time to accomplish the gas separation process? The answer is simple: *information*. What the demon has at its disposal is information about the system that, when used in a clever way, permits it to perform the otherwise energy-consuming operations necessary to accomplish the separation *without expending energy*. It is from this line of reasoning, as well as several other related ones, that the conclusion was first drawn that there is a relationship between information per se and energy. Though this argument straddles the boundaries of thermodynamics, statistical mechanics, and information theory, the result seems nevertheless to be intuitively obvious (at least in retrospect!).

Some scientists have expanded this line of argument as follows: even though there aren't any demons, it is possible—using the marvels of modern technology—to design extremely sensitive detectors, and these can be electromechanically coupled to small gate-openers to mimic the different operations of the Maxwellian demon—the purportedly sentient creature with the advantage of having information. If this is the case, then there is really nothing special about him. A non-sentient machine could also glean the same kinds of information and operate the gate in strict accordance with a set of decision-making rules to open and close it at just the right times. Of course, the construction of such a system—complete with sensors, detectors, actuators, etc.—would require the advance consumption of energy during its fabrication that would need to be accounted for. But this line of reasoning appears to beg the larger question that revolves around the fact that the demon's actions—or an equivalent machine's—seem to beat the system by creating energy in a *something-for-nothing* sort of fashion. Therefore, if some *equivalence* of *information* and *energy* were not posited, a perpetual motion machine would result.

If one follows this line of reasoning a bit further, then classic thermodynamic theory can be used to examine the relationship between energy and information. For a single *bit* of information (i.e., of *binary* yes-no type) at normal human body temperature (i.e., 310° Kelvin), the calculated result is that the amount of heat (i.e., energy) contained by a single bit of information is $\leq 3 \times 10^{-21}$ Joules (see appendix for an explanatory calculation[†]). This provides an upper bound for how much energy a bit of information is equivalent to (i.e., *worth*) within the context of any given system at the usual temperatures at which we operate.

This well-defined upper bound for the energy equivalent of a bit of information is exceedingly small, which means that it would be very difficult to measure experimentally. To put this value into perspective, it is instructive to consider how much (potential) energy would be expended if a liter of water (1 kilogram) fell to the floor from a table that was 1 meter high (a distance of about three feet). Since the force applied is equal to the mass of the water (1 kilogram) times the acceleration due to the earth's gravity (9.8 meters/second^2), and since the distance over which this force acts is the height of the table (1 meter), this can be calculated as follows:

[Force] x [Distance] = [1 kilogram x 9.8 meters/second^2] x [1 meter] = 9.8 Joules

This number is more than twenty-one orders of magnitude larger than the maximum amount of energy stored by a bit of information at room temperature (i.e., upon hitting the floor, the spilled pitcher of water dissipates an amount of energy that is a thousand billion billion times larger).

Nevertheless, the measurement of the very tiny energy equivalent of a single bit of information can be potentially overcome by simply "making it up in volume." Consider the following: if a human thought were to require something on the order of a billion billion bits of information for its representation (nobody currently knows how much this might actually be), then this amount of energy would be 9.8×10^{-3} Joules, which could routinely be measured using modern techniques.

The important result from all this is that there is a well-defined relationship between information per se and energy, which (effectively) makes them *interchangeable*—or essentially, two representations of one-in-the-same entity (just as the case is for mass and energy). Thus, if we were to follow this line of reasoning one step further, not only would information have an energy equivalent, but it would also have a mass equivalent associated with it in accordance with Einstein's mass-energy equivalence equation! Like the energy result, this mass per bit of information is also quite miniscule for a single bit of information, amounting to $\leq 3.3 \times 10^{-38}$ kilograms at room temperature (again, see the appendix for the details of this calculation).[†]

It is important to appreciate that it is not the very small size of the energy and mass equivalents of single bits of information that is crucial. It is that energy, mass, and information are all quantitatively related in a well-defined way that makes them *interchangeable*. This begs the question:

which of these interchangeable manifestations of energy-mass-information is *primary*? And, if they are all equivalent and essentially mirror versions of one-in-the-same-thing, *does it matter*?

The finding that energy-mass-information are all equivalent is quite an amazing—and unifying—result. In order to be consistent, this implies that the fundamental rules that apply to the storage, conversion, and transfer of energy (i.e., the laws of thermodynamics, as outlined in chapter 20, entitled "Thermodynamics: Laws Prohibiting the Spontaneous Reversibility of Physical Events") also apply to information—albeit with somewhat different formulations. Thus, when we consider the rules that apply to energy, which are well understood from a physical standpoint concerning both their operational considerations and limitations (i.e., that there is *conservation of energy*, that the creation of a perpetual motion machine is impossible, etc.), we also allude to equivalent rules that apply to information. They are simply two sides of the same coin.

The conclusion we can draw is that the *amount of information* contained by the universe is *directly proportional* to its *mass-energy content*. To determine the full extent of this information, we would need to know the total amount of mass-energy in the universe. In order to have complete knowledge, we would need access to all of this information, which would then provide us with the potential to develop a consistent understanding of everything. Although the estimates of the total amount of mass-energy in the universe are still uncertain, the figures are hugely in excess of the total amount of information that human societies currently possess. The implication is that we—as humans—are nowhere close to having all the information that we would need to be in possession of it all. Because of this informational deficit (i.e., incompleteness), both the knowledge and the understanding we have from it cannot be consistent (see chapter 11, entitled "Logic and Inference," for further discussion of the implications of incompleteness for consistency). Thus, we have no choice but to accept the fact that (1) the information we currently possess about the universe is enormously deficient and (2) that our understanding that arises from it is necessarily incomplete and, therefore, inconsistent.

* Harvey S. Leff and Andrew F. Rex, eds., *Maxwell's Demon 2: Entropy, Classical and Quantum Information, Computing* (2nd ed. Bristol; Philadelphia: Institute of Physics Publishing, 2003).

† For readers who are interested, an explanation of the relationship of energy-mass-information is presented in the appendix at the end of this book.

PART 4
CONSEQUENCES AND PRACTICAL IMPLICATIONS

CHAPTER 29
Modeling vs. Reality

Models provide schemas to help us understand the universe, but they are not reality.

Model: Definition (Merriam-Webster Dictionary)

- To produce a representation or simulation of
- To design or imitate forms: make a pattern

Real: Definition (Merriam-Webster Dictionary)

- Occurring or existing in actuality
- Having objective independent existence
- Of or relating to fixed, permanent, or immovable things
- Not artificial, fraudulent, or illusory: genuine

Reality: Definition (Merriam-Webster Dictionary)

- The quality or state of being real
- A real event, entity, or state of affairs
- The totality of real things and events

What is *real*? The preceding chapters have attempted to provide the philosophical and scientific groundwork for beginning to address this question, but they are by no means complete. Instead, they identify the signposts for where to begin to look further.

The general themes that have emerged from the discussions of the preceding chapters can be summarized as follows:

1. What we can view and analyze in an attempt to gain knowledge represents a *truncated* and, therefore, *incomplete view* of *all that is*.
2. Because the view we have is *incomplete*, it means that the information we have about objects and events is necessarily *inconsistent*.
3. Despite these limitations, what we repeatedly try to do—both as individuals and as human cultures—is to *build models* around the information we can access and then *evaluate* their *utility* based on their *predictive accuracy*.

Models are intended to be *abstractions* of the most *salient features* of *reality*. We define *reality* based on the *information* we obtain via *perception* followed by internal manipulations of these data (e.g., by *interpolation*, *extrapolation*, etc.). Preliminary *analyses* of this information allow us to generate *hypotheses* that we then develop into *concepts*. These concepts are then *operationalized* to serve as the basis of our modeling.

The primary method we use to assess the *veracity* of our models is the *accuracy* of their *predictions*. This determines if any of their predictions are violated and, consequently, over which domains they should be considered applicable. If a model appears to predict occurrences well (i.e., accurately), it is retained and considered to be a proper reflection of reality—at least over the domains where it has been tested. If it does not, then it is modified to conform to and encompass the additional (conflicting) observations. The adjusted model is then tested again to see if it can predict subsequent events accurately with its new modifications (i.e., those that occur either elsewhere or in the future, or both). This type of procedure for probing a model's veracity represents a version of what has been referred to as the *scientific method*. As such, these tests check the *operationalized view* of our *understanding* of reality. This is the only type of test we have for determining if the understanding we think we have is correct (see chapter 13, entitled "Understanding," for further discussion). Thus, by making multiple and varied observations, models can be *tested* to determine if they are accurate reflections of what they were constructed to represent.

But, by the very nature of testing procedures, fundamental issues arise that relate to both *measurement* and *perception* (see chapter 9, entitled "Measurement: How Circumstance and Change are Assessed," and chapter 5, entitled "Perception," for further discussion). This is because to perform a *test*, it is necessary to know

1. the *starting conditions* of the objects and events of interest (i.e., their *baseline states*);
2. the *nature* of any *predisposing influences* or *active interventions* that have an impact on them (e.g., their precise magnitudes, directions, etc.);
3. the *subsequent states* of the objects and events, which incorporate the *effect(s)* of the *predisposing influences* or *active interventions*; and
4. what would have happened if the predisposing influences or active interventions had not occurred.

These necessary elements for testing a model raise a key question: can models ever provide a *proper* vision of reality (i.e., what is *actually out there*), and if so, are the methods we have for testing them sufficiently accurate to permit us be certain of it?

To test a model, it is necessary to (A) *perform measurements* and (B) *perceive* the results. Thus, issues involving the *accuracy, precision*, and *completeness* of the information we use to check our models arise from the outset. These involve the limitations that have already been discussed regarding intrinsic errors associated with both measurement and perception (see chapter 9, entitled "Measurement: How Circumstance and Change are Assessed"; chapter 21, entitled "Quantum Theory: Uncertainties of the Very Small"; and chapter 5, entitled "Perception," for further discussion). These limitations are directly applicable not only to the reliability of the checks we use to assess the accuracy of our models, but also to the veracity of the information we use to construct them in the first place.

In modeling, the greater context of the surrounding environment is either (a) held completely at bay, which means that it is not even considered, or (b) held *constant* with respect to the isolated model, such that its influence is either obviated or minimized. Despite these attempts to establish *isolation*, the presumed advantages of this can never be completely realized, because there must always be some degree of cross-communication between different regions of the universe that are not at equivalent temperature (due to the unavoidable exchange of black body radiant energy—see chapter 25, entitled "Absolutes vs. Relatives: Relativity Theory," for further discussion). This absolute requirement calls the very idea of isolation into question (see chapter 19, entitled "Dynamical Certainty vs. Uncertainty: Trajectories"; chapter 20, entitled "Thermodynamics: Laws Prohibiting the Spontaneous Reversibility of Physical Events"; and chapter 22, entitled "Entanglement vs. Separability: The Locality Issue," for further discussions). The implication is that since models are a part of the greater universe, they cannot be entirely isolated from their surroundings.

This inability of models (and all subsystems) to be completely freed from the effects of their environment has a favorable consequence that obviates a far greater problem that would occur otherwise: an implicit admission of *incompleteness*. By definition, isolation means that there is a greater context within which a subsystem is imbedded, resulting in the information within the isolated system being truncated. This implies that any model (or any other subsystem) would be necessarily *inconsistent* if not for the unavoidable cross-communication with its environment (see chapter 11, entitled "Logic and Inference," for further discussion). Thus, this unavoidable cross-communication at least allows the possibility of completeness, which is a prerequisite for there to be consistency.

This brings up an issue with regard to modeling that illustrates the tension between context and isolation: with modeling, there is always at least one subsystem (e.g., the model of interest) within the greater contextual whole (i.e., the entire universe), such that the context—regardless of its degree of expansiveness—is intrinsically incomplete if it does not incorporate the influences of its imbedded subsystem (i.e., the model). Thus, if these two subsystems were actually isolated from each other—the *model* on the one hand and its *greater context* (i.e., the rest of the universe) on the other—both would be *incomplete* (and *inconsistent*), since each would fail to take the other into account.

This is the same type of tension that also exists in the realm of *empirical science*. For science to be possible, *isolated systems* are routinely approximated in order to permit variables to be *controlled*. This allows study designs to be standardized (at least to within certain practical limits). Despite the assumptions and limitations associated with the concept of isolation, the control of environmental influences allows the behavior of systems (and the performance of models) to be evaluated for reproducibility over repeated episodes of testing in different times and places. But this need for isolation calls into question the veracity of the findings of empirical science (and models), as well as the applicability of the results to any greater domain than the particular (isolated) venues in which they were derived.

Thus, if models are meant to establish a complete and proper understanding of reality, such that they represent the *Truth* (about *everything*—as denoted by a capital *T*), they are not designed to do this and will always be deficient! This is because models are *abstractions* by definition. They do not purport to incorporate all the information about the systems they describe but only the information and relationships that are considered to be *most important* for establishing an understanding of their trajectories. The information incorporated in such abstractions—as good as it may be at honing in on the most salient features of particular circumstances—can never provide *all* the information about the reality that it purports to model. (Otherwise it would actually be reality itself and not just a model!) Therefore, by eliminating various elements of reality—many of which would be *potentially destabilizing* to models if they were incorporated—they are necessarily subject to intrinsic errors (see chapter 18, entitled "Stability vs. Instability: System Inertia and Resiliency," and chapter 24, entitled "Chaos Theory: Implications for Macroscopic Predictability," for further discussions).

In summary, models are always *incomplete* and can *never* present a *comprehensive* view of reality that is entirely accurate. They sometimes behave in a stable fashion when the reality that they purport to model does not; often, this is due to the omission of small, nonlinear factors that are felt to be either extraneous or insignificant to the overall operation of the system being modeled, which they often are not (witness the wide-ranging effects of the so-called *butterfly effect*—see chapter 24, entitled "Chaos Theory: Implications for Macroscopic Predictability," for further discussion). But sometimes the opposite occurs: models can also behave in an erratic or unstable manner when the reality that they purport to model is actually more stable and more robust; this can occur because of "extra factors" that provide reality with more inertia and resiliency than were incorporated in the model. Thus, models—no matter how well-designed and all-encompassing they attempt to be—are prone to generating predictions that can vary widely from what actually occurs.

What this means is that all models are useful only in *operational* terms that pertain to their (*local*) view of *reality* (i.e., the "local" truth with a small *t*). Thus, their utility is applicable only over certain limited domains and some are better for particular purposes than others. If such models are valid at all, it is only for local circumstances, and they cannot be generalized or expanded into other domains with any predictable degree of accuracy (see chapter 15, entitled "Generalizability: Internal vs. External Validity," for further discussion). This is a severe limitation for anyone who purports to use a model to either know about or to understand anything about which there is no direct information.

The conclusion to be drawn is precisely what should have been obvious at the outset: *models* are *not reality*. Instead, they reflect only *facets* of *reality* that are *incomplete*. Sometimes they do this well and sometimes poorly, but always non-exhaustively and never with perfect accuracy. As a result, models are all intrinsically subject to *inconsistencies* that cannot be expunged (as a consequence of their *incompleteness*), making them vulnerable to *unavoidable errors*. This means that sometimes their predictions are simply wrong and that they can never be regarded as more than just a general guide in helping to predict the future. Although models can have utility for addressing certain well-defined problems under particular (i.e., narrow) circumstances, this is a far cry from the wide-ranging certitude that most of us would wish for them to have.

CHAPTER 30
Where We Fit and What We Can Know

What we know is limited by what we can perceive and how we process the information that is available to us.

Know: Definition (Merriam-Webster Dictionary)

- To perceive directly: have direct cognition of
- To recognize the nature of: discern
- To be acquainted or familiar with
- To have experience of
- To be aware of the truth or factuality of: be convinced or certain of
- To have knowledge
- To be or become cognizant
- To have a practical understanding of
- To have understanding of

We are in a unique situation as humans. We are not large, but we are also not small. We exist at the interface of two dimensional scales that makes us something of a bridge between them. At a functional level, we experience influences that impinge on us from both sides—from quantum effects involving submicroscopic particles (on the small end) to relativistic effects involving very large-scale objects and energies (on the large end). Because of our intermediate size, we represent an operational blend of both scales, which means that our existences do not comport purely with the rules of either.

The intermediate position we occupy may permit us to have some unique opportunities due to the integration of effects from our interfaces with both small and large scales. The question is: does our existence at this relatively unique size-energy interface allow us to have some degree of operational *freedom* that would otherwise be precluded within either of the adjoining domains?

To examine the ideas of the preceding chapters more closely, we can divide the concept of what we can know into three domains:

1. What can we know about the past?
2. What can we know about the present?
3. What can we know about the future?

For each of these domains, there are different types of limitations. But relativity theory has demonstrated that observers will have different views of the same events depending on their particular frame of reference. One consequence is that the idea of simultaneity does not apply universally. Thus, time-distance relationships (and, consequently, the ideas of past, present, and future) are different for observers located in different inertial frames of reference (see chapter 25, entitled "Absolutes vs. Relatives: Relativity Theory," for further discussion).

With respect to observers who evaluate events perceived (by them) to have occurred in the past, the only information available is what has been carried forward from the time in question until the present moment (i.e., when the events are being appreciated and considered). Therefore, if not all such information were properly transported and assembled in the present (i.e., in the future compared with the occurrence of the event itself), such that there is local access to it, these observers would necessarily be hamstrung by a local *information deficit* about the past. As outlined previously by the ideas of *light cones* and *event horizons* (see chapter 25, entitled "Absolutes vs. Relatives: Relativity Theory," for further discussion), this type of information deficit is both fundamental and insurmountable. Because of the incompleteness concerning the scope of information that is available about the past, the information that is available about it in the present is also inconsistent (see chapter 11, entitled "Logic and Inference," for further discussion). Additionally, the incomplete information from the past is limited even further by the lack of ability to perceive it in the present with complete accuracy and precision (see chapter 9, entitled "Measurement: How Circumstance and Change are Assessed," and chapter 5, entitled "Perception," for further discussions). Thus, our perceptions, measurements, analyses, knowledge, and understanding represent only limited approximations of the comprehensive "total" *Truth* over the domain that we refer to as the past—nothing more.

With respect to observers who evaluate events perceived (by them) to occur in the present, the only information available is what falls within the limits of observation, which is limited (once again) by *light cones* and *event horizons*. Thus, the information that is available in the present is also truncated and incomplete (with respect to what exists in the entire universe) and, therefore, it is also necessarily inconsistent (again, see chapter 11, entitled "Logic and Inference," for further discussion). Moreover, even the incomplete information that is available about the present is fundamentally limited—once again—in terms of both its accuracy and precision (because of the insurmountable limitations that pertain to perception, measurement, and analysis). Therefore, as was the case for events perceived to have occurred in the past, what can be known about the present is only a limited and potentially misleading glimpse of the "total" *Truth* for the set of observers who perceive what is occurring as being in the present.

With respect to observers who wish to evaluate events that have not yet occurred (i.e., those that will occur in the future), they must depend on the perception, measurement, analyses, knowledge, understanding, and projection of currently available information about the past and the present in order to make predictions about the future. As has already been outlined, the scope of the information available about the past and the present is incomplete and, therefore, also necessarily inconsistent. Moreover, once again, the incomplete information that is available about the past and the present is fundamentally limited in terms of both its accuracy and precision. Therefore, these can serve as the basis only for *approximations* regarding the present "total" *Truth*.

These approximations then undergo progressively more distortion and inaccuracy as they are projected into the future using blunt analytical techniques, which depend on average positions and trajectories. These cannot take the totality of system interactions (e.g., resonances) into account (see chapter 19, entitled "Dynamic Certainty vs. Uncertainty: Trajectories," for further discussion). Because of this, these projections generally incorporate underlying assumptions regarding smoothness and stability that are incorrectly founded (see chapter 17, entitled "Continuity (Smoothness) vs. Discontinuity (Roughness)," and chapter 18, entitled "Stability vs. Instability: System Inertia and Resiliency," for further discussions). Therefore, what we can know about the future is only a rough *approximation* of the *Truth* that is based on limited information, approximations, and inconsistencies about the past and the present, as well as unfounded assumptions (regarding smoothness and stability) and generalizations (that may or may not be valid) about the future.

So what can we be *certain* about in terms of what we know? Unfortunately, not much. And the degree of confidence we can have about what we know is paradoxically limited to a similar extent whether we consider closely defined, limited domains on the one hand or very large, broad-stroke domains on the other. This is because

- as the domains of interest shrink and become progressively smaller, we generally believe that we have a better understanding of local cause-and-effect relationships as a result of having isolated the systems of interest from other external effects associated with the greater context in which the system exists; however, by so doing, the effects of the (ever-changing) facets of the external context are not accounted for, which can often have major (but unappreciated) influences on the perceived cause-and-effect relationships within the local domains of interest; and
- as the domain of interest expands to become progressively larger, there are so many elements that need to be accounted for—all of them necessarily inexact with respect to their starting conditions and the influences that impinge upon them (with many of these being nonlinear, unsmooth (i.e., non-integrable), and chaotic in terms of their behavioral dynamics)—that there is (a) too little information and (b) too much approximation to have much certainty over the evolution of future states.

An important limitation is that the notion of *completeness* is *not testable*. We simply do not have any mechanism to evaluate objects and events that we don't know about. This can be summarized by the well-known catch phrase "*We don't know what we don't know.*" At a functional level, this means that there is no way to know when we are at the end of making new discoveries; this is because there is no way to know what exists unless we have a way of gaining access to the information about it.

Therefore, there is only one remaining idea that we can hope to use as a test to determine if what we believe to be true actually is: the idea of *consistency*. Importantly, if the overall system that we wish to know about (i.e., the universe) is incompletely known in terms of the information we have about it, this means that the limited information we have is necessarily inconsistent (see chapter 11, entitled "Logic and Inference," for further discussion). Under such circumstances, it is only a matter of time before we discover one or more *paradoxes*.

One of the most basic tests of consistency is the idea of *reproducibility*, which often constitutes one of the mainstays of the scientific justification we invoke for declaring something to be *true*. But, reproducibility is only one very limited type of test to investigate consistency. Of course, it is both desirable and necessary to observe the same outcomes in response to the same inputs in order to conclude that some type of a relationship is true (i.e., causal), but this is only a starting point with regard to ensuring consistency. It must also be that the inferences from each set of scientific tests are borne out by other scientific tests to ensure that there is *universal consistency* for all other test results that are possible.

As a practical matter, inconsistency is relatively easy to identify and, when it occurs, it is an undeniable indicator that what we think we know is flawed and intrinsically incorrect. However, *universal consistency* is much more difficult to establish. In order to make a claim of universal consistency—such that we can be comfortable believing in what we think we believe—the question is: must *all* tests be performed under *all* circumstances and in *all* contexts to have confidence that complete consistency has been demonstrated? To do so would require an infinite series of tests, which would consume an infinite amount of time to perform. If not, then where should the testing stop? And because *we don't know what we don't know*, what criteria should be adopted to decide when enough testing has been performed? These are all daunting questions without clear answers.

Under this type of a schema, the question becomes: *How much* inconsistency should be tolerated before deciding to discard the (mental) model that we have of the *Truth* concerning the universe? If our tolerance limit is zero—which would seem necessary to ensure that we had a proper understanding of everything—then we will be sorely disappointed on a regular basis, and we will be changing models interminably.

Perhaps not surprisingly, the ideas of *completeness* and *universal consistency* are both untestable due to the same fundamental constraint: we *don't know what we don't know*. This is a dilemma. Without being able to come to a definitive conclusion about these two crucial issues, it is not possible to decide if we should believe what we think we know. But, in both instances, they appear impossible to test to ensure that the criteria for their existence are fulfilled, either theoretically or practically.

This means that we are faced with a stark reality concerning our beliefs: we can continue believing whatever we think we know until or unless we are confronted with conflicting evidence (i.e., information) that would make our previous understanding of the universe inconsistent. At that point, we need to change our understanding to accommodate the newly conflicting information by constructing a new and consistent mental model of the universe. This model can then persist until some other piece of information comes along to challenge it by being again inconsistent. Then the mental concept needs to be revised again to establish consistency. There is a name for this process of sequential consistency testing: it is known as the *scientific method* for determining the validity of hypotheses. In itself, it is an incomplete and flawed process in terms of its scope and applicability, as well as the limitations of how it operates and what it can guarantee (see chapter 5, entitled "Perception"; chapter 9, entitled "Measurement: How Circumstance and Change are Assessed"; chapter 10, entitled "Associations vs. Causality"; chapter 11, entitled "Logic and Inference"; chapter 12, entitled "Analysis"; chapter 14, entitled "Deductive vs. Inductive Reasoning"; and chapter 15, entitled "Generalizability: Internal vs. External Validity," for further discussions). But unfortunately or not, it is the best that we have available to ensure that what we think we know should (continue to) be believed.

By now it should be clear that we have neither sufficient information nor the proper analytical tools to predict the future with any degree of certainty. We are all bound by the limited knowledge we have about both the past and the present, which means that we project our *best guesses* about reality into the future based on history, prior experience (both personal and collective), pattern recognition, analysis, comparison, analogy, and finally, *hope*. This final element of hope is key. Importantly, if we were magically able to predict the future with certitude, then there would be no room for hope even as a concept; the future would simply be completely defined, with no doubt about what it would bring.

With hope, however, comes something else that allows for its existence: the imbedded concept of alternative outcomes. For there to be hope, there must not only be the possibility of alternative outcomes (which arise naturally as a consequence of measurement indeterminacy [associated with Heisenberg's uncertainty principle], overlapping solutions to the universal wavefunction [associated with the superposition of alternate states at the submicroscopic level], and the chaotic behavior of unstable systems [at the macroscopic level]), but also an ability to *choose* among different actions at the present. The inescapable conclusion is that if hope exists, there must be *free will* (at least as perceived at a local level).

Thus, uncertainty about the future

I. arises because of *potential alternative outcomes*;
II. allows for the concept of *hope*; and
III. provides us with the *freedom* to *make choices* (at our local level).

The final result—the *freedom* to *make choices*—is the operational equivalent of *free will* itself. This makes us all more than simple pawns on a universal chessboard; it makes us agents of change (i.e., active participants), who help to shape the events around us, as well as the future. Of course, together with this free will comes accountability for our actions and, ultimately, responsibility—both in a personal and a joint sense—for all of the outcomes that ensue, with each being a means to the next that follows.

What a fabulous result from our *uncertainty* about the objects and events of our universe! It is because of this uncertainty that we are unable to predict the future with any degree of certainty, but it is also the reason that we are imbued with *free will* and, as a result, with *freedom*! What better result could be afforded to all humanity? Uncertainty is what has given us our freedom.

CHAPTER 31

Where Does All This Leave Us?

We are limited by what we are, as well as the information that the universe provides to us.

So what conclusions can be drawn from the discussions of the preceding chapters?

By now, it should be clear that the view we have of the universe is highly selected, being the result of fragmented and incomplete information. This is not to say that it is incorrect but only that it is *truncated*, both in terms of its scope on the one hand and its degree of accuracy and precision on the other.

Not only does the information we have access to via our senses give us a limited view of what we are and everything that surrounds us, but further uncertainties, approximations, and errors are introduced through its primary acquisition, transmission, and processing. Additional errors arise because of limitations associated with the methods we have for its analysis.

Our interpretation and understanding of the information we analyze is limited by the greater *context* within which we attempt to place it. The need for context arises because we do not know everything about the environment in which the systems we analyze are imbedded. Although context has an influence over what occurs locally, its full extent is unknown to us due to the lack of information we have about what exists beyond the scope of what we can access (e.g., inaccessible information that exists in hyperspace beyond the light cones that reach us, behind the event horizons of singularities, etc.).

These limitations are further compounded when the results of our analyses, which underpin our thoughts about the information we possess, are mobilized and translated into actions. Uncertainties regarding the effects of these actions are introduced through intrinsic physical inexactitudes that arise at two levels: (1) Heisenberg uncertainty at quantum scales and (2) chaotic dynamics at the macroscopic level. These uncertainties result in impacts that are not predictable in any more than probabilistic terms.

The outcomes of the actions we undertake generate new sets of consequences that are then communicated to us via the acquisition of new information from the environment—again with all of its associated limitations and imprecisions. This information then interacts with our perceptive apparatus and starts the whole cycle anew. This further compounds the errors and imprecisions that arise from our human perspectives, both individually and collectively.

If all of these errors and approximations were minor in both their extent and implications, they would have only a limited impact on our ability to predict the future. This would be the case if the effects were *bounded* (i.e., they could be predicted to within certain well-defined limits). But as has already been discussed (see chapter 24, entitled "Chaos Theory: Implications for Macroscopic Predictability"), the idea of bounded effects—which would permit accurate predictions to within certain well-defined limits—constitutes the exception and not the rule. Thus, although some of the errors and approximations may be "convergent" and of little importance (i.e., they will result in minor and transient deviations from predictions, but will ultimately *converge* on the same state), this is not the case for all of them.

Often, series of events diverge from the trajectories we expect. One reason is that their starting points cannot be defined with absolute accuracy and precision (due to Heisenberg uncertainty), and the other is that the influences (e.g., forces) that impinge upon them are similarly defined only imprecisely. In addition, single trajectories that begin adjacent to each other often diverge at rates that can accelerate. This leads to amplification of (cumulative) divergences when multiple events occur in sequence, either in space or over time. Such sequences can transit from zones of stability (smoothness) to domains of instability (where major discontinuities occur). These types of transitions from stable domains to unstable ones are not just rare anomalies in our universe; they happen all the time. This helps to explain why some events happen *unpredictably*. Under such circumstances, we should likely be satisfied that our species has managed to cordon off large portions of our (local) environments to make them behave in ways that are (generally) smooth and stable. This is a major triumph, but it cannot always be expected in all circumstances.

As discussed in the preceding chapters, the universe contains information that is unknown to us. However, because we all rely—as a collective set of *practically* oriented biological organisms—on our interactions with the environment to ensure both our successful survival and reproduction, we simply "fill in" the gaps in the types, scope, and precision of the information we have to allow us to process it and make the most informed decisions possible.

The preceding chapters outline the fundamental reasons for the gaps in our information and knowledge about the universe. The most important of these are:

1. our biologically based *senses* that transduce the information they receive incompletely or that are simply not designed to perceive certain types of information at all
2. physical quantities that are intrinsically *quantized*, resulting in *quantum uncertainties* that cannot be further defined
3. information that is *shielded* in areas of the universe that are not accessible to us (i.e., information in hyperspace beyond the light cones we have access to, behind the event horizons of singularities, imbedded within additional dimensions that we cannot access, etc.).

The implication is that because none of us, either individually or collectively, is capable of assembling a complete set of (precise) information about the universe at any one time, there is no hope that we will ever be able to analyze the universe as a giant *precision clock* that can be run forward and backward with impunity (as many influential rationalist thinkers had hoped). In addition, the reversibility of events is also precluded by fundamental thermodynamic constraints that routinely lead to universal entropy increases as events unfold spontaneously in the forward time direction.

So because we cannot know everything, there are missing pieces of the puzzle that delimit the perspective we can have about the universe and the context within which our knowledge is applicable. This means that we are all left to approximate our circumstances, to suboptimize the situations within our own limited contexts, and to hope that our knowledge and understanding are sufficient to maintain us within (local) domains that are both smooth and stable. This is a tall order, but—quite fascinatingly—it is one which we seem to accomplish very well most of the time.

Something unexpectedly positive arises from this universal knowledge deficit that we cannot surmount: no matter how much we think we know and understand about the universe, *human discovery* and *invention* will *never end*. Because *we don't know what we don't know*, it means that we cannot know what is yet to be discovered, which makes it unpredictable. Thus, our knowledge deficit means that humans will forever make new discoveries that had previously been unknown. This provides the impetus for us to continue searching, discovering, inventing, and adapting new ideas to our advantage. It would be hard to imagine a better consequence of our knowledge deficit: It provides us with the potential to have future lives that are better, more enriched, and more fulfilled. As such, it represents the best single cause for continued optimism about what the future holds.

But, there is also another consequence that arises from the incomplete availability of information: there *cannot be* any *certainty*. The preceding chapters have outlined why certainty is a physical impossibility when there is an information deficit—for the past and the present, as well as the future. We simply do the best we can within the limits of what we can know, constrained by the bounds of the inaccuracies and the imprecision of our available information. Given this limitation, it is a significant tribute that we humans are as successful in controlling our circumstances as well as we do. But in actuality, we are very far from in control. We often think we are, but we may be nothing more than unwitting participants on a grand stage, most of which is shrouded in darkness around its periphery.

Because of this, we have only two floodlights to guide us—our *intellect* and our *intuition*. Our intellect depends on gleaning information from the environment as the substrate for analysis, but it is intrinsically limited for all the reasons already discussed. Our intuition seems to be linked to the very root of our *consciousness*, but its origins constitute a great unknown. Is it a phenomenon that each of us possesses individually, or is it (somehow) part of a greater collective "universal" understanding that we simply all have access to? The answer is that it could be either. But perhaps because of its origin, our instinct often appears to serve as a better guide than either our intellect or past experience. Where and how this arises is still a mystery, but it is not to be minimized. So, at least until more is known, it is probably best to pay close attention to it.

Despite the fact that our understanding of the universe arises as the result of a *truncated, incomplete,* and, therefore, *inconsistent view* of *reality*, these seemingly daunting limitations actually present us with an opportunity. Consider this: The alternative would be that we would know everything about the universe and the rules that govern all interactions. If this were so, the consequence would be that (a) all of the past, present, and future would be laid out for us without ambiguity, and (b) there would be no opportunity for *discovery, intervention, creativity, hope,* or *optimism*.

Thus, as a result of our information deficit, the paradigm that we are left with and that we can employ operationally with regard to new discoveries that influence our knowledge, understanding, and overall "dealings" with the universe is as follows:

1. **Make new discoveries**
2. **Check** for **reproducibility**
3. **Evaluate** for broader **consistency** with other known information
4. **Establish** the **scope** of **validity** by **exploring** the **limits** of **applicability**
5. **Probe** to "**invent**" **new uses** with **novel purposes**
6. **Apply** to generate **other novelties** that have **utility**
7. **Repeat** the process after **incorporating** the **new information**

This is analogous to what has previously been termed the *scientific method*, but the underlying concept is different. The traditional scientific method represents a set of methodological standards for interrogating the reproducibility and consistency of information concerning objects and events, with the goal of identifying inconsistencies (i.e., to serve as a test for the potential falsification of the validity of particular concepts). But, the system outlined here is less stringent and more realistic, with goals that are less grandiose and more flexible. This is because, instead of trying to discover the *Truth* (in an overall sense) that the scientific method strives for but which our universal information deficit renders impossible, the metric used here is instead *utility*. As a result, there is no presumption of universal Truth being discovered from the application of this system. Instead, its goal is *utility*, which is *locally defined* and *purpose-dependent*. Thus, whereas the *Truth* requires *complete information, complete consistency,* and *universal applicability*—all of which are impossible from our human perspective—*utility*, which is based on a particular purpose, requires none of these. This makes it both locally useful and attainable.

We have concluded in previous chapters that objects and events appear to be inescapably connected to each other, thereby causing all objects and events to have an effect on the outcomes of everything else (see chapter 19, entitled "Dynamical Certainty vs. Uncertainty: Trajectories"; chapter 20, entitled "Thermodynamics: Laws Prohibiting the Spontaneous Reversibility of Physical Events"; chapter 22, entitled "Entanglement vs. Separability: The Locality Issue"; and chapter 25, entitled "Absolutes vs. Relatives: Relativity Theory," for further discussions). This has the effect of making the distinction between a *system of interest* and its *surrounding environment* a moot point. It also reduces the question concerning our individual control of and the predictability of the future to the following:

What is more important in terms of the level of impact exerted on objects and events?

1. We as *individuals* (with all of the capacities and capabilities that we have been designed to embody as humans), or
2. *Everything else* in the universe (i.e., all of the other objects and events that exist as part of it)?

From a quantitative standpoint, there is no contest: the universe is much more vast, energetic, and massive than we are as individuals, and, therefore, it must have a greater impact than we do on the overall course of events as they progress into the future. But, what does this mean in terms of the rest of the universe's impact on local objects and events compared with our own? Even if it has more of an impact overall, what is the *balance* between the two effects at a *local level*, and how much of an impact on future events do we as individuals actually have as *agents* of the universe? The answer to this question holds the key to identifying how much control over the future we have as individuals.

The obvious objection to this type of formulation is the following: the idea of universal connectivity means that all individuals are an inextricable part of the greater universe (i.e., it is impossible to negate the myriad of connections that we as humans have to it), thus making the ability to divide the impacts of the two (i.e., humans versus the rest of the universe) an impossible and irrelevant exercise. However, at a practical level, we might still choose to make this artificial distinction of individual humans on the one hand versus the rest of the universe on the other. Then it becomes not just a question of the size, scope, energy, mass, and informational content that is brought to bear by each, but also issues of *proximity, timing, degree of force*, and the *smoothness* (or *roughness*) of the local *input-response profiles* to establish what the outcome of any composite-input situation will be.

If this is the case, then for us as humans, the following practical considerations should prove important with regard to the issue of control over sequences of events and our ability to predict the future: the *closer*, the *more forceful*, and the *more well-timed* our inputs are to the outcomes of interest, the more consequential our inputs should be for determining the course of future events compared to those of the remaining aspects of the universe. Even in cases where the universe provides tremendous inertia and resiliency with respect to change, if we (as humans) provide incremental input that constitutes the "straw that breaks the camel's back," these may have disproportionately large effects that can lead to tremendous system changes. These depend on encountering "tipping points" where discontinuities are reached and where even large systems are subject to changing their direction based on incremental differences in inputs. When this occurs, system changes may occur that are very large even though we provide only a relatively tiny impetus for change. Witness again the so-called *butterfly effect* where a minute input (the motion of a butterfly's wings) can materially change a much more massive system (the earth's overall weather pattern). What this means is that there is always a chance that very small changes can result in very large consequences. We just don't know where and when such types of disproportionate responses will occur, but we know that they can—and that they do all the time.

But the issue of how much (relative) impact can be attributed to individual human actions compared to that of the rest of the universe is only the first question. An equally important one follows that involves the issue of *human volition* (i.e., *free will*): do we possess an independent ability to exert a *choice* over the actions that we undertake, or are we simply bound to execute our roles as agents of the universe (of which we are an intrinsic part) to accomplish its purpose (i.e., essentially as imbedded instruments)? This brings the argument concerning relative impacts full circle. Because, if we are significantly involved as individuals in directing the course of future events, but if we are bound to do what we do despite our best (internal) efforts and our belief that we have a choice among many alternative actions, then we do not actually have control over anything. If that is the case, it is unclear that we can have an influence over *changing* the course of future events at all.

Thus, the question concerning whether we can predict the future can be divided into three. The first is:

"Can we *influence* the course of *future* events via *individual actions*?"

The second is:

"Do these actions arise as a result of *free will*?"

And the third is:

"Can we *predict* the *consequences* of *current events* with regard to their effects on future outcomes and circumstances?"

These questions are fundamentally different and may have divergent answers. For instance, it may be that we *can influence* the course of *events* locally via our actions (i.e., a positive answer to the first question), but that this does *not* arise as a result of *free will* (a negative answer to the second question). Or, it may be that we actually *do not have free will* to be able to independently direct the course of events locally (i.e., a negative answer to the second question), but that we believe that we *can predict* the *outcomes* of current circumstances reasonably well (i.e., a positive answer to the third question). Thus, the idea of *influencing* the future, doing it *volitionally* (or not), and *predicting* it are all different questions.

Based on what has already been presented, most readers are likely to conclude that the answer to the third question is negative (i.e., that we *cannot predict* the events of the *future* with absolute *certainty*). But the answer to the first and second questions may be more nebulous. From the arguments presented in the preceding chapters, I will leave it to the reader to form his or her own judgment concerning the issues of whether individuals have have the ability to (a) *influence local events* on the one hand and to (b) exercise *free will* in doing so on the other. These are the key factors that define and delimit our potential *freedom* as *agents* to *effect change* in the universe and to *redirect* the course of *future events*.

CHAPTER 32
Potential Theological Implications

We can be comforted that we were always meant to be here to do what we do, and that none of us is ever alone.

Theology: Definition (Merriam-Webster Dictionary)

- The study of religious faith, practice, and experience; especially the study of God and of God's relation to the world
- A theological theory or system
- A distinctive body of theological opinion

As has been discussed in previous chapters, there are *holes* in our information base, our knowledge, and our understanding about the universe that we cannot fill. This is the case not only in a practical sense but also theoretically. This book has attempted to provide an outline of what and where the holes are and what it is possible for us to know.

The view that we all have of the universe is necessarily *incomplete* because our collective information about it is *truncated*. As we have seen in the preceding chapters, this means that our knowledge about the universe must also be *inconsistent*. Based on our current understanding, there is no hope of our ever being able to correct this limitation: it exists as a fundamental part of the structure of the universe in which we live. We can never hope to have a complete vision of the entire universe because we are all only an imbedded part of it with a truncated view of all that exists.

What this means is that we cannot glimpse something very fundamental about the universe: its *purpose*. And, because we cannot know the purpose of the universe in its entirety, we similarly cannot know the purpose of our own roles in it. All we can do to console ourselves is to live with the reassurance that we all do indeed have a role. But, exactly what each of our purposes is, we cannot know with any degree of certainty.

So where does this leave us with regard to what is left (i.e., the other objects and events that exist "out there" in the universe, in particular those that are beyond the reach of all our collective perceptions)? Quite simply, we cannot know about them. This leaves room for speculation and, accordingly, for some kind of faith. By this, I mean neither blind faith (i.e., something that is without regard for what we know about the objects and events around us) nor allegiance to something akin to the euphemistic "God of gaps" (i.e., where gaps in our understanding that appear to require a divine explanation can change and narrow as a function of our increasing level of scientific knowledge). Instead, what I mean is that our lack of understanding of what constitutes the whole universal system leaves room for a fundamental capitulation: that we are only a portion of a much larger system that has somehow created us as a part of its need for its greater and ongoing *evolution*. As such, we all play key and irreplaceable roles within it, but precisely what they are meant to be is beyond the grasp of each of us, both individually and collectively.

Something else must be mentioned explicitly: with regard to our understanding, we are all starting from the same position on the playing field. In other words, all of the *holes* that exist in our knowledge and understanding of the universe (i.e., the ones that create room for faith) are the same for all of us. This means that all modes, flavors, and varieties of faith are predicated upon the *same* knowledge deficits and the *same* intrinsically unanswerable questions. Accordingly, any differences in faith that may arise among us are merely nuances in the speculations arising from these various holes in our knowledge and understanding, such that they create a different superstructure for a *belief system* within our societal realm of human existence. But the key is that these superstructures are *not real* in any physically meaningful sense. Instead, they are simply created (by us) as part of a construct that many people over thousands of years have spent much time and effort imagining and conjuring.

It is impossible to verify which of these competing *belief systems* (i.e., *models*) might be more *true* than others, because they are all predicated on *local views* of reality, and, beyond that, they all involve speculation rather than any information that we can interpret as facts. Thus, the inescapable conclusion is that none of them has a preferred position over others. They are all merely attempts to fill in information and knowledge deficits that we all have, albeit by way of generally thoughtful analysis by well-meaning people. Thus, although we may arrive at different conveniences in an attempt to provide explanations, we are actually all "captives" of the same lack of information which underpins our collective lack of knowledge.

If we imagine that the universe "knows where it is going" but that no one else does (or can), what does this mean? Does it mean that the universe actually *knows* anything about what it is *doing* (thereby meaning that it has some equivalent of *consciousness* even at its level), or is it simply a *complete, consistent,* and *coherent* system that is *executing* its prescribed evolution (much like an entirely deterministic system that is automatically *cranking through* its preprescribed plan)? The reality may be either, but it is difficult to imagine another alternative. If this is the case, then it would seem problematic to admit that the universe has conscious, thinking beings imbedded within it (such as ourselves, thereby demonstrating that it has the capacity to foster consciousness), but that it has no larger sense of consciousness itself (i.e., in its totality). The universe may, of course, be doing all that it does in a higher dimensional space than we currently have direct evidence about—the full scope of which is still uncertain—but this type of dimensional expansion does not change any of the fundamental issues at hand.

If this is a reasonable representation of what we are left with, then two corollaries emerge:

1. We are all part of (and beholden to) the *same system* that has both created us and assigned us *unique* and *irreplaceable roles*.

2. If there is a *master plan* to which we are made and meant to conform by something larger than ourselves (i.e., "the universe," "nature," "God" by any name, etc.), then that power is the *same* for *all of us*.

Therefore, if there is a *higher power* to which we must all ultimately answer regarding the proper execution of our roles within the universal system of which we are all an integral part (assuming, of course, that there is room for *free will* to make actual *choices* within it), then our allegiance must necessarily be to the *same* higher power. It would seem absurd to think that differences in nuance concerning our limited perspectives about what we *cannot* know should precipitate discord, argument, or contemptuous unrest over what amounts to superficial disagreements regarding competing human models and trappings. These types of differences must be appreciated for what they are: feeble human attempts to provide order and completeness to our *limited human perspectives* and *myopic human interpretations* of *incomplete* and *inconsistent information* rather than anything more.

Given this, there is no defensible justification for significant human discord when it pertains to what we *cannot know* within the limited framework of what we do know. What can be known is the same for all of us and what *cannot be known* is *equally unknowable* for *all of us*. The result is that there is no preferred position in the realm of ignorance.

PART 5
OVERVIEW

CHAPTER 33
Summary and Conclusions

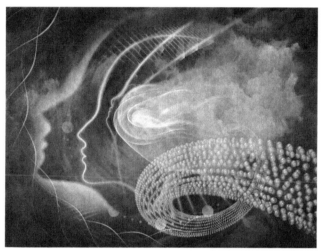

Highlights and core messages from each of the preceding chapters are presented in summary form below.

1. The Past, the Present, and the Future

- The *present* depends on the *past* and acts as a *launching point* for the future.
- Without stability there is no *benchmark* for assessing change.
- *Stability* is necessary to make predictions.
- *Limitations* concerning the ability to *predict* the *future* include:
    o The types and scope of *information* that we can access
    o The intrinsic *accuracy* and *precision*—as well as the *consistency* and *completeness*—of the *information* that we have to work with
    o The *accuracy* and *precision* of the *methods* we use to *process* and *analyze* the *information* we possess

- o   The *accuracy* and *precision* of our *interpretations* of the *information* that is available to us
- o   How well we can place the *information* we have into *context*
- o   The opportunities we have for *acting on* the *information* that we possess, and
- o   How well the *results* of our *actions* can be *predicted*.
- Related are the following issues:

  a. How much information about the universe do we have access to?
  c. How much can we *know* about the information we are able to access?
  d. How much of what we know concerning this information can we *understand*?
  e. What is the *domain* over which we have our understanding?
  f. How much of what we know and understand can we *act on*?
  g. How much *choice* do we have over our actions?
  h. How *precise* are the *actions* that we undertake?
  i. How *predictable* are the *consequences* of the events we trigger by our actions? and
  j. What are the *limits* (i.e., *scope*) of the *effects* of our actions?

2. Predicting the Future: What We All Strive To Do

- Everyone has wants and needs:
  - o   These impel us to *assess current circumstances, establish future goals*, and *devise plans* (i.e., *actions*) to make the *future* unfold in ways that we want.
- We attempt to make *predictions* by projecting *past events* through the present and into the future:
  - o   Accurate *projection* depends on:
    - *Continuity* (i.e., *smoothness*), and
    - *Stability* (of the wider *platform* where everything occurs).
- Expectations about the future assume that:
  - o   The *present* is *well-characterized* and well-known
  - o   *Initial conditions* can be used as a *starting point* for prediction
  - o   *Causality* is the *universal instrument of change*

- o The universe is *intrinsically stable*, and
- o We *know* and *understand* both the *initial conditions* (i.e., the starting points) and the *rules* (i.e., the laws of change) where we operate.
- We assume that if we *know* the *present conditions accurately* and if we *believe* that *causality* is the universal "instrument of change," we can predict how the present will evolve into the future.
- Real predictions about the future are based on:
  - o *Imprecise* and *incomplete information* collected in the past
  - o *Analyses* of *past objects and events*, and
  - o Our belief that *projections* of *past trends* can be made into the future.
- Our ability to predict the future is limited by:
  - o *Information* that is *unknown* and/or *inaccessible*
  - o The *scope* and *sensitivity* of the *apparatuses* we have for obtaining *information*
  - o *Quantum uncertainty*
  - o *Analytical inexactitudes*
  - o *Extreme sensitivity* to *starting conditions* (*chaotic behavior*)
  - o *Discontinuities*, and
  - o *Threshold effects*.

3. Agency: Free Will vs. Determinism

- *Agency* refers to particular actions that are used to achieve certain ends.
- *Determinism* implies that once the universe was set into motion originally, its future trajectory was completely *defined*:
  - o *Causality* is required—the notion that one set of events causes the next, which causes the next, and so on
  - o *Future predictions* are reduced to an exercise in *calculation* once *all* the *information* in the universe is assembled at any particular instant and all the *rules* concerning the interactions of physical objects are known
  - o It makes the *future* (and the *past*) both *transparent* and *predictable*.

- *Free will* presupposes a *freedom to operate* that is *unconstrained* by *physical precedents* that arise from physical interactions.
- If the universe is *deterministic*, and we believe that we have the *free will* to make choices, then when we make a choice, how can it ever be made freely (i.e., is it ever more than an *illusion* of free will)? Two complementary questions arise:
  o If the universe is *deterministic*, how can there be any type of *choice*, (i.e., *free will*), and
  o If *free will* exists, how can the universe be *deterministic*, as there would be choices that if made differently would unavoidably alter circumstances, trajectories, and the future?
- *Free will* depends on *thought*:
  o If *thoughts* are *deterministic* in character, then there is an *iterative regress* of completely predictable precedent thoughts (to a *first thought*), as well as to future "new" thoughts
  o If all our thoughts result from a first thought and a *highly scripted* set of subsequent *deterministic processes*, these might include a predisposition toward the mind-set (or a set of *illusions*) that creates a *belief* in *free will* when, in actuality, no such free will exists.
- *Determinism* and *free will* may be flawed *idealizations* of a more complex reality:
  o *Information deficits* exist because *all* the *information* in the universe is *not accessible* at a local level.
    - *Local information deficits* may deny us access to information that would permit us to recognize the deterministic nature of the universe.
  o *Decision points* encountered at a *local level* may arise from *local indeterminacy*, at least part of which results from local information *incompleteness* and not because of any lack of universal determinism.
    - On a universal scale, reality might be entirely deterministic while local views might create a seeming need for *decision making* due to a *locally perceived need* to *choose*.
    - Despite *local myopia*, no actual need to choose exists, because outcomes are already determined on a universal scale

despite being *unknown* at more truncated scales until they actually occur.
- Misunderstandings may arise due to our *idealized* views of the universe including:
  o *Mathematical idealizations* (such as the concepts of *points, integers*, etc.)
  o An ability to *measure* to within *arbitrarily high limits of accuracy and precision*, and
  o Presumptions of *smoothness* and *continuity* in the relationships among objects and events.
- *Deterministic trajectories* likely represent *idealizations* that have no single corresponding physical incarnate; rather, they are *sets of trajectories* that simply *average* to the single values that we measure:
  o Our inability to *measure* and define initial conditions *precisely* results in *inexact predictions* of *system trajectories*.
  o Due to our *inability* to *resolve underlying spectrums* of what appear to be single trajectories, we do not recognize them as composites with separate underlying components.
  o Because *single trajectories do not exist*, there is *no single deterministic set of interactions* arising from a series of prior interactions; rather, an *ever-increasing number* of *expanding possibilities* occurs with the unfolding of events, which become progressively *amplified*.
- A *panoply* of underlying *trajectories* may result in outcomes that:
  o Reduce to a statistically-defined version of single trajectory determinism, or
  o Produce *non-normalizable* divergences that create entryways into *uncertain* (i.e., incalculable) or chaotic domains, which may open the door for *free will*.
- *Universal determinism* and *local free will* may not be contradictory due to:
  o The physical constraints and limitations concerning the *incompleteness* of *available information* about the universe in any *one place and time*, and
  o The *inability* to *process information faster* than the *universe* itself *evolves*.

- The conflict between *free will* and *determinism* only holds if two things occur, but neither is possible:
  - There is complete access to all the information about the totality of the system (i.e., the universe) in which agents operate, and
  - Information can be analyzed at faster than light speed.
- If silos of information exist within the universe such that not all information is available at the local level, then:
  - *Future states* are *not locally knowable* until they actually occur
  - *Local decisions* (i.e., local choices) need to made in *real time*, and
  - *Deterministic* (i.e., *causally-based*) *systems* of interaction can still *permit* the *local existence* (i.e., *perception*) of *free will*.

4. Causality: Linking Events Separated by Time and Space

- The idea of *causality* is that one event (or object) has an effect on another.
- Without causality, there is no basis for *connections* between objects and events.
- For a causal relationship to be present, the causally related events (or objects) must be *separate*:
  - *Discrete events* (and *objects*) are *separated* by *time* and/or *space*
    - When events (or objects) are separate in *time*, the first (the *cause*) necessarily precedes the second (the *effect*).
    - When events (or objects) are separated in *space* but are contemporaneous, the lack of a temporal relationship makes it uncertain which should be considered the cause and which the effect.
- Relativity theory posits that differences in *time* can be *traded* for differences in *space* and vice versa, depending on an observer's point of view (i.e., their *inertial frame* of *reference*):
  - The *speed of light* (in a vacuum) is the one universal constant for all observers.
  - Events can be *simultaneous* in one inertial frame of reference and *sequential* in another.

- o As long as the *speed of light* is not transited for any observer, it is not possible to view any event that occurred prior to another as occurring afterward in another frame of reference.
- If events were to occur in *reverse order* for different observers, it would be impossible for an event to be causally related to another from a temporal standpoint:
  - o If events could be *reversed*, this would make the past changeable (i.e., *temporal causality loops* could occur), creating potentially irreconcilable *paradoxes* and *inconsistencies* for subsequent states (i.e., the future).
- Two events (or objects) may simply be *associated* with each other rather than causally related; a stringent set of criteria must be satisfied for there to be a causal relationship.
- It is often assumed that an event's largest impact occurs *locally* (i.e., nearby in time and space), even though the full extent of the effects is unknown:
  - o The idea of *locality* would appear to be self-evident; however, it may be an ill-founded vestige of pre-quantum mechanical thought.
- A single event is seldom the only one to have an effect on other occurrences; many events (and objects) can have influences on others, generating a *web* of interacting causal factors that can *converge* as a *causal nexus* to produce a resultant effect.
- *Physical laws* (such as the *second law of thermodynamics*) impose directionality on temporal sequences of events:
  - o Whenever (real) processes proceed *spontaneously* in the *forward time direction*, there is always the creation of *increasing amounts* of overall *disorder*.
  - o *Entropy* can be likened to a measure of *disorder* or *homogenization*.
  - o When events occur *spontaneously, more entropy* is created (an increased state of overall disorder for the *combination* of a thermodynamically isolated *system* plus its surrounding *environment*).
- Real processes (i.e., events) are *not spontaneously reversible* because *increased order must be generated* to re-create the original state;

this requires the expenditure of outside *energy*, which violates the condition of spontaneity.
- There may be an infinite number of branching, non-communicating universes (i.e., so-called *parallel universes*), such that every version of mutually exclusive trains of events exist *somewhere*; because of the inability to communicate with these other universes, it is impossible to either verify or refute their existence.
- If causality were wrong as a concept, our universe would allow "anything to happen," such that nothing could be reliably predicted about the future or the past.

5. Perception

- Objects and events must be *perceived* in order for us to know about them.
- We only perceive what we have been *designed* to recognize; everything else is beyond our capacity to detect:
  o If objects and events exist, but there is no way to perceive them, it is as if they do not exist (i.e., they are effectively *invisible* to us).
  o The only objects and events we can know about in a non-speculative way (i.e., one not part of our imaginations) are those presented to us though *information* that we can access about them.
- *Information* that we receive about objects and events (i.e., their *phenomenology*) is not the same as the entirety of what they *are* (the *things-in-themselves*):
  o *Perception* involves the reception of *information* that is *phenomenological* in nature.
  o Discrete pieces of information (*representations*) reach us and allow us to construct a mental image of what *things-in-themselves* "look like."
- A *receiver* (i.e., detector) of some type is necessary for *perception* to occur:
  o *Receivers* transduce *information* into a form that can be recognized.

- o Humans perceive *information* via biological detectors (i.e., *senses*), after which *stimuli* (i.e., *signals*) are *communicated* internally (i.e., *transmitted*).
- All *detectors* are *non-continuous* in their ability to receive *stimuli* (i.e., *signals*):
  - o For a *stimulus* to be *recognized*, a *detection threshold* must be exceeded.
  - o If stimuli are received that are *below* the *detection threshold* for generating a signal, they necessarily go *unrecognized*.
- A *signal* is either a *sum* or an *average* of the incident stimulus received over both space (i.e., the *finite dimensions* of each receiver element) and time (i.e., the *finite time* over which the incident signal is *integrated*):
  - o *Primary data* (i.e., *stimuli*) are discrete and arise from *intrinsically discontinuous* packets of *information*.
  - o Detectors transduce *stimuli* onto *grids* with *local* on-off type recognition (i.e., yes or no *signals* that are spatially and temporally defined); accordingly, they are received and represented as a *mosaic* of *discrete* points that are *granular* (i.e., "*digitized*").
  - o Each of the "*tiles*" of a *sensory mosaic* represents only a *sampling* of the total spectrum of *incident inputs*, being generated by less-than-completely-efficient receptive mechanisms that are triggered by only a fraction of the total stimulus that bears upon them.
  - o *Signals* undergo *primary interpretation* at the level of the apparatus that receives them; our *minds* then *interpolate* (and sometimes *extrapolate*) information to *fill in gaps* that exist routinely in the primary data.
  - o *Signals* are communicated (often via an *all-or-none digital* signal) from the periphery more centrally for further processing.
  - o *Stimuli* are typically perceived as *continuous* by being internally *smoothed* with the *imputation* of *missing* (i.e., *intervening*) *data*.
  - o The representation of information as *continuous* allows for its easier analysis; this is a *convenient idealization* but a *construct* that is fundamentally *incorrect*.

- *Biological detectors* (i.e., *senses*) have well-defined *operating ranges*, and their degree of *accuracy* and *precision* is limited (*finite*); they provide only an *incomplete view* of our environment due to:
    - Intrinsic *design constraints* that *limit* the scope of their *ability* to *detect signals*
    - *Incomplete* and *integrated* (i.e., time- and space-summed or averaged) representations of only *a portion* of the particular *signals* that bear upon them
    - Detecting only signals that *exceed* a *threshold* to permit their recognition
    - Producing a fragmented (i.e., *pointillist*-type of *grid*) of what is ultimately perceived as a more fine and continuous representation of the external *emitter* of the information (i.e., the *thing-in-itself*)
    - Because they are *blind* to phenomena that are beyond their operating limits, detectors "miss" the great majority of what is "out there".
        - Sensory recognition is incomplete and imprecise, making it impossible to perceive all there is to know about objects and events.
        - Other characteristics of objects and events may remain unrecognized (i.e., functionally "*shielded*"), leaving them unknown.
- We simply "*don't know what we don't know*":
    - External or *auxiliary detectors* can be made to respond to information beyond the capability of our native senses, but it can *never be certain* if *everything* has been *covered*; other items may always remain uninvestigated beyond the (extended) domains of such devices.
- Our *senses* are ultimately the only means for us to glean *information*, which forms the basis for our *perceptions*; in all cases, these are:
    - *Detector design-constraint dependent*, and
    - *Incomplete* (i.e., non-exhaustive).
- Despite the fact that the information we receive is *limited*, we must:
    - Make the *best use* of the *fragmented* and *incomplete information* we obtain
    - *Draw conclusions* from it, and
    - *Use* the *resulting constructs* that we devise to *best advantage*.

6. Consciousness
- *Consciousness* is a *baseline state of being*; it acts as a platform against which *inputs* of various sorts can be *registered* and *compared* to other states:
    - It exists only in *sentient entities*.
    - It is *experienced*.
    - It depends on the maintenance of a *quasi-steady state* as a *point of reference* (i.e., a *well-defined* "baseline" *internal state of order* must exist, which depends on *internal system (pseudo)stability*).
    - It allows *comparisons* to be made between a *stable benchmark* and other *states*; these can either be contemporaneous or historical in nature.
- *Subjective experience* depends on *consciousness*:
    - It is what it is *internally* "known about" by *individuals*.
    - It is necessary for an *appreciation* of anything.
    - There must be *internal change* for it to occur
        - Without *changes* in *internal physical states*, there would be no physical correlate of informational change and, therefore, no internal *register* to serve as the basis for experience.
- *Consciousness* is often equated with *awareness*, which is closely linked to the notion of *self-identity*:
    - *Internal system stability* provides *continuity* for what is appreciated as a *single conscious entity* over time (i.e., a single *self*).
    - *Self-identity* serves as a *de facto division* (i.e., limiting barrier) between sentient beings and their surroundings (the outside environment).
- For consciousness to have utility, there must be a concomitant ability to be *aware*:
    - This depends on the idea of being a "central entity" to appreciate "other things," such as the *objects of perception*.
    - From this, there is the potential to influence objects and events outside of ourselves (i.e., manifest *agency*) and also to (perhaps) exercise *free will*.
- *Consciousness* is a prerequisite for *thought*:
    - *Thought* is an *internal phenomenon* that is fundamental to defining who we are and how it is ultimately possible for us to know about anything.

- *Consciousness* is a necessary antecedent for *volitional acts*, though it does not require that any *external* actions actually occur:
  - There is no requirement for the *external representation* of subjective experience.
- *Consciousness* must exist to *recognize* perceived sensory *information*, as well as to channel and *integrate* the information for *analyses* of more than just vegetative type:
  - Perceived *information* serves as the initial substrate for pathways that establish *knowledge* and *understanding*.
- The *location* of consciousness is of only limited consequence with regard to what we can know and how it can help us to predict the future:
  - *Quantum entanglement* posits that "everything-is-connected-to-everything-else" and this may have profound implications for the localization of consciousness as a phenomenon.
  - Although consciousness may appear to exist at a particular place (and time), its actual location may be more diffuse.
- *Sentient entities* have an *effect* on their *environment* as a consequence of their internal changes; these are small and occur irrespective of any desire (or lack thereof) to do so:
  - The *cross-communication* of *black body* (or *gray body*) radiation exists for all objects at non-equivalent temperature; this implies that absolute *thermodynamic isolation* is an *idealization* that can never be realized.
  - Complete thermodynamic isolation would violate a primary condition required to support the *maintenance* of a sentient being's *internal homeostasis* and *internal organization* (i.e., its *pseudo-steady state*)—the necessary acquisition and *consumption* of *external energy resources*.
- *Consciousness* is an *absolute prerequisite* for being able to *know* about anything, to gain *understanding*, to have *free will*, and to establish *agency* through actions.

7. Thought

- *Thought* spans a wide range of mental activities involving the *representation* and *manipulation* of *mental objects* and their *relationships*;

these can pertain to physical *objects* or *events* (either outside or inside of us), or to wholly mental constructs (e.g., unicorns).
- Only *conscious beings* have the capacity for *thought*.
- Thought presupposes notions of *space* and *time*.
- *Thoughts* constitute *internal phenomena*:
  o They are *internal representations* of information with no routinely measureable outward manifestations.
  o Not all objects and events that thoughts encompass have a separate, physical existence (i.e., some are wholly mental constructs).
- *How much information* is necessary to define a *single thought*?
  o *Differences* in the *informational content* of *thoughts* may depend on their *complexity*, but this is not known.
- Regardless of whether the *objects* of thought have an external existence, they must be *coded* into *mental representations* of objects and events in our minds.
- It is unclear if thoughts are:
  o Represented as a *diffuse type* of *brain phenomenon* (analogous to the way holographic representations are constructed, stored, queried, and reconstructed), or
  o *Confined* to *specific brain areas*.
- If thoughts are confined to specific brain areas, it is not clear:
  o How many neurons (brain cells) are involved in their representations
  o Where these neurons are located (precisely)
  o If thoughts depend on specific functional connections among neurons
  o If different thoughts are represented solely by variable patterns of neuronal excitation
  o If other relevant phenomena are required for thoughts to become manifest, such as:
    - More global types of brain processes and/or representations
    - Processing that resides deeper within the physiologic structures of individual neuronal cells (e.g., within microtubules)
- Although thoughts can arise de novo, they can also be the subject of *recall*:

- o *Memory* is likely to represent a separate and subservient function that provides substrates (i.e., mental objects) for thoughts (e.g., as do the inputs of perception), but is *not intrinsically required* for thought itself.
- The connection between *tangible information* of *sensory inputs* and the types of more *abstract representations* that constitute *thoughts* is uncertain.
- Thoughts require more than mere perception; they must be *appreciated* by a sentient being.
- Thoughts must be placed into a larger *context*, because only then do they have the potential to have *relevance*.
- *Thought* is a *complex phenomenon* that requires the presence of all the following:
  - o *Information* (whether it originates externally or internally)
  - o *Coding* (i.e., internal representation of available information)
  - o *Processing* (i.e., manipulation of the information)
  - o *Awareness* (i.e., "*viewing*" of the information), and, finally
  - o *Consciousness* (i.e., which allows for the *appreciation* of the information).
- Often, the *process* of thought *uses* the *substrates* of *thought* (i.e., *ideas*) to compare some objects (or events) to others:
  - o The mental objects of thought are often checked for *consistency*—or lack thereof—with other information.
  - o This other information may be either contemporaneously received or historical in nature (i.e., the result of recall).
- *Thought* occurs only in *conscious beings* and constitutes a *higher-level function* that:
  - o Is necessary to establish *knowledge*
  - o Serves as the basis for our reaching what we call *understanding*—both about the universe as well as ourselves.

8. Knowledge

- *Knowledge*:
  - o Refers to the available information appreciated by a sentient being about *objects* and *events* and their *relationships* (e.g., *facts*)
  - o Exists as circumscribable *objects of thought*

- o *Informs* our decisions.
- The origin of knowledge is either *native* or *acquired*, or both:
  - o If it is *native* (e.g., inborn *instincts*), it is derived exclusively from the internal structures and associated functions that exist *within* conscious beings themselves (i.e., it is *hard wired*).
  - o If it is *acquired*, it appeals to information that is available from the *outside* (i.e., information external to the conscious being itself).
- *Knowledge* is unlikely to be derived exclusively from either native or acquired sources; instead, it is likely to be a blend of both that depends on
  - o the *abilities* of the *receivers* of information (i.e., conscious beings)
  - o the types of inputs *capable* of being received (i.e., ones for which the properly sensitive sensory apparatuses are available), and
  - o what conscious beings are *prepared for* and can *accept* (i.e., what they are capable of *recognizing, incorporating, processing,* and *interpreting*).
- Being-specific factors "filter" available information that then results in *changes* to *internal states*, which form the basis of *knowledge*:
  - o Such information is *received* via a *perceptive apparatus* (senses) that are *granular* in their ability to detect specific signals because they
    - *integrate* information over *spatial* and *time dimensions*, and
    - must exceed certain *thresholds* for a *stimulus* to be *recognized*.
- *Limitations* apply to both the *veracity* and *scope* of our *knowledge* because of:
  - o The *discrete nature* of the *information* comprising it
  - o The *restricted ability* of our *perceptive apparatuses* to *acquire* the *full scope* of the information that is available
  - o The *limited accuracy* and *precision* of the information to which we have access
  - o *Intrinsic limitations* associated with both internal and external *mechanisms* for *processing* and *interpreting* the information.

- As a result of these multiple constraints, the *knowledge* that we can have about the universe is fundamentally *limited*, as well as our interpretation of it.

9. Measurement: How Circumstance and Change Are Assessed

- *Measurement* forms the basis of all we can know, first by *identifying* objects and events, then by *categorizing* and *cataloging changes* in them and their relationships.
- *Accurate* measurement of objects and events is necessary for us to *know* about them.
- *Absolute accuracy* in measurement is *not possible*; the *accuracy* and *precision* of a *measurement* depends on the:
  o *Measuring instruments* used
  o *Methodology* for making the measurement
  o *Limits* dictated by *quantum uncertainty*.
- *Accuracy* and *precision* are different:
  o *Accuracy* addresses how well a measurement reflects the *true state* of an object or event.
  o *Precision* addresses the idea of how good a measurement is.
- *Very small quantities* can *fall below* the *discrimination threshold* of the methods used to measure them:
  o *Detection* is *not possible* if the methods for making a measurement are too *coarse* compared with what is being measured.
  o Anything *undetectable* necessarily goes *unrecognized*.
  o Technological advances may improve the ability to measure small quantities, but very small scales exist below which differences cannot be resolved (i.e., *quantum scales*).
- *Repeat* measurements assess *reproducibility*, but they *do not improve accuracy*:
  o Measurements can be *repeatedly precise*, but still *inaccurate*.
  o Measures of *central tendency* (e.g., a *mean, median, mode*, etc.) say very little about the *real* values of any collection of measurements; they are summary statistics that represent *idealizations*.
  o Meaningful *accuracy* is not possible without acceptable *precision*.

- - If precision is so poor that repeated measurements are "all over," then any attempt to define a *central tendency* is too inexact to be an accurate reflection of reality.
- For any measurement, the *tools* and *methods* used need to be specified, including:
  - The *type* and design of the measuring device
  - Its intrinsic *precision*
  - *Who* (or what) is doing the measuring
  - *How* the measurement is *performed*
  - *How* the result is *recorded*
  - How many times the measurement is *repeated*, etc.
- "*Gold standard*" techniques for making measurements represent "the best methods available," but are still flawed:
  - All methods of measurement have *intrinsic limitations*.
  - Each method provides a result that has some degree of practical *utility*.
  - The *utility* of a measurement depends on the *intent* for its use.
  - "Gold standards" for measurement do not exist in an absolute sense.
- All *raw data* requires *measurement*:
  - Raw data provides the *substrates* for testing the validity of scientific *hypotheses*.
  - It can be derived either *externally* or *internally*
    - For *external data* (i.e., information arising beyond ourselves), there must be an energetic interaction between our biological receptors (senses) and outside objects and events.
    - For *internal data* (e.g., *a priori* "analytic" thoughts), there is no appeal to outside objects or events.
  - The information comprising raw data must be *quantified* to be *recognized*, then *compared* and *contrasted* to other data.
- *Empiricism* refers to information derived from *experience*; it is not required to conform to any underlying theory.
- *Empirical information* is gleaned from *perception* and relies on *measurements*:

- The practicality of conducting empirical investigations depends on the *accuracy* and *precision* with which measurements can be made.
- *Changes* are assessed by *comparing* future to starting *values*.
- In *observational* studies, objects and events are *measured*—together with their relationships—typically in *cross-section* with respect to *time*; these are *tracked* (without intervention) to observe system *evolution* (*changes*).
- In *interventional* (i.e., *experimental*) *studies, measurements* are made of objects and events before the superposition of an (external) *intervention* and follow-up measurements are made. A *control* experiment is also performed without the intervention; the *difference* between the changes in the interventional and the control experiments are *compared*, and this is *attributed* to the *intervention*.

- The key differences between *observational* and *interventional studies* are:
  - *Observational* studies document *associations* between objects and events but cannot determine if relationships are *causal*; they simply catalog the evolution of a system from a starting condition to some subsequent state and describe the trajectory of change.
  - *Interventional* studies provoke system changes via *external interventions* that *perturb* them; together with a *control experiment*, they quantify the extent of the *causal effect* attributable to the intervention.
- The *existence* of any object or event is determined by:
  - Defining something *unique* about it that can be identified (i.e., a special attribute) and
  - Making a *measurement* to determine if that attribute is present
    - If it can be *detected*, it is said to *exist*.
    - If it cannot be detected (i.e., if it is *not present* or it falls *below* the level of *detectability*), it is said *not* to *exist*.
- *Models* based on empirical data are often constructed post-hoc to organize observations (i.e., make sense of them); subsequent *predictions* of the *models* are either verified or disproven by further measurements made in follow-up studies.

- Data can be classified as either *quantitative* or *qualitative*:
    o *Quantitative* information is considered of *higher quality* (i.e., more precise, more finely *localizable*, and more *granularly definable* on *smaller time-distance scales*, etc.); it is often regarded as *continuous* and as one of the following
        ▪ An *interval variable* (where the interval between values has a well-defined meaning), or
        ▪ A *ratio variable* (where the ratio between numbers has a well-defined meaning).
    o *Qualitative* information is considered *less precise, less well defined*, and of *lower quality*; it is something that is either *nominal* or *ordinal*, being defined as follows
        ▪ *Nominal* (something that can be placed into a distinct category)
        ▪ *Ordinal* (such that there is an order to the variable, but the precise magnitude or significance of differences associated with the order is either not consistent or not well defined).
    o A "middle category" (i.e., *semi-quantitative* data) is sometimes said to fall between the other two, but this presents a contradiction in terms.
- The distinction between qualitative and quantitative data is *arbitrary*:
    o The difference is that *qualitative* measurements are performed with a *lesser degree* of *accuracy* and *precision* compared with *quantitative* ones.
- Traditional data categorizations do not account for *quantum uncertainty* and make implicit assumptions about the *discreteness* and *locality* of information; these may not comport well with modern interpretations of quantum theory.
- Once primary measurements are made, the values generally undergo *processing* to deliver *useful information* via *analyses*:
    o *Errors* (i.e., *inaccuracies* and *imprecisions*) imbedded in the original measurements that create data are *compounded* by additional downstream manipulations; these errors typically become *magnified* with increasing distance from their origins.

- *Analyses* using *inexact* or *improperly quantified* values cannot generate more determinate (i.e., clearer) information when the original information is *incompletely determinate* (i.e., unclear).
- If the *methods* used for measuring objects and events are *flawed*—or if they are a function of other *connections* that stand outside of what is being measured—then by measuring, we may simply be generating context-dependent approximations that are *misleading* at best and delusions at worst.
- The *predictability* of systems and their *understandability* depends on the degree of *accuracy* and *precision* in *measurement*:
  - Due to *limitations* in our ability to *measure quantities*, there is a fundamental *limit* to what we can *know* and, therefore, what is *predictable*.

10. Associations vs. Causality

- *Associations* represent *concordances* of objects and events (in *space*) or *sequenced aggregations* (in *time*) that "run together":
  - They can either exist in *space* (i.e., being arrayed *around* each other in *clusters*) or in *time* (by having some type of *sequence*, so that whenever one occurs, something else follows).
  - There is *no dependence* of one object or event on the others for it to exist or to occur (i.e., they do not influence each other).
- Often, *clustering* and/or *sequences* of objects or events can be misunderstood to suggest that one gives rise to another.
- *Causation* implies that one object, circumstance, or event has an effect that is *responsible for* (or engenders a *predisposition to*) another:
  - It often occurs over *time* (i.e., an object or event occurring now has an *impact* on others that occur later).
  - It can also occur among objects or events that exist *simultaneously* (i.e., something *existing now* has an effect that fosters the *contemporaneous existence* of something else).
- Causality is rooted in a mechanistic view of interactions (i.e., that *chains of events* or *causal webs*) operate that are either spatially or temporally related:
  - With causality, temporal *sequences of events* generate *trajectories*, such that one event determines the next, which determines

the next, and so on; this makes causality a requirement for *determinism*.
- o Without the occurrence of antecedent causal event(s), objects and events that are further "downstream" (in time) will not occur.
- The possibility of a causal relationship is typically gauged via its *plausibility* (i.e., "How is object (or event) *A* capable of causing object (or event) *B*?"):
  - o This evolves quickly into the idea of *mechanism*, which is addressed by *empirical science*.
  - o Causal relationships are often considered unproven until a *mechanism of interaction* between objects (and/or events) is identified.
- A *mechanism* of *interaction* is neither an absolute requirement for the presence of a causal relationship nor proof of it:
  - o Mechanisms that *connect* objects (or events) can be
    - *Unrecognized* (because the sensory apparatuses—either biological or mechanical—are simply not available to detect them)
    - *Inapparent initially* (despite being elucidated subsequently)
    - Ultimately determined to be *incorrect*.
- A *sequence* of *causal interactions* extends in *both temporal directions*—back into the past as well as into the future:
  - o *Mechanistic models* of causality imply chains (or webs) of events that
    - Extend backward in time in an *iterative regress* to a *first cause*
    - Extend forward in a sequence that is unbounded except for time itself.
- *Patterns* help us to anticipate what is *most likely to occur* in the future:
  - o We *learn* about our surroundings (and ourselves) by making *associations* between different objects and events and recognizing *patterns*.
- Depending on the *consistency, uniqueness,* and *persistence* of an *association* (i.e., a *pattern*), *sequences of events* can become very strongly ingrained *expectations*:

- o Rising *expectations* for patterns to repeat themselves can make us *conditioned* to accept them as the norm (e.g., Pavlovian-type conditioning).
- o *Consistent associations* can be characterized as a "habit"—a habitual set of associated objects or events.
- o Concluding that an antecedent event *caused* subsequent ones to occur from *patterns* alone would be wrong; patterns merely represent consistently repeated sequences.
- The *predictive value* of *associations* is *less* than for *causal relationships*.
- If two objects (or events) are intrinsically interdependent for their existences, but neither of them causes the other, they could be regarded (depending upon definition) as either:
  - o *Two separate objects* (or events), or
  - o *A single object* (or event) with multiple (internal) components.
- *Contemporaneous* objects or events that are *separate* and *not causally related* may still act *interdependently* to give rise to other objects and events (i.e., a greater combined structure).
- *Associations* and *causal relationships* are often *confused*, resulting in *errors*:
  - o Distinguishing associations from causal relationships can be difficult.
  - o If we rely only on empirical *observations* instead of testing specific hypotheses in an *interventional* fashion, distinguishing the veracity of one hypothesis over the other (association vs. causality) is often impossible.
  - o The *testing* paradigms of *empirical science* are crucial for making this distinction (i.e., using *interventional experiments* to *test hypotheses* that are *potentially falsifiable*).
- To distinguish (temporal) causality from associations, a rigorous schema has been developed to reflect the minimum evidence required to infer a causal relationship; nine considerations are derived from the criteria of Sir Austin Bradford Hill:

  A. **Temporal relationship** (the cause must precede the consequence)
  B. **Strength of association** (the correlation, relative risk, odds ratio, etc. should be large)

C. **Consistency** (the consequence should be seen to follow the cause repeatedly)
D. **Response gradient** (the strength of the consequence should be related to the strength of the cause, e.g., there should be an *intensity-response relationship*)
E. **Experimental evidence** (well-controlled experiments should support the cause-and-effect hypothesis)
F. **Specificity** (the consequence does not occur when the cause does not occur)
G. **Plausibility** (a mechanism—or pathway—can be envisioned whereby the cause could result in the consequence)
H. **Coherence** (the cause-and-effect relationship is consistent with other existing knowledge or evidence)
I. **Analogy** (the cause-and-effect relationship is similar to other known relationships that have been proven previously).

The first five criteria are most important and the remaining four are weaker. *Specificity* is reassuring, but it seldom occurs (i.e., there is often more than one "cause" that can precipitate a particular "outcome"; if it is absent, it does not necessarily weaken the case for a particular cause-and-effect relationship). *Plausibility* (i.e., a mechanism of interaction) can be falsely reassuring if present, and falsely undermining if it is undetectable or not yet discovered. *Coherence* and *Analogy* are both reassuring when present, but they are only inconsistently applicable because they cannot be present if a newly discovered relationship is "first-in-class".

- Associations do not permit the idea of *agency* (i.e., the capacity for *acting* to *exert influence* to achieve a particular end), whereas causality does.
- Dangers arise if *associations* (e.g., *clusters* or *patterns*) are mistaken for *causality*:
    o Relationships can be misconstrued, precipitating a flawed understanding.
    o Connections between objects and events can be presumed that do not exist.
    o A lack of connection between objects and events can be believed when one actually exists.

The consequences are:

- o We might believe that we can act to influence a downstream event when no such impact is even remotely possible.
    - We might commit time, energy, and resources to accomplish something that is impossible without even recognizing it—and be surprised when the outcome isn't what we thought.
- o We might believe that there is no causal relationship between objects or events and act to influence what we consider to be only an "innocent bystander" (i.e., one without any potential for downstream impact on the event of interest), only to precipitate unintended and distressing consequences.
- Before choosing to *act*, it is essential to determine if the *relationships* between objects and events are *causal* or simply *associations*:
    - o Otherwise there is a risk that we may go astray with an intervention, which might make *downstream iterations* of events evolve in ways that *cannot* be reasonably *predicted* or *controlled*.

11. Logic and Inference

- *Logic* is the term used to denote the process for making *inferences* from *two* or more *premises* (also known as *statements* or *axioms*).
- *Premises* are statements that comprise the substrates of arguments.
- *Logic* focuses on the *structure* (i.e., form) of arguments, *not* the *content* of the statements used as substrates (i.e., what the premises state).
- *Logical systems* are meant to ensure that inferences (i.e., *conclusions*) are *consistent* with starting *premises*:
    - o *Inferential systems* operate as follows: "If we accept these premises as true (at the outset), we can infer these *additional truths* as a result."
    - o This implies that the *additional truths* are *imbedded within* the greater truth of the original premises.
- For a logical system to be *valid*, if the *premises* are *true*, then the *inferences* derived by using them must also be *true*.

- *True premises* are *required* for a logical system to draw *legitimate conclusions* (these must be "fed in" at the *start*):
  o The *truth* of *starting premises* is left *unaddressed* by logical systems.
  o The *truth* of premises is established by methods external to the logical system itself; they are *assumed* to be *true* without proof (i.e., *given*).
  o The term *self-evident* is often used to establish the *truth* of *axioms*, meaning "evident without proof or reasoning"; but, self-evident to whom, under what conditions, within what context, etc. is left unspecified.
  o The question arises as to the reasons for our initial beliefs, as they fall beyond the realm of logic.
- If the truth of *premises* is *flawed*, then the truth of the *conclusions* derived by using formal logic will also be *flawed* (except if, by chance, we are very "lucky").
- Three *principles* allow *inferences* (i.e., *conclusions*) to be *derived mechanically* from *rules*, which are the underpinnings of classical (Aristotelian) logic:

   a. **Identity**: An object is the same as itself (i.e., "If a statement is true, then it is true") [a tautology].
   b. **Excluded middle**: For any proposition, either the proposition is true, or its negation is true (i.e., a statement must be either *true* or *false*).
   c. **Non-contradiction**: A statement cannot be both true and false at the same time (e.g., the two propositions "*A is B*" and "*A is not B*" are mutually exclusive).

- Optimally, logical systems should be able to generate *all true inferences* from (a minimal but *complete set* of) *true premises*.
- At a minimum, logical systems should ensure that all *conclusions* are *consistent* with starting *premises* (i.e., formal logic should not lead us incorrectly from an initial set of true premises to conclusions that are false):

- o If untrue conclusions were generated from true premises, this would lead to *paradoxes* (i.e., *contradictions*) that would undermine the system's validity.
- *Mathematics* is our most relied-upon system of formal inference:
  - o *Theorems* are *formal mathematical statements* that are *proven* based on previously accepted *axioms*.
  - o Tests have been performed to see if mathematics can generate *contradictions* (i.e., if it would violate the third rule of Aristotelian logic).
- *Paradoxes* have been identified that call into question the consistency of mathematics:
  - o To address this, the twentieth-century mathematician David Hilbert proposed that mathematical proofs be developed to
    - ensure that all mathematical *theorems* are based on a *finite* and *complete set* of *axioms*, and
    - demonstrate that *all* of the axioms are *consistent*.

  The goal is to assure the following minimum elements, which are viewed as essential to establish mathematics as an unassailable system of formal logic

  Formalization: All mathematical statements should be written in a *precise formal language* and manipulated according to a well-defined set of *rules*.

  Completeness: A proof is needed to demonstrate that *all* true mathematical statements are *provable* within the formalism.

  Consistency: A proof is necessary to show that *no contradiction* is possible within the formalism; this proof should use only *finite* reasoning (preferably) about finite mathematical objects.

  Decidability: An *algorithm* is necessary for deciding the *truth or falsity* of any mathematical statement.

- In 1931, Kurt Gödel showed via his *incompleteness theorems* that *any consistent theory* powerful enough to encode for the underpinnings of mathematics *cannot prove* its *own consistency*:
  - o Gödel showed the following with regard to Hilbert's goals

Formalization: It is *not possible* to *formalize all* of *mathematics*; any such attempt *omits* some *true mathematical statements*.

Completeness: Mathematical theories are necessarily *incomplete*; there is no complete, consistent extension of a recursively enumerable set of axioms.

Consistency: Even a simple mathematical theory (such as *arithmetic*) *cannot prove* its *own consistency*; a restricted finite subset of it cannot prove the consistency of any more powerful theories (e.g., set theory).

Decidability: *No algorithm exists* that can decide the *truth* (or *provability*) of statements in any consistent extension of arithmetic.

From this, it can be concluded that:

- *No consistent set* of *axioms* whose *theorems* can be listed by an *effective procedure* (i.e., an *algorithm* of the type that might be executed by a computer program) is *capable* of *proving all* the *facts about them*; there will *always* be *statements* that are *true* but that are *not provable* within the system (Gödel's first theorem).
- If such a system is also capable of proving certain basic facts about the premises, then a *particular truth* that the system *cannot prove* is the *consistency* of the *system itself* (Gödel's second theorem), meaning that there is a theoretical limit to the utility and applicability of logical systems.

What this implies (for all nontrivial logical systems) is:

- *If* a *logical system* is *consistent*, then it *cannot be complete* (i.e., there are true statements that lie outside of the system's ability to prove them).
- *If* a *logical system* is *complete*, then it *cannot be consistent* (i.e., there are statements that are both true and false within the system at the same time).
- Gödel's *theorems* undermine the validity of all known systems of formal logic:

- *Logical systems* used to infer (or deduce) additional (i.e., imbedded) truths about premises are fundamentally limited in their scope and applicability; they *cannot* be *both complete* and *consistent* at the same time.
  - If they are *consistent*, the implication is that they must necessarily be operating over a *limited domain* that does not consider outside factors.
  - If they are *complete*, they necessarily *embody intrinsic inconsistencies* that can lead from true premises to false conclusions.
- The Aristotelian premise of *exclusion of the middle* contends that everything can be dichotomized into either yes or no, true or false, is or is not, or this or that, etc.; it deliberately leaves no room for anything to bridge the gulf and to be *BOTH* this *and* that at the same time:
  - If there is *useful information* contained within the *excluded middle* (e.g., as might be the case for continuous variables), then the process of dichotomization into two opposing *big bucket* categories *discards* the *intervening information*.
  - There may be instances where objects and events are *both* "this and that" at once under the same conditions, without any contradiction, such that *exclusion of the middle* is an inaccurate reflection of reality.
- *Errors* can be *unrecognized* and *multiplied inadvertently* through subsequent (i.e., *iterative*) usage, making them larger, especially if there are no external standards (i.e., benchmarks) by which to judge outcomes:
  - Discarding even small amounts of information—as is done by *excluding the middle*—can result in unpredictable *downstream effects*.
  - For systems that are *unstable*, even small perturbations can *tip them over the edge* without warning, producing large effects that may be discontinuous.
- *Logical systems* of inference are often *useful*, but they are *flawed*:
  - All are prone to *errors*.
  - They can break down quickly and unexpectedly.

- They ultimately result in *uncertainty* in how we *assemble, categorize,* and *process* the *information* we are able to access about the universe.
- The ability of formal *logical systems* to make *accurate, unique,* and *complete predictions* based on starting premises is limited due to:
  - The uncertain means by which the *truth* of *initial premises* are established
  - The *incompleteness* of the *information* available for inference
  - *Inconsistencies* imbedded within the formalisms of logical systems themselves.

These factors, among others, severely limit the confidence we can have in all formal systems of logic.

12. Analysis

- *Analysis* dissects objects and events into their *component parts* to gain a better appreciation of how they behave by:
  - *Breaking them up* (either physically or mentally) into smaller parts (i.e., *constituents*), and
  - *Assessing* the *intrinsic nature* of the *components*, as well as their *relationships* and *interactions.*
- The process of analysis is designed to help us learn:
  - *How* objects and events are *internally organized*
  - *How* they *operate* and the nature of their *interactions* with other objects and events.
- Analysis can be used as a starting point to address *why* objects and events *exist* (i.e., *what* they *really are,* what they are *supposed to do,* and, ultimately, what they are *here for*—more than in only a functional sense).
- The intent of analysis is to provide a *launching point* for *understanding* by predicting system behavior and being able to construct like systems, so that they exist and behave similarly to what has been previously analyzed.
- Analytical approaches vary widely depending on the type, size, scope, and quality of available data, but for any type of *formal analysis,* a *set of rules* or *procedures* must be adopted:

- o *Formal analysis* requires the *step-by-step prescription* of a *well-defined list of procedures* (or operations) that describe how to proceed from a starting point (i.e., *inputs*) to an end result (i.e., *outputs*); this set of instructions is referred to as an *algorithm*.
  - o *Different* sets of rules are used as the working frame for different types of analyses, depending on the level of sophistication, degree of precision, and intent for the use of the outputs.
  - o *Different analytical rules* have the potential to generate *different results*.
  - o The rules that are chosen *define* the *scope* and *limitations* of analysis, as well as its *applicability*.
- Despite being *algorithmic, formal analysis* often *does not provide* well-defined *results* that are *stable, reproducible, reliable,* and *generalizable*:
  - o As a result, formal analysis often *cannot provide additional insights* to materially assist in making *accurate predictions* about the *future*.

13. Understanding

- *Understanding* has no completely satisfactory definition, but it can be tested functionally:
  - o We suppose that we have an *understanding* of objects and events and their relationships when we can *think them through* in advance of their actual occurrence and *predict* them correctly.
  - o The *functional assessment* of *understanding* requires the practical assessment of its *predictive utility*.
- *Functional tests* to assess if understanding is present depend on *observations* that are made *over time* and/or *space*:
  - o *Functional tests* provide an ongoing suggestion (but not a proof) of *validity* over the *local* domains that are tested (in both time and space).
  - o The *soundness* of understanding is based on a *rolling assessment* of predictive *accuracy*
    - This makes it transient and limited to domains that have been investigated in the past, rather than permanent and universal.

- It always has the potential to be undermined by the next test, making it both temporally and spatially constrained.
- *Predictions* flow from the application of *rules* to previously abstracted information, followed by projections to as-yet-uninvestigated circumstances; this relies on:
  o The application of *deductive reasoning* to known objects and events to establish *patterns* and *generalizations* to support overarching *concepts*
  o The use of *inductive reasoning* to apply predefined *concepts* to *like types* of objects and events at other times and/or places, and under different circumstances.
- *Understanding* is presumed if events can be *predicted* by:
  o The use of *prior knowledge* together with
  o The application of some type of a *process* (i.e., *analysis*).

To do this, two elements are required:

  o An *understanding* of *prior information*, and
  o *Application* (i.e., sound extension) of this understanding to *like situations* (in other places and/or at other times).
- When predictions concerning objects and events are *accurate*, we believe that we have a *proper understanding*; when predictions describe them *incorrectly*, we surmise that our understanding was *insufficient* (either wrong or incomplete).
- Understanding relies on consistent and interlocking (or interfacing) *concepts*, which provide the basis for *models* (i.e., *schemas* that can be *operationalized*).
- *Models* invoke *mechanisms* as *explanations*; these are typically reduced to a set of interaction *rules* within a prescribed domain:
  o *Models* are evaluated for their predictive *accuracy* with respect to objects and events that are *testable* and yet to be evaluated.
  o When predictions are inconsistent with observations, we no longer believe in a model's consistency and completeness (i.e., that at least in some circumstances it is incorrect), thereby undermining our presumption of proper understanding.
- To know if our understanding is *correct* (i.e., consistent and complete), an *infinite set* of *tests* would be necessary for all circumstances

in all potential environments to ensure its validity over all venues; unfortunately, this is not possible due to the constraints of both:
    o   *Limited time*, and
    o   The *ongoing evolution* (i.e., ever-changing nature) of the universe.
- *Human understanding*, no matter how broad we believe it to be, is always *local* and *limited*, with its validity extending only as far as the scope of its previous testing allows:
    o   It can be characterized as a set of *not-yet-violated beliefs, hypotheses,* and *operating principles* that are derived from, and limited in applicability to, *directly accessible realms* that are known—both in terms of spaces that have been interrogated, as well as to times that have already occurred.
    o   It is established by functional tests that can only be evaluated for validity with respect to local knowledge about *past* objects and events.
    o   It is not necessarily applicable to "other places" that we do not have access to or have not yet come across (i.e., inaccessible spaces and future times).
    o   Its validity with respect to future applicability—where we would like it to apply—is always in question and cannot be tested before the future actually occurs.
- *Algorithms* provide a formal approach to information processing and the manipulation of preexisting data:
    o   They represent sets of *rules* (or *procedures*) that embody *well-defined steps* (i.e., a structure) for the execution of processes to manipulate information that is "fed into" them.
    o   *Algorithmic processing* unfolds rigidly, but it may result in the ability to gain additional insights about preexisting information.
    o   The *outputs* from *algorithmic calculations* must be *appreciated* and *interpreted* by *sentient beings* outside of the rigid algorithmic framework.
- *Algorithmic calculations* can extend to domains that are *chaotic* (i.e., where the result could not have been predicted before executing the algorithm), thereby revealing something *new* that was not known previously:

- - Despite unveiling previously *unforeseen* results (from a *local perspective*), algorithms merely represent tools for doing so.
  - *Algorithms do not* themselves *understand* anything by having *cranked through* their processes, regardless of their level of sophistication.
- Attempting to extend *human understanding* into realms *other than local* ones (such as *inaccessible spaces* and *future times*) constitutes nothing more than *unfounded conjecture*—a mere *hope* of universalizability based on the assumption that what we already know will have applicability to other realms that we don't:
  - This presumption—no matter how consistently applicable our understanding might have been to other places and to times past—is always *without adequate foundation* for places and times that have not yet been investigated.
  - The *applicability* of our understanding to *other places* and *other times* can *never be proven* or guaranteed until they are actually reached.

14. Deductive vs. Inductive Reasoning

- *Deduction* (also called *deductive logic*) involves the construction of arguments to demonstrate that particular *conclusions follow necessarily* from a *set* of (*preexisting*) *premises*.
- *Deductive arguments* are based on information regarding events and circumstances that have *already occurred*.
- *Deduction* uses *logical connectives* that *combine, contrast, order,* and/or *equate* the *information* contained in premises; these connectives are presumed to be *inert*.
- Deduction is *valid* only if *conclusions follow properly* from its *premises*.
- A *deductive argument* is either *valid* or *invalid* (which relates to its *structure*) and, if valid, either *sound* or *unsound* (which relates to both its *structure* and *content*).
- The *conclusions* of an argument are *sound* (i.e., *true*) only if:
  - It is *valid* (in terms of its *structure*), and
  - Its *premises* are *true* (in terms of their *content*).

- *Deductive logic* provides nothing *new* in terms of *additional information*:
    - The *total pool* of *information* of a deductive argument is *fixed* and *imbedded* in its *premises*, which provides the *content* for its conclusions.
        - A deductive argument's *pool* of *information* in is either *flat* (i.e., does not discard any of the original information contained in the premises) or *diminished* (i.e., it may discard some of its original informational elements to *focus* on a more limited *subset*).
        - When any of the original information is *discarded*, it necessarily *adversely affects* the *consistency* of what remains.
- *Deduction* is entirely *algorithmic*:
    - The process of deduction *recasts* or *reformulates* the information contained within the original premises into *alternative formats* that can be *more readily interpreted* and/or *applied* to particular situations.
    - Nothing new can be invented by invoking the deductive process; therefore, it *cannot be used* to *gain new knowledge*.
- Deduction *organizes* information about objects and events into *classes* that can be teased apart into independent elements:
    - *Classes* are defined by sets of *properties*, regardless of whether they are real (i.e., physically measureable) or imaginary.
    - *Classes* can be *deconstructed* and then *reconstructed* to fit some newly devised sets of categories by *reshuffling* the preexisting information into other categories that are consistent with the original ones (i.e., the information can be mapped from one set of categories to another).
    - *Consistency* is assumed because of the *process*, which depends on the *validity* of the logical constructs and the *truth* of the *premises*.
- *Deductive logic* is *sound* only for what is already *known*:
    - Deduction has *no direct applicability* to the *future*, which is necessarily *unknown* because it has not yet occurred.
- *Inductive reasoning* (also known as *inductive logic*) is essentially identical in structure to deduction, but its *substrates* (i.e., its premises) are fundamentally *different*:

- In *deductive* reasoning, the *substrates* (i.e., contents) arise from *specifics* that are *observed* and *well-investigated*.
- In *inductive* reasoning, the *substrates* arise from *general concepts* derived from *past trends* and *patterns* (i.e., they are gleaned from and summarize previously observed individual instances).
- *Inductive reasoning*:
  - Begins with *generalizations* (i.e., *patterns* based on *previous experiences* and *past trends*)
  - Applies its arguments to *hypothetical specifics* (i.e., premises) that have *not yet been encountered* and for which there is no direct evidence of their applicability.
- *Inductive reasoning* is philosophically nuanced:
  - The *premises* of an inductive argument indicate *some degree* of *support* (*inductive probability*) for the *conclusions*, but they *do not* entail them (i.e., they *suggest* the truth, but they *do not ensure it*).
  - *Probability* is invoked as the justification for moving from generalizations to (hypothetical) individual instances; this process is less rigorous than for deductive logic and depends on two additional beliefs about what has not yet been observed for "like occurrences"
    - That they will be *qualitatively the same* (or similar) to those that were *already investigated*
    - That they will be *quantitatively the same* (or *similar*) to what was *previously observed* to within a certain *degree of likelihood* (i.e., *probability*).
  - In essence, it assumes that the future will be very much like the past, which must be accepted *without proof*.
  - *Predictions* are ultimately predicated on a belief that past and current circumstances can be reliably projected forward into the future.
- *Inductive logic* reaches different types of conclusions than deduction:
  - Its *conclusions* are founded on the *likelihood* that what is already known about the universe will *remain stable* for what is yet to be investigated.
  - It attempts to place *confidence limits* around predictions concerning objects and events that have not yet been observed.

- o The *assumptions* made by *inductive reasoning* can be summarized as follows: "If the *universal platform* upon which we operate is *more-or-less the same* in the future as it was in the past (i.e., there is *"platform stability"* that can be counted on despite ongoing changes in the universe), then we can assume that some types of objects and events that we observed in the past will be *likely to happen* in the same or a *similar way* again in the *future.*"

This line of argument is circular—it does nothing more than predict the stable behavior of events in the future by making an assumption of future stability in the first instance.

- *Inductive logic* does not provide much insight or comfort when used to predict the future; at best, it can be used as a guide to state that: "Circumstances in the future will unfold with this type of a *pattern* and with this degree of *probability* if they are anything like what has been observed in the past."
- *Inductive reasoning* represents a *hope-filled extension* of the methods employed by deductive logic:
  - o It reduces to an *appeal to wisdom* for *projecting past trends* into the *future* with some *degree of confidence* (i.e., a reasonable *likelihood* or *probability*).

15. Generalizability: Internal vs. External Validity

- *Proving* anything about the universe necessarily entails *isolating* a portion of it for examination.
- *Isolation* involves taking a *sample* of what we are interested in:
  - o *Isolation* provides a *tractable scope* of investigation.
  - o If what we want to investigate is connected to everything else, the required scope of interrogation would be limitless, making it impossible.
- When a *sample* is taken, the hope is that it will be representative of more than just what has been subdivided off; if so, it provides the potential to *generalize* the results that are uncovered to other *like systems.*
- *Internal validity* vs. *external validity*:

- o *Internal validity* refers to our *confidence* that the *measurements* of objects and events in an *isolated sample* of a *system* of interest are *accurate, correct,* and *reproducible* (i.e., not serendipitous), such that we believe that what has been demonstrated is *true*.
- o *External validity* refers to our *confidence* that the *results* found for an *isolated sample* of a *system* are *generalizable* to the entire (original) system as well as to *other like systems* (those that are separate and similar, but not identical), despite that they
  - Have *not* been *measured directly*, and
  - May *still* be *connected* to their *surrounding environment*.
- *External validity* depends on the concept of *generalizability*, which can be thought of functionally as precisely the *opposite* of sampling:
  - o Whereas *sampling splits apart* larger entities into smaller parts that are hoped to be representative of their larger wholes, *generalization aggregates* smaller and often disparate pieces together to create larger wholes (generally assuming that the rules and relationships that applied to the different pieces are preserved).
- When results are externally valid, it means that local findings can be *generalized*, so that *outcomes* for systems of interest can be *predicted* when *no direct measurements* about them are *available*:
  - o This is not only for the like systems at the present time, but also for such systems that existed in the *past* (about which we typically have no direct knowledge) and for those that will exist in the *future* (for which measurements cannot yet be made).
- *Generalization* is a *powerful tool* if its limits are properly appreciated:
  - o The accuracy and precision of generalizations can only be guaranteed through the present time (i.e., to where the last test system was examined); the findings will *not necessarily hold* for the *next sample* from *another place* or in the *future* (i.e., they may not be time and space invariant).
  - o *Generalization* encompasses the idea of *external validity*.
    - It cannot be justified theoretically.
    - It is prone to *error* in a practical sense.
- The *ability* to *generalize* (i.e., to infer *external validity*) should be considered *most applicable* at a *local level*; when objects and events are farther away—either in space or in time—generalizations can be misleading (at best) and sometimes frankly incorrect (at worst):

- The *closer* an *untested system* is to *one* that has been *measured* and *well-characterized*—in terms of its *design, size,* and *energy,* as well as its *temporospatial proximity* to systems that have been tested—the *more likely* the *generalization* of *known results* to the *untested system* will be.

16. Computability: Algorithmically Definable Calculations

- *Computability* and *determinism* are different, but they are often confused:
  - It is *possible* that the universe is entirely *deterministic,* but that its *future* and *past states* are *not computable* (i.e., cannot be *calculated*).
- *Determinism* is framed by the question: "Given the current state of the universe, is every prior state and every future state *completely determined*?"
  - If so, regardless of whether we know the precise rules governing the progression of events from one set of circumstances to the next, *everything* is completely *immutable*—the *past, present,* and the *future.*
  - If not, then there is room for *variance* in the *phenomena* and *events* that occur from *one well-defined juncture* (i.e., *state*) of the universe to *another.*
- *Computability* is framed by the question: "Given the current state of the universe, is its state at any future (or past) point in time *calculable*?"
  - To determine if the states of the universe are *calculable* depends first on whether it is describable *algorithmically.*
    - *Algorithms* are *step-by-step procedures* for making *calculations* that are expressed as a *finite list* of *well-defined instructions.*
- If the universe is *algorithmic,* then:
  - It is possible to describe a set of *steps* (i.e., *procedures* or equations) to *crank through* a *process* that (mechanically) allows for the *precise description* of any *past* or *future state,* starting from a description of only its current *state* (i.e., its present condition).
  - If this is so, it *may* be *computable,* but if it is not algorithmically describable, then its computability is *not a possibility.*

- If there is an *algorithmic set* of *operations* that can be *executed* to arrive at a description of the universe's past and future states, the next question is: "Can this be accomplished within a *finite period of time?*"
    - If so, then it *may* be *computable*; but if not, then the results of the calculation will never be available, and computability is *not a possibility.*
- If an algorithmic set of calculations can be executed to arrive at a description of the universe's *future states* within a *finite period* of *time*, then another question arises: "Is it *possible* to arrive at these results *before* the *universe gets to those points* itself?"
    - If so, then the results are *computable* and (at least potentially) *knowable* before the events occur, making them practically as well as theoretically relevant
    - If not, then the results will be *impossible* to compute *before* they *actually unfold*; this would obviate their having any predictive value, such that they would have no practical utility.
- The utility of computations depends on the *speed* with which *calculations* can be *made* relative to the speed at which the universe advances from one state to the next:
    - *Both* may be defined (and *limited*) by the inviolable *speed of light*.
    - It is possible that *no calculation* regarding *future states* of the *universe* is *possible* at a *speed faster* than the *universe itself evolves*.
- *Parallel processing* (i.e., performing multiple *simultaneous calculations*) at *sub-light speeds* might be considered to arrive at calculated results for future states at *faster than light speed*; however, two limitations preclude this:
    - *Summing* the results of *multiple operations* that occur at *sub-light speeds* can *never exceed* the *speed of light* in their composite (i.e., the *speed of light* is an *inviolable absolute speed* for *all observers* that *cannot be exceeded*).
    - Even if sufficient resources could be focused to perform a *faster-than-light calculation* using *parallel processing* in a *particular venue* (i.e., to "win" by performing a calculation to predict particular aspects of the future faster than they unfold), this approach is *not universalizable*.

- - The use of resources to perform such a calculation in one venue necessarily *limits* the *remaining resources* to perform other such calculations elsewhere
    - There aren't enough "duplicate resources" to "go around" and execute the parallel processing approach everywhere.
  - This makes it impossible to process all the information we have at *faster-than-light* speed to predict everything about future states simultaneously everywhere.
  - Since *faster-than-light calculation cannot be universalized*, this makes all predictions of future states *incomplete* and, therefore, necessarily *inconsistent*.
- If the universe is *deterministic* but its precise set of past and future states is *not calculable*, this would have the effect of rendering the idea of determinism to predict the future *moot*:
  - Despite being *deterministic*, *past* and *future states* would be *unknowable* to anyone aside from those *actually present* (i.e., those with the capacity to make direct measurements of the particular state of affairs at the time).
- *Calculation*, although possible and sometimes quite practical, often provides little insight for predicting the future in ways that we want: *in advance*, with a *high degree* of *certainty*, and with the *ability* to *manipulate current circumstances* to *change future outcomes* so that they will better comport with our wishes.

17. Continuity (Smoothness) vs. Discontinuity (Roughness)

- *Continuity* encompasses the notion of incremental change and, with that, *predictability*.
- *Discontinuity* encompasses the notion of rapid change and (the potential for) *unpredictability*.
- *Accurate predictions* depend on the *universe's* natural predisposition toward *continuity* (smoothness) versus *discontinuity* (roughness):
  - If the universe behaves in a *continuous* fashion, then sequences of events have the potential to be *predictable*.
  - If the universe harbors *discontinuities*, then sequences of events have the potential to be *unpredictable* wherever these occur.

- Any *pockets* of *continuity* necessarily exist over only certain *limited domains* of *space* and *time*; beyond these, discontinuities naturally predispose toward *unpredictability*.
- *Empirical data* suggest that *discontinuities* are *widespread* in the universe:
    o There are sudden *breaks* in system behaviors—social, economic, scientific, personal, etc.—that are characterized by abrupt and irrevocable transitions.
    o Examples range from earthquakes, to erupting volcanos, to buildings destroyed by tornados, to the disjointed actions of unstable governments, to financial markets that lose value precipitously, to exploding supernovas, to people who die from one moment to the next.
- An important discovery regarding the *smoothness* of the universe was made by Jules-Henri Poincaré in the nineteenth century:
    o *Energetic descriptions* of a large portion of ordinary *dynamical systems* (i.e., those described by Newtonian mechanics) are *non-integrable*—meaning that they are *not smooth*; this implies that
        - *Discontinuities* in our universe are *commonplace*.
        - The idea that *sequences of events* evolve according to smooth and predictable transitions applies only in a *subset of cases*.
    o The *trajectories* of systems with discontinuities through *space* and *time* are *not predictable* in any mathematically precise way.
        - The *behavior* of many systems describable by classical dynamics is *incapable* of *being predicted* in a well-defined, accurate way.
- *Discontinuities* undermine the *validity* of our attempts to *project trends* (i.e., *trajectories*) from the past through the present and into the future.
    o Because of *widespread discontinuities* in our universe, there is an *endemic potential* for *unpredictability*.

18. Stability vs. Instability: System Inertia and Resiliency

- *Stable systems* are those where *perturbations* may *disturb* their *organization* and *dynamics temporarily*, but the *tendency* is for them to *return* to their *original state* over time.
- *Unstable systems* are those where *small perturbations* result in even *larger changes*, such that the *final state* of the system is *different* from where it began.
- Many mathematical functions describing the evolution (i.e., *trajectory*) of classic *dynamical systems* (i.e., those defined by Newtonian mechanics) are *non-integrable*, meaning that they have *discontinuities* that predispose them to *unpredictability*:
  o *Trajectories* (i.e., paths) can be categorized as either *nice* (i.e., *integrable* and *deterministic*) or *random* (i.e., *non-integrable* and *irregular, wandering*, and *unpredictable*).
  o *Non-integrable trajectories* are often a consequence of *system resonances*.
    - These arise due to the *internal interactions* of different *system components*.
    - As the *energy* of a system increases, the number (and density) of *system resonances* is also increased, augmenting the probability that *immediately neighboring trajectories* will *diverge*.
    - Adjacent *trajectories* that *diverge* can give rise to discontinuities and *unpredictable behavior*.
- *System resonances* constitute an *emergent phenomenon*; they are intrinsically *non-local* and arise from the entire system, not from any one portion of it (i.e., they constitute an overall system phenomenon of *complex systems*):
  o *System resonances* provide *feedback* at the *local level* of all the *individual internal system trajectories* that gave rise to it.
  o This effectively *couples* all *system elements* into a *single whole*.
  o *Feedback* at the local level places a *limit* on the *precision* with which the *position* and *momentum* of *any individual system element* can be known.
  o This *limits* the degree of *confidence* we can have for making *predictions*.

- *Complex systems* are ubiquitous in the universe, making *system resonance* widespread:
  - Attempting to analyze the *multiple trajectories* of *interacting components* in a *complex system* in an individual fashion is bound to failure.
  - Whenever system resonances occur, the result of any sequence of events can be thought of as targeting a zone (i.e., a *zone of probability*) rather than any particular point.
- Success in making accurate *predictions* about the future depends on whether systems are *stable* or *unstable*; to establish this, the following must be assessed:
  - The *stability* of the current system
  - What the *effects* of *system resonances* will be (i.e., if they will direct trajectories in a convergent or divergent manner)
  - If *current trajectories* will *remain stable* when projected into the future.
- With *stability*, there is at least a *chance* that the *evolution* of events will be *predictable*, whereas with *instability*, no *accurate predictions* concerning the future are possible.

19. Dynamical Certainty vs. Uncertainty: Trajectories

- *Dynamics* describes the *evolution* of *physical systems* over *time*; it requires knowledge of the *positions* of *objects*, as well as the *forces* that act upon them.
- *Trajectories* describe the *positions* of physical bodies as they change over *time*:
  - They are *predicted* based on the application of *physical laws* (i.e., universal rules) to physical entities (i.e., *bodies*).
- *Dynamics* represents an example of a *deterministic model* for describing the *evolution* of *events*:
  - *Dynamical certainty* depends on *infinite accuracy* and *precision* in defining the *starting conditions* of system elements (i.e., their positions and momenta).
    - *Small changes* in *initial conditions* can lead to increasingly exaggerated *deviations* from expected trajectories over

time; with multiple iterations, these errors may compound, leading to increased *dynamical uncertainty*.
- For systems that are intrinsically *unstable*, if starting conditions are not certain, this can lead to *nonlinear divergences* in *trajectories*.
- *Classical dynamical formulations* have *no preferred direction* in time:
  o This is *inconsistent* with our collective observation of an *arrow of time* that monotonically directs the unfolding of events in a forward direction.
  o It *violates* a cardinal tenant of *causality*: that specific objects and events (*causes*) serve as antecedents to other events (*consequences*) and not the other way around (i.e., that consequences are responsible for precipitating the objects and events that caused them in the first place).
  o Reversibility in classical dynamics arises because of three major *idealizations*.
    - *Bodies* that occupy space are represented as mere *points*
    - *Masses* and the *forces* that act upon them are defined with *absolute certainty* (i.e., with *absolute accuracy* and *precision*), and
    - *Energy* is treated as a *continuously variable* quantity (i.e., something that is not quantized).
    All of these are approximations that cause the accuracy of dynamical models to break down.
- *Higher-level* (i.e., *non-local*) *effects* must be accounted for to describe the evolution of *real events* instead of appealing to only single, isolated trajectories:
  o These arise from unavoidable *interactions* among system components that give rise to *resonances* that have *non-local* system effects.
  o They *entangle* every system component with every other.
- The following pattern of *internal interactions* occurs in all real *systems*:
  o Single (i.e., intrinsic) component trajectories combine with
  o Other system component trajectories to create
  o Resonant effects that influence the whole system and provide
  o Individualized feedback to all the contributing system elements

- o Each of which contributed to originating the overarching system-wide resonant effects in the first place.

This pattern generates *temporal asymmetry* and *time directionality* in a natural way, preventing events from being spontaneously reversible.
- *Classical dynamics* relies on *idealizations* that are not a proper reflection of the universe; this makes it *incapable* of *predicting future events* with the *level of certainty* we would like.

20. Thermodynamics: Laws Prohibiting the Spontaneous Reversibility of Physical Events

- *Thermodynamics* deals with the relationship between *heat transfer* (a form of energy exchange) and the amount of *energy* that can be *extracted* from a physical system to do *work*.
- *Spontaneous heat transfer* results in the liberation of *free energy* (i.e., energy that is not bound up in any other form), so that it is *available for use* by other systems:
  - o *Free energy* derived from one system can be used to *drive* sequences of *events* energetically "uphill" elsewhere (i.e., in a direction that would not occur spontaneously otherwise).
  - o Liberated *free energy* has the potential to perform *useful work* on the *surroundings*.
- Real *events* (i.e., those that are *spontaneous*) occur because they produce new states that are *energetically favored* (i.e., *contain less energy*) relative to past ones:
  - o When systems make the *spontaneous transition* from a *higher-energy* to a *lower-energy state*, there is the unavoidable production of *entropy*.
- *Entropy* arises naturally as a concept from the *second law of thermodynamics*:
  - o It occurs because there are *many more ways* for system components to be *disordered* than ordered.
    - This makes the *probability* of finding a set of *system* components in a spontaneously *ordered state* lower than for a more *disordered* one.

- *Ordered states* (those with *lower entropy*) contain more extractable energy compared with more disordered ones (those with *higher entropy*).
    - Since *ordered states* are a relative rarity, they are *energetically more difficult* to *create* and *maintain* compared to those that are *disordered*.
    - A portion of the *energy contained* within *ordered systems* is *liberated* when they become more disorganized; this allows *ordered states* to act as an effective *reservoir* for *free energy*.
    - It is relatively easy for ordered states to become disordered (with the *release* of *free energy*), but the opposite requires *work*; it takes the *expenditure* of (external) *energy* to arrive at *organized states*.
- The amount of *work expended* to *create* the degree of *organization* inherent to a system is reflected by the sum of its *potential energy* and *internal energy*.
- The *difference* in *energy content* between an *ordered* and a *disordered* system *prevents it* from *spontaneously evolving* from a *disordered state* to an *ordered* one:
    - The "*spontaneous organization*" of real systems is possible, but it requires that even more disorganization be created in the surrounding environment (i.e., that there is an *overall net entropy increase* for the entire universe).
- *Entropy ensures* that the *forward progression* of *time* cannot be reversed:
    - As *real events* unfold spontaneously, the total amount of *entropy* in the universe *increases* (i.e., the sum of the entropy for *all* systems, including the surrounding environment).
    - All real systems *evolve spontaneously* from *lower to higher entropy*, making it impossible for them to collectively run in reverse to make events occur backward; this constrains *time* to *advance* in only *one direction*—forward.
        - Because there is a *monotonic increase* in the *overall entropy* of the universe, there is no way to make everything exactly as it was in the past; *something must always be different*, which collectively constitutes the universe's spontaneous forward evolution.

- The *complete isolation* of any real system *cannot be realized*:
    - There is always *cross-communication* between different regions of the universe that are not at *equal temperature* due to the unavoidable exchange of *black-body radiation*; this makes *complete system isolation impossible.*
- The *second law of thermodynamics* ensures that the *arrow of time* (i.e., *time directionality*) remains intact:
    - *Entropy increases* with the occurrence of *all spontaneous real processes.*
    - This ensures that all *future states* of the universe must necessarily be *different* from *past states.*
    - This is comforting, because it *prohibits reverse causality* (i.e., the *reversibility* of *real events*) from ever being a possibility.

21. Quantum Theory: Uncertainties of the Very Small

- *Very small physical quantities* come in minimally sized units or *packets* (called *quanta*) that are *discrete* and *not further divisible*:
    - *Quanta* exist only in one *well-defined amount* or in the next available *step* that is either above or below that level—nothing in between.
- Items that are *quantized*:
    - Can only take on values that are *separated* from each other by an *intervening gap* (i.e., in space, time, energy, etc.).
    - Behave in a *jerky* way in terms of both their quantities and transitions from one value to the next, because they "*jump*" from one value to another.
- "Quantum is to continuous" what "digital is to analog":
    - In both cases, the former is *discrete* with a *distinct boundary* to define its full extent, whereas the latter varies in a *flowing, non-disjointed, smooth,* and *subdividable* way.
- *Quantum mechanics* is a widely tested theory of very small, discrete quantities:
    - It accurately predicts the otherwise inexplicable experimental results that involve submicroscopic objects and events.
    - It is the *most consistently correct theory* ever developed.
    - It results in a number of baffling *paradoxes*.

- The *Heisenberg uncertainty principle* posits that there is a *fundamental limit* to the *accuracy* with which certain *pairs* of *physical properties* can be *known simultaneously*, such as the position and momentum of a particle:
    - The *more precisely one property* is measured, the *less precisely* the *other* can be known, determined, or controlled.
    - This limitation is *intrinsic* to the fabric of physical reality and not a mere artifact of the incomplete information that we have about it.
    - It *limits* the *accuracy* of *predictions* concerning *future events* because
        - The *knowledge* we can have about *physical quantities* is fundamentally limited, making them *intrinsically uncertain*.
        - *Trajectories* can *never* be *predicted more accurately* than the *original accuracy* of a system's *initial conditions*.
- *Quantum theory* provides an additional explanation for the *irreversibility* of *natural processes* (i.e., the *forward direction* of *time's arrow*):
    - Because of the *intrinsic uncertainty* in the specification of the *initial conditions* for any physical system, there is *uncertainty* in the *forward trajectory* of *events* as well as for *trajectories* that operate in the *backward direction* (i.e., if one would try to reverse the sequence step by step).
        - With any attempt to reverse the direction of events, there are *many more non-overlapping trajectories* compared with the one set that overlaps the forward-and-reverse trajectories precisely.
        - Accordingly, the *likelihood* of the *forward* and *backward trajectories overlapping perfectly* to reestablish the initial conditions (which due to Heisenberg's uncertainty principle cannot be precisely defined in any case) is *extremely low*.
    - It is not possible to spontaneously reverse series of events precisely without adding external energy to a system (i.e., to constrain the reverse trajectory to one particular pathway rather than to others), which violates the premise of spontaneity.
- Due to *quantum uncertainty*, there is a limit in our ability:
    - To *know* beyond a certain *degree of accuracy* the *precise state* of the *initial conditions* for any *physical system*

- o To *know* the precise *magnitude* and *direction* of the forces acting upon any system element
- o To *define trajectories* that *can accurately predict future events,* and
- o To *intervene* to *influence events* in a way that is *predictable.*

22. Entanglement vs. Separability: The Locality Issue

- *Quantum theory* posits that persistent *quantum entanglement* exists for *particles* that have *interacted* and then separated:
  - o *Quantum entanglement* asserts that there is a (*non-local*) *connection* among seemingly separate (i.e., locally discrete) objects and events.
  - o This precludes any object or event from being separate from everything else.
- To address the issue of *non-locality,* John Bell derived what is known as *Bell's theorem* in 1964:
  - o Two basic *assumptions* underpin *Bell's theorem*
    - *Reality exists* (i.e., microscopic *objects* have a *definite state* that *defines* the *values* of *all real properties* determining the outcomes of quantum mechanical measurements, which is independent of their being observed), and
    - *Objects exist locally* (i.e., *reality* is *not influenced* by *measurements performed* simultaneously at *large distances*); if observers are sufficiently far apart, a measurement made by one can have no effect on a measurement made by the other.
  - o If the degree of *correlation* between the *properties* of *distant particles* stems from *local random variables,* there is a *limit* to *how much correlation can exist* unless they somehow continue to interact (in a way that is not known).
    - This is assumed because general relativity states that objects *cannot exchange information* at *faster* than the *speed of light.*
- All potential *hidden variables* are encompassed by *Bell's theorem* (i.e., including those that are unknown or inapparent).

- Experiments have shown consistent *violations* of the inequality of *Bell's theorem*:
  o These *violations* indicate that *at least one* (or both) of the *two assumptions underlying* Bell's theorem is *wrong*, meaning that
    - *Reality* is somehow *observer dependent* (i.e., the *physically measurable properties* of *objects* are *not intrinsic to them*, but are somehow *dependent* on their *being observed*), or
    - *Objects* (and *events*) are not *separable* (i.e., all objects—and events—are somehow *connected*).
  o Accordingly, the *concreteness* of *physical reality* (as most of us think of it) seems *untenable*, and the probabilistic description of reality provided by *quantum theory* appears to be more correct.
- Most physicists interpret the experimental results that violate Bell's inequality as *undermining* the *validity* of *local realism*; this is disturbing, because it means that:
  o An *objective local reality does not exist* independent of its being observed (which is a standard interpretation by quantum theory), and
  o *Everything is connected to everything else* (in a way that is not understood)—regardless of *where* it is (i.e., no matter how far away it is in terms of distance) and *when* it is (no matter how far distant it is in the past or into the future!).
  o This implies that functionally, everything in the universe is part of a *single, inseparable,* and *non-subdividable* system that *encompasses everything* that exists (i.e., all objects and events) in *all directions* and at *all distances* of *space* and *time.*
- This means that *attempting* to *investigate* any part of the universe in *isolation* with the hope of drawing conclusions about any *local reality* is only an *approximation:*
  o Such *local approximations* generate artificially *truncated, incomplete,* and *inconsistent views* of *reality* that are ultimately bound to *misinterpretation, misunderstanding,* and *failure* (in both a conceptual and functional sense).

23. Many Worlds: Parallel Universes as an Explanation for Quantum Paradoxes

- The *many worlds* interpretation of quantum theory hypothesizes that many other *parallel universes* exist in addition to our own.
- *Parallel universes* have no connection:
  - There is *no way* for them to exchange *energy*, *matter*, or *information* (i.e., *nothing can get there from here* and vice versa).
  - Because there is *no physical ability* to *communicate* with objects and events in these other space-times, they are *outside of our universe* due to their total inability to influence anything that we can access.
- Each *parallel universe* has a different history and can evolve in divergent ways due to the *alternative unfoldings* of events:
  - *Alternatives* result from *decoherence* of the superposition of solutions to the universal *wavefunction* (the *Schrödinger equation*) at each point in time.
- The *many worlds* interpretation asserts that the *universe we know* is an *objective* and *real consequence* of the quantum mechanical *universal wavefunction*, but:
  - There is *no necessity* for *observation-triggered collapse* of the wavefunction, as each alternative solution is realized in a parallel universe.
  - It *avoids* the *collapse* of the *wavefunction* into a *single reality*.
  - It accepts that *all possible realities* (i.e., all alternative past histories, all presents, and all futures) are *real*, with each of them embodied in an actual universe (i.e., a *world*) that *exists objectively*, but *entirely separately*.
- The set of parallel universes constitutes a fantastically large number of all possible permutations of the solutions to the Schrödinger wavefunction over time:
  - Each universe embodies an *objective reality* that is *different* but *just as real* as every other—they simply exist in parallel.
- The *many worlds* theory eliminates the difficulty that quantum physics has in explaining the collapse of the wavefunction into a single reality:

- o It is one of a number of *decoherence theories* that has become a mainstream interpretation of quantum theory along with the longstanding Copenhagen interpretation.
- o It removes both randomness and observer-dependence as explanations for the reduction of the wavefunction into a *single reality*.
  - ▪ For every quantum event with a non-zero probability of being an alternative outcome, *all* of these outcomes *actually occur*, with each occurring in a *different parallel universe*.
- o We are only *aware* of the *one outcome* that occurs in our universe, because it is the one to which we have access.
- The *many worlds* theory reconciles the observation of apparent *non-deterministic events* with the *deterministic equations* of *quantum physics*, all *without* employing any notion of *chance* or *probability*:
  - o This *resolves quantum correlation paradoxes* (such as the EPR paradox and Schrödinger's cat), since *every possible outcome* of *every event* actually *exists* in its own *world*.
- The *many worlds* interpretation changes quantum theory's view of reality:
  - o Before *many worlds*, quantum theory viewed reality as a *single past*, a *single present*, and a *single future yet to unfold*.
  - o With *many worlds*, quantum theory views reality as being analogous to a *branching tree*, where *every possible quantum outcome* has actually *been realized* (in the *past*), *is realized* (in the *present*), and *will be realized* (in the *future*).
  - o Despite this, there is *only one* universe that we have *access to* and that we know about: the *particular one where we find ourselves*.

24. Chaos Theory: Implications for Macroscopic Predictability

- *Chaos theory* addresses the idea that *very small changes* in the *inputs* to a *complex system* can *drastically change* its *outputs*.
- *Chaotic behavior* was first discovered in 1961 by the meteorologist Edward Lorenz; its implications are wide-ranging and apply to the majority of real systems:

- *Chaotic behavior* occurs routinely in *complex systems* that have numerous components, especially those having nonlinear interactions.
- Even if the trajectories of complex systems can be calculated, they are still *not predictable* in advance of their computation.
- Because it is completely deterministic, the type of chaotic behavior referred to here is called *deterministic chaos*.

• *Chaotic behavior* occurs due to the *extreme sensitivity* of complex systems to their *initial conditions*:
- It *does not* arise from either *random variation* or *random inputs* that are unpredictable or unknown.
- *Everything* about chaotic systems is *accounted for* (at least to within the physically allowable quantum limits of accuracy and precision).

• *Nothing is confused* about *chaotic systems*; despite this, *long-term predictions* are *impossible*, except in a *general way*:
- To describe their behavior, chaotic systems have *broad targets* called *attractors* (these are essentially *weighted probabilities* that describe where system outputs will most likely *hover*).
- The *rules* for *estimating how complex systems* will *evolve* represent a macroscopic analogue of what quantum mechanical probability densities are on a submicroscopic scale.
- Exactly where the system will wind up at any given juncture is not predictable until either a direct observation or a complete calculation is made.

• *Chaotic systems* represent an *extreme example* of dynamic *instability*:
- In such systems, the *trajectories* associated with distinct initial conditions *diverge*, no matter how close they are to each other.
- *Small changes* in *initial conditions* become exaggerated and are *amplified* over time.

• *Dynamical chaos* can be encountered in systems that are otherwise stable when particular *thresholds* have been exceeded in a system's initial conditions, such that a newly entered starting domain is different from the one that preceded it on the other side of the *small difference*; in such cases:
- Dynamics are *smooth* and *predictable* on one side of the starting threshold, but on the other side a *chaotic domain* is entered

where the *effect sizes* associated with the small changes are *unsmooth* and *unpredictable*.
  - *Outputs* and behaviors may *fluctuate wildly*, but always in a deterministic fashion.
- *Chaotic behavior* has the potential to occur in all *complex systems*:
  - Most *real systems* are *complex*.
  - *Chaotic domains* are *widespread* and *routinely affect* the *behavior* of *real systems*.
- *Chaos theory* is necessary to *understand complex systems*:
  - In direct analogy to what occurs at quantum scales, the *degree* to which *macroscopic trajectories* can be *projected forward* (into the future) or *backward* (into the past) is *limited* by *chaotic domains* where the smoothness and *continuity assumptions* about real systems *break down*.
- *Chaotic domains* pose a *fundamental limit* to what can be *predicted* by projecting the *trajectory* of prior *event sequences* into the future:
  - They *reduce* our *knowledge* concerning the universe to only *generalities* and *trends*.
  - This is instead of anything approaching the level of certainty that most of us would like to have regarding our ability to predict the future.

25. Absolute vs. Relative: Relativity Theory

- *Relativity theory* began with Albert Einstein's famous formulation of the *special theory of relativity* in 1905; he expanded it to a broader theory of *general relativity* in 1915:
  - It provides a universal framework for *consistency* by asserting that the only inviolable metric is the *speed of light*, which is the same for all observers, regardless of their inertial frame of reference (i.e., their velocity and acceleration).
  - *Space* and *time*, which were both previously thought to provide a firm and immobile stage for the occurrence of events, are *interrelated* and *interconvertible* in calculable ways; perspectives based on absolute measures of space and time are replaced by *relativism*.

- o *Time* can be either *dilated* or *contracted* and *length* can be either *stretched* or *foreshortened* to provide a consistent view of the same events for different observers; this prevents events from being observed in reverse order from different points of view, which allows the crucial idea of *causality* to be preserved.
- o Experiments have confirmed the theory's predictions to an extraordinary degree of accuracy; to date, no significant violations have been found.
- The *speed of light* (in a vacuum) is *finite*, *absolute*, and identical in all frames of reference:
  - o This serves to cement together the *evolution* of *events* throughout the universe by maintaining their *consistency* from every point of view.
- Relativity theory demonstrates that some regions of the universe contain information that is *not* accessible:
  - o The scope of information that any particular observer can access is *truncated*; this is because observers cannot communicate with objects farther away than can reached by a signal traveling at the speed of light, and
  - o Very dense bodies can create *event horizons* beyond which any information is inaccessible to any outside observer.
- The truncation of information for particular observers is illustrated by the idea of a *light cone*, which demarcates the limits over which a signal can be disseminated by the *speed of light*:
  - o Anything falling *within the cone's boundaries* has the *ability* to *communicate* via signals that travel at light speed or slower, while anything falling outside cannot because the signal would need to travel faster than the speed of light to do so.
  - o Since we exist at a particular point in space-time, there is a *limited spatial field of information from the past* that can "get to where we are" via the speed of light (the fastest speed possible); anything *farther away cannot catch up* to us, making information from those regions *out of reach*
  - o Similarly, there is a limited *sphere of influence* that *current actions* can have on objects and events of the future in *different spatial domains*: if a *spatial region* is *far enough away* that it *cannot be reached* by a light-speed signal emitted locally, it has

no way to ever get there and to have any influence on events that occur at that location.

Thus, the *speed of light* serves as a *barrier* between different regions of the universe that are too far-flung to communicate (at least within the confines of our four-dimensional space-time).

- *Black holes* result from dense collections of matter where the *gravitational field* is *so strong* that it *precludes* the *escape* of anything *beyond* their *event horizons*—even light:
  - *Event horizons* serve as a *barrier* to the *outward egress* of any *useful information* about what exists within black holes; this information cannot be known to anyone outside.
  - They act effectively as *one-way trap doors*—energy, mass, and information are pulled into them from the ordinary space-time of the universe that surrounds them (thereby being *lost* to the rest of the universe), but nothing inside them can ever return in any useful way to the surrounding portions of the universe in which they are imbedded.
  - They *limit* the *scope* of *information* available to observers in our universe.
- What we can observe *locally* is what guides us:
  - We *cannot access all* the information in the universe; consequently, we sometimes infer that there are associations between objects and events that may be due to other phenomena that we simply cannot know about locally.
  - Relativity theory explains why we are limited to *local perspectives* that are *incomplete* and represent mere *approximations*.
- The *truncated communication* implications of relativity theory demonstrate that we *cannot have complete information* about *everything* in the universe:
  - Without a complete set of information about the universe, we *cannot* attain the necessary level of consistency and *clarity* to *predict the future* with certainty.

26. Energy

- *Energy* is what enables systems to do *work*:
  - Physical systems contain energy.

- o Some fraction of it may be extracted to do *useful work* (elsewhere).
- A *system* is defined as any physical entity that can have a boundary drawn around it to separate it from its surrounding environment (at least imaginarily):
  - o *Systems* can be anything within a circumscribable volume of interest.
- *Work* is defined as a *force* exerted over a *distance*.
- *Force* is the *change in momentum* (i.e., [mass] x [velocity]) of an object over *time*.
- The amount of *energy expended* by a system is *equal* to the *amount of work done* by the system on its external environment (barring dissipative losses).
- *Energy*:
  - o Can be *transferred* from one place to another or *interconverted* from one form to another, including being represented by mass (i.e., according to Einstein's famous mass-energy equivalence equation $E = mc^2$)
  - o *Cannot be* created de novo or destroyed.
- All (real) systems have *internal energy*:
  - o At the *low-energy extreme*, internal energy is *zero* and *no external work can be done*; such systems are *entirely homogeneous*.
  - o Systems that are *inhomogeneous* (at *non-zero temperature*) contain a quantitatively definable amount of *internal energy*.
  - o Some fraction of *internal energy* is *tied up* as an essential part of real systems due to
    - The *internal motion* of the system's constituents
    - The intrinsic *non-equilibrium nature* of the system's *components*
    - The *organized relationship* of the *system components* to one another
    - An *inaccessible portion* of the system's *internal energy* that is *non-retrievable* unless the system components are completely degraded to a state of total randomness (i.e., a homogenous state).
  - o Another fraction of *internal energy* is (potentially useful) *free energy* (according to a variety of definitions)

- - This energy can be retrieved (or *extracted*) from the system to *do work* on the environment outside of the system.
- If the universe (i.e., everything that exists) were *entirely homogeneous*:
  - It would be in *equilibrium*.
  - There would be *no energetic differences* among *different regions*.
  - It would be entirely *disordered* (there would be a complete lack of system organization, meaning *maximum entropy*).
  - It would be unable to *self-organize*.
  - *Non-equilibrium* (i.e., *organized*) *structures* would be precluded (including sentient beings).
  - There would be *no potential* for it to perform *useful work* (i.e., there would be *no free energy*).
- *Conservation of energy*—the idea that *energy cannot* be *created* from nothingness or *destroyed* without a trace (i.e., erased)—is an inviolable concept:
  - This prohibits the creation of "something of meaning from nothing".
    - If we could *create* energy, we would be able to construct *new* items at whim, like genies conjuring up anything they wanted.
  - It applies to every known physical relationship, both classical and relativistic.
- According to the principle of *conservation of energy*, our universe *started* with a *certain amount* of *energy*, and that is *all there is*:
  - Since the beginning of the universe, *no energy has ever been created or destroyed*; it has only been *transferred* from one place to another and *interconverted* from one form to another.
    - The term universe includes *everything that exists, everywhere*—whether accessible or inaccessible, known or unknown, including energy that may be included in potential extra dimensionalities in addition to ordinary four-dimensional space-time.
- *Conservation of energy* has an important implication concerning the *amount* of *information contained* in the *universe*:
  - Anything with a *non-equilibrium physical existence* embodies some amount of *internal energy* that gives it *meaning*, reflecting its *information content*.

- o The *amount of information* in the universe depends on—and is proportional to—the total *amount of energy* the universe contains.
    - This *amount of information* is defined by a *relationship* between *energy* and *information*.

27. Information

- *Information* is the *substrate* of all *knowledge*:
    - o Without information it would be impossible to know about anything.
- To be *useful*, *information* must be assembled, placed into appropriate *context*, and *interpreted*.
- *Information* is *not free floating*:
    - o To *exist*, it must be *represented* in some type of a *physical medium*.
- *Physical media* are *organized, non-equilibrium structures*:
    - o They cannot exist in a universe of maximal *entropy* (i.e., one that is maximally disorganized and homogeneous).
- A *thermally (energetically) homogeneous universe* is completely *disordered*:
    - o It has a complete lack of system organization, resulting in *maximal entropy*.
    - o All *sentient beings* capable of *processing information* would be precluded, as they represent organized structures.
    - o As a result, *knowledge* is *not possible* in a *uniform universe*.
- In a universe of *ultra-high energy density* (i.e., one that is extremely hot):
    - o Different forms of electromagnetic energy are interconverted, but matter is not stable enough to create robust physical systems; the universe was likely this way in its early stages.
    - o The *lifetime* of any particular *state* of the universe is *extremely short*, resulting in *time-dependent instability*.
        - Even if it were possible for information to exist under these conditions, its *half-life* before erasure would be so *brief* as to make it *transient*.

- The *storage* of information in any region of the universe could only be maintained *very briefly* before being *drowned out* by *thermal noise*.
- By the time any such information could be *recognized* by a sentient being (assuming that one could exist under such hostile conditions), it would be *changed* or *erased*, making its *processing* impossible (i.e., it would have *no utility*).
- In an *ultra-low energy density* universe (i.e., one approaching *thermal equilibrium* near *absolute zero*), there is:
  - *Sufficient stability* over time to both *represent* and *store information*, but
  - *Insufficient free energy* to *transfer* and *process* it to make it of any practical use.
- *Useful information* (i.e., information that is *persistent* and *stable* enough to be *stored* and *recognized*, as well as *analyzed* and *knowable*) can only exist between the conditions of the two extremes of an *ultra-low* and an *ultra-high energy density* universe:
  - This intermediate range is where our universe currently exists, making *conditions suitable* for the *representation*, *maintenance*, *storage*, *retrieval*, *transmission*, and *processing* of *information*.

28. Energy and Information: Maxwell's Hypothetical Demon

- In the nineteenth century, James Clerk Maxwell described what would occur if a gas mixture of two components—one of higher energy and the other of lower energy—could be *separated* into its *constituent parts* using *information alone* (having originated from two chambers *A* and *B*):
  - "*A being whose faculties are so sharpened that he can follow every molecule in its course ... would be able to do what is impossible to us ... without expenditure of work,* [he could] *raise the temperature of B and lower that of A, in contradiction to the second law of thermodynamics.*"
- Maxwell's "being" (i.e., the so-called *demon*) could use *information alone* to open and shut a (frictionless) gate at the proper times to *separate* a *gas mixture*:

- o   *Information* about the system would permit otherwise energy-dependent operations to be performed without consuming energy, thereby violating the principle of *conservation of energy* by *creating energy* from *nothing*.
- o   A *perpetual motion machine* would result if not for the *equivalence* of *information* and *energy*.
- A *well-defined relationship* between *energy* and *information* arises from thermodynamics, statistical mechanics, and information theory that addresses the *conservation of energy* violation that Maxwell's demon would otherwise create:
  - o   A single binary *bit* of information (the most basic yes-no type) has a heat equivalent (i.e., *energy*) of $\leq 3 \times 10^{-21}$ Joules at human body temperature (i.e., 310° K).
  - o   Einstein's mass-energy equivalence equation ($E = mc^2$) implies that a *bit* of information also has a very small mass equivalent ($\leq 3.3 \times 10^{-38}$ kg at room temperature).
  - o   Both quantities are difficult to measure because they are exceedingly small.
  - o   *Energy, mass,* and *information* are all *interchangeable*; which should be considered the *primary* manifestation of the underlying phenomenon they represent is irrelevant, because all are equivalent.
- The *rules* that apply to the *conservation, storage, conversion,* and *transfer* of *energy* also *apply* to *information*:
  - o   They are well understood from a physical standpoint as they apply to *energy*.
  - o   Because of the equivalence of energy and information, they also apply to *information*, albeit with different formulations.
  - o   *Energy* and *information* are two sides of the same coin.

29. Modeling vs. Reality

- We repeatedly try—both as individuals and as human cultures—to *build models* around *information* that we can access concerning reality.
- *Models* are *abstractions* that attempt to capture *reality's* most *salient features*:

- They incorporate only what we consider the *most important* elements of the systems under consideration.
 - They are always *incomplete*.
- A model's *veracity* is assessed based on the *accuracy* of its *predictions*:
 - If *accurate*, a model is considered to be a *proper reflection* of *reality* (at least over the limited domains where it is tested) and it is retained.
 - If *inaccurate*, it is modified to encompass conflicting observations and tested again to see if the new model predicts events properly.
- When a model is *tested*:
 - Reality is cast into *operational* terms.
 - The *accuracy* and *precision* of *measurements* is crucial.
- With modeling, the *greater context* of the surrounding universe is either held:
 - *Constant*, such that *outside influences* are either *obviated* or minimized, or
 - *Completely at bay* (i.e., not even considered).
- Models *do not incorporate all elements* of *reality*:
 - Many of the omissions made by models would be *destabilizing* if they were incorporated.
   - Models often behave in stable ways when the reality they purport to model does not.
 - They are subject to *errors* because of their *incompleteness*
   - Models are prone to generating results that are *predictable* but that *vary widely* from what *actually occurs*.
- *Models* necessarily provide an *improper view* of *reality* because:
 - They are *isolated* from the greater universe that they attempt to describe.
 - Their *incompleteness* makes them necessarily *inconsistent*.
- Models *cannot* be *generalized* to other domains with predictable accuracy:
 - They have only *limited applicability* to systems where there is *no direct information*.
- Using a model to establish the *Truth* about everything (with a Capital *T*) cannot be achieved:

- All models are useful only in *operational* terms concerning their (local) view of the truth (with a small "t").
- They are an *incomplete* reflection of realty and *never perfectly accurate*.
- They are all intrinsically subject to *inexpungible inconsistencies* (due to their *incompleteness*).
- Because they *never* present a *comprehensive* view of reality, they are subject to *unavoidable errors*.
• Models can never be regarded as more than a *general guide* in helping to predict the future, which is a far cry from the certitude that most of us would wish for them to have.

30. Where We Fit and What We Can Know

• As humans, we exist at an *interface* between two dimensional scales: the *quantum level* (small) and the *relativistic level* (large):
  - We *experience influences* and have *interactions* with *both*.
  - Our existence at the *interface* may allow us some degree of *freedom* to operate that otherwise deterministic effects would preclude.
• For events that have not yet occurred, we must rely on our *perceptions, analyses, understandings*, and *projections* of currently available information about the past and the present to make predictions about the future.
• The *information available* about the *past* and the *present* is:
  - Limited in *scope, accuracy*, and *precision*
  - *Incomplete*
  - Only an *approximation*.
• *Approximations* about the *past* and the *present* undergo progressive *distortion* as they are *projected* into the future:
  - *Analytical methods* are *prone* to *error* because they are intrinsically *incomplete* and, therefore, *inconsistent*.
  - *Trajectories* are improperly calculated due to *incomplete information*, including but not limited to
    - *Inaccurate* and *imprecise positions* and *momenta* of objects
    - The *inability* to take the complete set of *system interactions* (e.g., *resonances*) into account.

- *Projections* into the future rely on not only past and present *approximations, inconsistencies, assumptions,* and *generalizations,* but also on the presumption of *smoothness* and *stability,* both of which are improperly founded.
- *Completeness* is *not testable*:
  - It is impossible to evaluate objects or events about which there is *no way* to *gain information.*
  - There is no way to know when there are no more objects or events to discover.
- Besides completeness, *consistency* is the only other metric we have for assessing if we can believe in what we think we know:
  - *Inconsistency* is a clear indicator that what we think we know is *flawed*.
  - However, *universal consistency* is *untestable* because it would require *all* tests to be performed under *all* circumstances and in *all* contexts.
    - This would necessitate an infinite number of tests, which would require an infinite amount of time.
    - If fewer tests are performed, it is unclear what criteria should be used to decide when a sufficient number have been done (i.e., since *we don't know what we don't know*, where should the testing stop)?
- If neither *completeness* nor *consistency* can be definitively established, it is not possible to decide if we should believe in what we think we know.
- If *universal consistency* cannot be established, *how much inconsistency* should be tolerated before deciding that a model should be discarded?
  - If our tolerance limit is zero, we will be changing models interminably.
- The *scientific method* is designed to *evaluate hypotheses* that are *potentially falsifiable* by using *consistency testing* to *determine* their *validity*:
  - We believe in whatever we think we know until testing generates conflicting information that makes our previous understanding inconsistent.

- At that point, we construct and test a new model that changes our understanding to adjust for the newly conflicting information.
- This model then persists until some other information arises to challenge it by again being inconsistent.
- Because it cannot be certain that the truth has been arrived at until all possible tests have been performed, and because all possible tests cannot be completed, the process is *flawed*.

Despite its *limited scope* and *applicability*, the *scientific method* is the best we have to ensure that what we think we know should continue to be believed.

- We are all bound by *limited knowledge*:
  - All we can do is project our *best guesses* from the *past* and the *present* into the future based on *history*, *prior experience* (both personal and collective), *pattern recognition, comparison, analogy, analysis*, and finally, *hope*.
- *Hope* would not be possible if the future could be predicted with certitude:
  - *Uncertainty* about the future allows for
    - Potential *alternative outcomes*
    - The concept of *hope*, and
    - The *freedom* to make *choices*, which constitutes *free will*.
- If *hope* exists, we must possess *free will* (at least as it is perceived locally).
- *Uncertainty* means that we are *unable* to reliably *predict* the future, but it is also the reason that we have *free will* and, ultimately, our *freedom*.

31. Where Does All This Leave Us?

- Our view of our universe is highly selected, being the result of *fragmented* and *incomplete* information; although it is not intrinsically incorrect, it is *truncated*, both in terms of scope as well as its degree of accuracy and precision:
  - *Incomplete information* gleaned from our senses is further confounded by *uncertainty* and *approximations*, as well as by errors in its *acquisition, transmission*, and *processing*.

- Additional *approximations* are introduced through the *analysis* of the information we receive; these result in *errors* because of the limitations associated with the *methods* we use for processing it.
- The *interpretation* and *understanding* of our analyses is limited by the *context* in which we place it; it may be applicable locally, but the full context is truncated because of *missing information* about what exists beyond what we can access (i.e., behind event horizons and in hyperspace).
- *Uncertainties* and *limitations* about the *understandings* we have are compounded when the results of our analyses (i.e., our thoughts about the information) are mobilized and translated into *actions*.
- *Uncertainties* regarding the *effects* of our *actions* are introduced through physical inexactitudes, which arise at two levels
  - Heisenberg uncertainty (at the quantum level)
  - Chaotic dynamics (at the macroscopic level).

  Both have impacts on the results of our actions that are not predictable.
- *Actions* generate new sets of *consequences* that are communicated to us via new information that we glean from our environment—again with its associated limitations and imprecisions.
  - This information interacts with our senses and starts the whole cycle anew with the (further) compounding of imprecision and inexactitudes, at least from our (local) human perspective.

- As *practically* oriented biological organisms, we simply "fill in" *gaps* in the *types* and *scope* of the incomplete and inexact information that we have:
  - This allows us to process it and interpret it subjectively.
- No one, either individually or collectively, is capable of assembling a complete set of (precise) information about the universe at any one time; without this:
  - We are left to *approximate, optimize local situations* (within *limited contexts*), and *hope* that our *knowledge* and *understanding* is *sufficient* to *maintain* us within (*local*) *domains* that are both *smooth* and *well-defined*.

- o This means that the universe cannot be *analyzed* as a giant *precision clock* that can be run forward and backward with impunity.
- Making *precise predictions* in *unstable domains* is *not possible*:
  - o *Instability* is fostered by *discontinuities*, which occur commonly.
  - o *Discontinuities* predispose to *unpredictably*.
- *Errors* in the *acquisition, processing, interpretation, understanding of,* and *reactions to* information can:
  - o be of little importance, or
  - o lead to *cumulative divergences* that result in their *amplification*.
- *Intellect* and *intuition* are the only two methods available to guide us:
  - o *Intellect* depends on gleaning information and *analyzing, interpreting,* and *understanding* it; the processes for doing so are intrinsically *flawed*.
  - o *Intuition* is different
    - It depends to some extent on *instinct*.
    - It is linked to *consciousness*, but its origin is unknown.
    - It may be a better guide than intellect and past experience.
- Is *consciousness* a *being-specific phenomenon* that each of us possesses, or is it part of a *greater collective* "universal database" of understanding that we all simply "tap into"?
  - o The answer is unknown; it could be either.
- Because of our *universal knowledge deficit*:
  - o No matter how much we think we know and understand about the universe, *human discovery* and *invention* will *never cease*.
  - o *We don't know what we don't know*, which means that we *don't know* what is *yet to be discovered*; as a result, it *not predictable*.
  - o Humans will forever make discoveries that had previously been unknown, allowing for continued searching, inventing, and adapting of new ideas to our advantage.
  - o This is the best single cause for continued *optimism* about the future.
- The paradigm that we are left with and that we can employ operationally with regard to our knowledge, understanding, and overall dealings with the universe is:
  - o Make new *discoveries*.

- o *Check* for *reproducibility*.
- o *Evaluate* for broader *consistency* with other known information.
- o *Establish* the *scope of validity* by *exploring* the *limits of applicability*.
- o *Probe* to "*invent*" new uses with novel purposes.
- o *Apply* to generate *other novelties* that have *utility*, and
- o *Repeat* the process after incorporating the new information.
- This schema is a variant of the *scientific method*, but the concept is *different*:
  - o The *scientific method* represents a set of *methodological standards* for *interrogating* the *reproducibility* and *consistency* of information, with the goal of identifying inconsistencies (i.e., *testing* propositions that are *potentially falsifiable*).
  - o The goals of the *new system* are *less stringent, more flexible,* and *more realistic*.
    - Instead of trying to discover the *Truth* (about everything, with a capital "T"), the goal is instead *utility*, which is *locally defined* and *application-dependent*.
    - Whereas the *Truth* requires *complete information, consistency*, and *universal applicability* (which cannot be ensured), *utility*—which relates to a particular purpose—does not; this makes the metric of *utility* both locally *useful* and *attainable*.
- The issue of *individual control* and predictability can be reduced to the question of what is more important in terms of *extent of impact* on objects and events:
  - o *Individuals* (with all the capabilities that we have been designed to embody), or
  - o *Everything else* (i.e., the rest of the universe)?
- The *universe* is much more *vast, energetic,* and *massive* than we are individually:
  - o Accordingly, it should have a *greater impact* on the *occurrence of events*.
  - o But even if the universe has more of an impact *overall* than individuals, what is the *balance* between the two effects at a *local level*?

- How much of an impact do *individuals* have on *locally-occurring events* as *agents* of the universe? The answer dictates how much control we have over the future.
- If all objects and events in the universe are *connected*, then they all *affect each other*:
    o This makes the distinction between *systems-of-interest* and their *surrounding environments* both artificial and moot.
- Even though *individuals* are an *inextricable part* of the *universe* (i.e., it is impossible to negate the myriad of connections that we have to it), at a practical level, we might still choose to make the (artificial) distinction of *individuals* on the one hand versus the *rest of the universe* on the other:
    o It is not just the *size, scope, energy, mass,* and *informational content* that is brought to bear by each, but also issues of *proximity, timing, force,* and *smoothness* of the *input-response profile* that establishes what the *outcome* of any composite-input situation will be.
    o The *closer, more forceful, more well-timed,* and *nearer* to the *outcomes* of interest are our human *inputs*, the more consequential they should be in determining the course of future events compared to those of the remaining aspects of the universe.
    o The idea of *impact* (or *influence*) is different than that of *predictability* of effect.
- *Free will* is the *independent ability* to exert *choice* over the actions we take:
    o Do we have it, or are we simply bound to execute our roles as agents of the universe (of which we are an intrinsic part) to accomplish *its* purpose (i.e., essentially as imbedded instruments)? No test exists to distinguish between the two alternatives.
    o If individuals have impact in directing the course of events, but if we are bound to do what we do despite our belief that we have a choice among many alternative actions, then we do not actually have control, and it is unclear whether we can influence the course of future events at all.
    o Whether we can *influence the future* can be divided into three separate questions

- "Can we *influence* the course of future events via our individual actions?"
- "Do these actions arise as a result of *free will?*"
- "Can we *predict* the consequences of current events with regard to future outcomes and circumstances?"

These are fundamentally different and may have diverging answers, for instance:
- It may be that we *can influence* the course of events locally via our actions (i.e., a positive answer to the first question), but that this does *not* arise from *free will* (a negative answer to the second question).
- Or it may be that we actually *do not have free will* to be able to independently direct the course of events locally (i.e., a negative answer to the second question) but that we *can predict* the *outcomes* of current events with regard to the future (i.e., a positive answer to the third question).

The ideas of *influencing* the future, doing it *volitionally* (or not), and *predicting* it are all different:
- Based on the arguments in this book, the likely answer to the third question is negative (i.e., we cannot predict the future with certainty); but, the answer to the first and second may be more nebulous.

- Far from being in control, we may be nothing more than *participants* on a *grand stage*, the majority of which is *shrouded*.
- A triumph of our species is that we have cordoned off portions of our (local) environments to make them behave in ways that are *smooth* and *stable*, such that some degree of *prediction* is *possible*.
- There is *no certainty*; we simply *do the best we can* within the limits of what we can know.
- Each reader will need to form his or her own judgment concerning the issues of whether individuals have the ability to:
  - *Influence local events* on the one hand, and
  - Do so by *exercising free will* in on the other.

32. Potential Theological Implications

- *Holes* exist in our *information base*, our *knowledge*, and our *understanding* about the universe that we cannot fill.
- Our view of the universe is *truncated* by *immutable physical constraints*, including (but not limited to):
    - Our *limited ability* to *perceive* signals, as well as our restricted ability to *appreciate* the complete nature of the *information* we receive (due to the limitations of our biological senses)
    - Fundamental *quantum uncertainties*
    - Our *limited catchment* of information (as defined by *light cones*)
    - *Inaccessibility of information* that resides behind the *event horizons* of *black holes*, etc.
- All of this makes our perspectives concerning the universe *incomplete*.
    - Because our perspectives of the universe are incomplete, they are also *inconsistent*.
- We cannot glimpse the entire universe, as *we exist* as *only a part* of it:
    - Because of this, we cannot have a vision of its overall *purpose*.
    - As a consequence, we *cannot know* the *purpose* of our *own roles* in it.
- Our *lack of understanding* of what constitutes the *whole universal system* leaves room for capitulation:
    - We are only a portion of a much larger system that has somehow created us as part of its need for *ongoing evolution*.
    - As such, we all *play key and irreplaceable roles* within it, but precisely what they are meant to be is beyond the grasp of each of us individually and collectively.
- We cannot know about what exists "out there" in the universe *beyond the reach* of all our collective perceptions:
    - This leaves room for *speculation* and, accordingly, for some type of *faith*.
- The *holes* that exist in our *knowledge* and *understanding* of the universe (i.e., the ones that create room for *faith*) are the *same* for all of us:

- o All modes, flavors, and varieties of faith are predicated upon *identical knowledge deficits*, making us all captives of the same intrinsically unanswerable questions.
- o Any differences in faith are merely *nuances in speculation* arising from holes that exist in our knowledge and understanding.
    - These allow for the creation of different *belief systems*.
- o Belief superstructures are *not real* in any physically meaningful sense.
    - They are simply created (by us) as part of a construct that people over thousands of years have spent much time and effort conjuring.
- It is impossible to verify which competing *belief system* might be more *True* than others:
    - o They all attempt to address issues that we *do not know* about.
    - o Because of this, *none* has a *preferred position* over others.
    - o They all attempt to fill in information and knowledge deficits by providing different conveniences in an attempt to provide explanation.
- The universe may "know where it is going," but *no one else can*:
    - o Does the universe actually *know* anything about what it is *doing* (implying, in essence, that it has *consciousness* even at its level), or
    - o Is the universe simply a *complete, consistent,* and *coherent system* that is *executing* its prescribed evolution (much like an entirely deterministic system that is simply *cranking through* a pre-prescribed plan)?
- The universe may extend into *higher dimensional spaces* than we have access to:
    - o Even though the full scope of the universe's dimensionality is uncertain, its precise dimensionality does not change any of the issues at hand.
- Two corollaries emerge:
    - o We are *all part of* (and beholden to) the *same system* that has both created us and assigned us unique and irreplaceable roles in it, and
    - o If there is a (universal) *master plan* to which we are made and meant to conform (i.e., "the universe," "nature," "God" by

any name, etc.), then that *larger, guiding power* is the *same for all of us*.
- There can be *no preferred positions* in the realm of *ignorance*:
  o There is *no justification* for significant *human discord* pertaining to *what we don't know* within the limited framework of what we do.
- What it is *possible to know* is the *same for all* of us and *what can't be known* is *equally unknowable* for *all of us*:
  o If there is a *higher power* to which we must all answer regarding the proper execution of our roles within the universe (assuming, of course, that there is *free will*), then our allegiance must necessarily be the *same*.
  o It is absurd to imagine that differences in nuance concerning what we *cannot* know should precipitate discord, argument, or contemptuous unrest over superficial disagreements regarding human trappings.
  o *Differences in faith* must be appreciated as nothing more than *limited perspectives* and *interpretations* of *incomplete* and *inconsistent information* by us as humans rather than anything more substantive.

*APPENDIX (FOR CHAPTERS 20 AND 28)

Some readers may be interested in a more detailed explanation of the results presented in chapter 20 ("Thermodynamics: Laws Prohibiting the Spontaneous Reversibility of Physical Events") and chapter 28 ("Energy and Information: Maxwell's Hypothetical Demon"). The following is a derivation from first principles of the equivalence of energy-(mass)-information.

For any closed physical system, the principle of conservation of energy must be satisfied. According to the first law of thermodynamics:

$$\Delta Q = \Delta U + \Delta W \tag{1}$$

where:

ΔQ = quantity of heat added to the system

ΔU = change in the internal energy of the system

ΔW = work done by the system

The second law of thermodynamics, which arises as a natural consequence of the first, states that for any change in the state of the system:

$$\Delta S \geq \Delta Q / T \tag{2}$$

where:

ΔS = change in the entropy of the system

ΔQ = quantity of heat added to the system

T = absolute temperature

Equation 2 can be rewritten as:

$$\Delta Q \leq T \, \Delta S \tag{2a}$$

Statistical mechanics has shown that the entropy change associated with any macroscopic system can be expressed as:

$$\Delta S = k \ln \Delta P \tag{3}$$

where:

k = Boltzmann's constant

P = Statistical probability that the system will exist in an allowed system microstate that gives rise to a particular and indistinguishable system macrostate (Planck complexions)

For the case of information represented in a binary format, the change in physical system entropy associated with the representation of a single bit of information reduces equation 3 to:

$$\Delta S_{bit} = - k \ln 2 \tag{4}$$

Substituting this expression for ΔS into equation 2a yields:

$$\Delta Q_{bit} \leq - T k \ln 2 \tag{5}$$

An explicit energy calculation can then be made per bit of system information that becomes irretrievable as a function of temperature. For instance, at normal human body temperature (310° Kelvin), the result is:

$$\Delta Q_{bit} \leq - (310 \,°K) \times (1.38 \times 10^{-23} \, J/°K) \times (0.693) \tag{6}$$

$$\leq - 2.96 \times 10^{-21} \text{ Joules}$$

Appeal to Einstein's famous mass-energy equation then results in an estimate of the mass deficit to be expected for each bit of information that becomes irretrievable:

$$\Delta E = \Delta m \, c^2 \tag{7}$$

where:

ΔE = change in energy
Δm = change in mass
c = speed of light

Substituting the energy deficit value per bit of information lost at 37 degrees Celsius and solving for Δm, this becomes:

$$\Delta m_{deficit/bit} \leq -2.96 \times 10^{-21} \text{ J}/(3.00 \times 10^8 \text{ m/sec})^2 \tag{8}$$

$$\leq -3.29 \times 10^{-38} \text{ kg}$$

CPSIA information can be obtained
at www.ICGtesting.com
Printed in the USA
FFOW02n2032261214
9849FF